THE LAST

THE SEVEN WONDERS OF THE CROSS

WILKIN VAN DE KAMP

WHITAKER
HOUSE

THE SEVEN WONDERS OF THE CROSS
The Last 18 Hours

(Originally published in Dutch in 2005 as *Het wonder van het kruis*)
English translation by Hope Visser

Wilkin van de Kamp
www.wilkinvandekamp.com/www.crosslight.eu

ISBN: 978-1-64123-071-1
eBook ISBN: 978-1-64123-072-8
Printed in the United States of America
© 2005, 2018 by Wilkin van de Kamp

Whitaker House
1030 Hunt Valley Circle
New Kensington, PA 15068
www.whitakerhouse.com

Library of Congress Cataloging-in-Publication Data (Pending)

1 2 3 4 5 6 7 8 9 10 11 ⊔⊔ 24 23 22 21 20 19 18

TABLE OF CONTENTS

Overview of the Seven Wonders of the Cross

Dedicated to my father, who
—while I was writing this book—
unexpectedly went to our heavenly Father.
He went home to be at the feet of his Master.

PREFACE

As a professional translator, I am used to speaking and writing the words of others. When I was asked to share my experiences, emotions and thoughts while translating this book, I had to stop and think hard. Translating this book was not easy. As I worked my way through the chapters of what Jesus' sacrifice really meant, I was forced to take a long, hard look at my own beliefs, ideas and how they influence my life.

I came away from this book a changed woman. The realization that I have yet to fully grasp how far God's love is willing to go to get a hold of my heart, has made me bow down in awe and worship.

The Almighty traded His place in Heaven for unimaginable suffering, for me. Unworthy, yet loved. Wanted. It is my hope and prayer that Wilkin's words will touch your heart, your life, as you read how the God of the universe paid the ultimate price to show you His love. He wants you. He loves you. He wants to free you from all that is preventing you from becoming the person you were designed to be, vibrant and full of life. He has a plan for you. And He is willing to go to great lengths just to show you how much He loves you. He thinks you are worth it. And you are.

Hope Visser

THE WONDER
OF THE CROSS

Think of what he went through;
how he put up with so much hatred from sinners!
So do not let yourselves become
discouraged and give up.

(Hebrews 12:3, GNB)

A few years ago, I was invited to speak at a Christian summer camp for children and teenagers. I have a background in teaching and have taught children of all ages for many years, so they must have thought that I would easily be able to handle a group of some eighty children, varying in age from six to sixteen. I spontaneously said yes and accepted the invitation. But as the date drew closer, I started to dread it. How could I grab and hold the attention of a group that size, with such a variety of ages? How on earth was I going to do it? I started to pray and had the impression that God said this to me: "Have a Cross built of wood and set it up in front of the kids. Tell them in simple words about the wonder of the Cross. Give them paper and markers and tell them they can write down all the sins they've committed in their lives and all the bad things they've experienced, and give them to Jesus. Bring a hammer and nails so they can nail these things to the wooden Cross." I took this to be God's word and asked a church member to build a transportable wooden Cross for me. I collected hammers from everyone in the neighborhood and purchased old-fashioned nails that were about ten centimeters long.

When the first morning of the camp came, I began in simple words to tell the young people about the wonder of the Cross. I told them they were allowed to write down or draw pictures on a piece of paper of all the bad things they had done and all the bad things they had been through. To my amazement, nearly all of the children started to fill their sheet of paper right away. I walked around as they worked. I saw what some of them had written and was deeply touched. I couldn't believe some of the things I read and saw, the things some of the children had gone through at such young ages.

HAMMERS AND NAILS

Then came the moment that the children had been waiting for. They were allowed to start using the hammers and nails. Each youngster took his or her sheet of paper filled with words or pictures and started to nail it to the Cross, and before long you couldn't see the wood of the Cross any longer: all you could see was a jumble of paper sheets filled with confessed sins and bad experiences. The children went back to their seats. Then I told them they were not yet rid of their sins, even though they had been nailed to the Cross. I started to share once again about the blood of Jesus that takes away our sins. And that is a wonder, a supernatural wonder. I told them that only the blood of Jesus could take away their sins and that, if they wanted to experience that, they could come forward. At first only a few came, but soon they all came. The summer camp leaders joined me in praying for the children. We took them to the Cross of Jesus. We were able to do what Jesus told His disciples: "If you forgive anyone's sins, they have been forgiven them."[1] Together, we were able to share the forgiveness of God with them. Then something happened that I will never forget. The miracle occurred.

Every time someone goes to the Cross of Jesus, a miracle takes place. A miracle that cannot be performed by a doctor, a psychologist or a psychiatrist nor any counseling session. It is the wonder of the Cross, which can only take place when you go to Him and confess with your mouth: "Father, I have sinned, I need your wonder in my life."

The kids had done this, and then the Holy Spirit came upon all the children in the room. It was the first time in my life that I had witnessed the outpouring of God's Spirit on a group of people. I had heard and read about such things, but I had never experienced anything like it, let alone with children. The Holy Spirit descended on those children and I did nothing at all.

I had no control over what was happening. I said: "Lord, what is going on here?" Little children started to cry; teenagers were touched by God's hand. Children started to pray for each other. Jesus started to heal and deliver. At the back of the room, there was a boy of about twelve years old who had started to cry, a desperate cry from deep within. All of a sudden the crying turned into screeching. Without anyone having prayed for him, demons started to manifest themselves and to leave this young boy. No one had to say: "Be gone in the name of Jesus." No one. Why? That is the wonder of the Cross. When our sins are removed and we have been cleansed by the blood of Jesus of all the sins in our lives, the devil has no more power over us.

THE WONDER OF GOD'S LOVE

Yes, I love to speak about the wonder of the Cross because it has totally changed my life. And not only mine but those of millions of others as well. The wonder of the Cross has completely taken hold of me. My whole life is centered on it. For me, the wonder of the Cross is the wonder of God's love. It is God's supernatural intervention in this world, in my world. The story of the Cross is a story full of wonders. Wonders on earth and wonders in heaven. All wonders are supernatural wonders; they transcend human capabilities. The wonder of the Cross is the greatest wonder of all.

Medical experts, historians and archeologists from all over the world have studied in depth the crucifixion willingly suffered by Jesus. It is good to listen to them to discover what exactly happened and to become aware of the immense price Jesus paid so that we can be a part of the wonder of the Cross. All experts agree that what He endured was one of the most horrific and painful forms of capital punishment ever conceived by man. But how do we view the story of the crucifixion? If we look at the crucifixion with our

The wonder of the Cross is the greatest wonder of all.

natural eyes only, much of what really happened in both the visible and the invisible realm will be lost on us. It's good to ask ourselves, How much do we really know about what happened in and just outside Jerusalem during those last eighteen hours leading up to Jesus' death? For example, have I ever taken the effort to look at the crucifixion of Jesus through the eyes of God the Father?

The story of the Cross is a story that has to be seen "from above" as well as from ground level. Jesus hung on a wooden cross between heaven and earth, abandoned by both God and man. If we really want to fully understand the wonder of the Cross and what it means to us, we must explore what happened in that space "between heaven and earth." Then we will discover the wonder and receive the faith to become a part of the resurrection power of Jesus.

UNDERSTANDING THE
WONDER OF THE CROSS

In this book, I want to try to answer the question of what went on during the crucifixion of Jesus of Nazareth, the Son of God. Did the people who were more or less personally involved in the judgment and crucifixion of Jesus understand exactly what was happening and why He died? Did they know that the course of history would be totally changed within the space of a few hours? The Bible says that "none of the rulers of this world knew."³ By looking at these men and women, who were eyewitnesses, I am confronted with the question of whether or not I myself really understand the wonder.

A preacher once told me that he was at a loss as to how to handle the story of the Cross. "Jesus did not have to die for me. I want to be held responsible for my own actions. Another person— and especially Jesus—should not have to pay the punishment." If church leaders do not understand the meaning of the wonder of the Cross, how can they lead a church? The apostle Paul probably had a similar experience, judging by what he wrote to the Corinthians:

> *For the message about Christ's death on the cross is nonsense to those who are being lost; but for us who are being saved it is God's power.* (1 Corinthians 1:18, GNB)

BRINGING THE MESSAGE OF THE CROSS (BACK) INTO FOCUS

We have seen several Muslims come to faith in our church. Initially, many of them struggled with the thought of God allowing His Son, who was innocent, to die for the guilty. What kind of father would do something like that, letting his child take the blame for other people's faults? The number of Muslims is growing rapidly in Europe. Who will tell them of the wonder of the Cross? Who can explain to them what the wonder of the Cross can mean to them? I've noticed that these people yearn to be freed from their sins. I see the same strong desire among the adherents to every other religion. I see people who would give anything to be freed from their sins: they torture themselves (in the Philippines, men literally get themselves crucified for several hours); pilgrims undertake long journeys to holy places, bring costly sacrifices (that they really can't afford) and take annual ritual baths in holy rivers. Who will tell them how they can truly find redemption by allowing the wonder of the Cross into their lives?

What about Europe and the rest of the world? The world needs the wonder of the Cross now more than ever. Thousands have turned their backs on God and gone their own way. The consequences are visible everywhere. Official statistics tell us that one out of every five Dutch people needs psychological help. The actual numbers are probably much higher, given the numbers of people seeking help from alternative healers. And yet the church has the answer to these problems. It is time for the church to bring the message of the Cross back into focus, just as Paul said:

> *For I determined not to know anything among you, except Jesus Christ, and him crucified.* (1 Corinthians 2:2, WEB)

THE MAJESTY OF THE CROSS

When the film "The Passion of the Christ," about the last twelve hours of Jesus' life, directed by Mel Gibson, was released, one of the responses was as follows: "It is a true torture film. The entire movie is really only about the useless torture of Jesus. I think it is awful to watch someone die in vain like this! What was the point of it? It makes me so angry that they let nice people die in such a completely useless manner!" This is what many people think when they consider Jesus' suffering on the cross. They see someone who meekly endures suffering and a tragic fate; a man who has been beaten to a pulp, his life coming to an end on the cross. This is what happens to anyone who would be king in the dominion of the emperor: they nail him to a cross, as a king without clothes. A pathetic show that no one wants to see. To unbelievers, the story of His suffering is just fiction. For Muslims, it is a farce; according to the Koran, another person was tortured and crucified in Jesus' place.

This book is my attempt to give people a different insight into the last eighteen hours of Jesus' earthly life. Jesus was not a Jewish martyr, who went to the cross with the courage of despair. God did not send His Son and force Him to die, but meticulously prepared Him for every last detail of the last eighteen hours of His life. The evangelist John testifies that Jesus knew *everything* about what would happen to Him (John 18:4). Six months before Jesus died, God sent Moses and Elijah from Heaven to prepare Him for His death, which would take place in Jerusalem (Luke 9:30–31). They spoke with Him about each step in the great master plan, the painful suffering, but also the joy that lay before Him. (Isaiah 53:10; Hebrews 12:2). Jesus spoke the following words in the Garden of Gethsemane to Peter, who was very confused: *"But all this was done that the Scriptures of the prophets might be fulfilled"* (Matthew 26:56 NKJV).

The last eighteen hours form a majestic Easter saga in which we see a sovereign Jesus who reveals Himself as both the Lamb of God and the great High Priest, who regally endured humiliation and ridicule. The last eighteen hours of Jesus' life testify to exceeding courage, love and strength. Jesus was not a victim of His own success. They did not murder my Jesus. Before He left for Jerusalem, where He would die, He said: *"Therefore My Father loves Me, because I lay down My life that I may take it again. No one takes it from Me, but I lay it down of Myself. I have power to lay it down, and I have power to take it again. This command I have received from My Father"* (John 10:17–18, NKJV).

Jesus showed us on the cross what perfect love is and God's greatness was revealed, as Jesus prayed several hours before His death: *"Father, the hour has come. Glorify and exalt and honor and magnify Your Son, so that Your Son may glorify and extol and honor and magnify You. [Just as] You have granted Him power and authority over all flesh (all humankind), [now glorify Him] so that He may give eternal life to all whom You have given Him"* (John 17:1–2 AMP). Just a little later an angel appeared from Heaven to give Jesus supernatural strength so that He might reveal the greatness of God's love through His suffering (Luke 22:43). Years later, John, who was an eyewitness to it all, would write: *"Having loved his dear companions, he continued to love them right to the end"* (John 13:1, MSG). It was pure love that held Jesus nailed to the cross, a love the like of which had never been seen and never will be again. He gave His life so that He could rise again three days later and beat Death at its own game.

Let this book take you back to the seven specific moments when the blood of Jesus flowed, so that the seven wonders of the Cross can take place in your life and you may receive forgiveness, salvation, cleansing, healing, freedom, reconciliation and you can be born again. The seven wonders of the Cross together form one amazing gift from God the Father to His children in this world.

At the end of each chapter, you will find a prayer. This book is not meant just to inform you about the wonder of the Cross, but to allow you to experience that wonder in your own life. That is my prayer. I am convinced that, if you pray these prayers out loud, with an open heart and faith in God the Father, the wonder of the Cross will take place in your own life. Let's discover together what the fullness of the wonder of the Cross has to offer us.

Wilkin van de Kamp

THE MAN WITHOUT SIN

For him who knew no sin he made to be sin on our behalf;
so that in him we might become the righteousness of God.

(2 Corinthians 5:21, WEB)

CHAPTER 1

When I was growing up I had a neighbor, a single guy who was passionate about collecting stamps. He had an impressive collection with several highly valuable stamps, and all the kids in the neighborhood were very impressed. He loved sharing his passion with us, and it will not come as a surprise that many of the children started their own stamp collections. To this day I still have an album filled with Dutch stamps I collected in those days. People who are passionate are attractive people. Their passion controls their life, determines their agenda. They know what they're talking about and want to share it with you. Passionate people attract other people. Passion is contagious and highly transmissible.

ATTRACTIVE

Above all else, the church of Jesus needs a renewed passion for Jesus Christ.

Our love for Him can be compared to the early, pure and un-
containable passion between two people who are madly in love
with each other. They cannot and will not be without each other
for even a moment. They think of nothing and no one else but each
other. That's passion. It's ardor; it makes people around them smile
and even feel envious of their happiness.

This is what our passion for Jesus should be like. We've been
captivated by His unconditional love for us. This is not some mys-
tical experience, or an escape from reality. It is a deep assurance
that God has revealed Himself to this world in the form of a person: Jesus Christ, who gave His life because of His love for us, so
that we might receive eternal life and know God as our Father in
heaven. A church that is full of that kind of passion is an attractive
church.

LOVESICK

The Bible book Song of Songs is the book of love. In a very
moving way, it tells of two lovers and how they long for each other,
describing their innermost feelings and how they rejoice in being
together. The story can also be seen as a picture of the love that
Jesus (the bridegroom) has for His church (the bride).

At one point in this Bible book, the bride calls out to the young
women of Jerusalem:

> *I adjure you, daughters of Jerusalem, if you find my beloved,
> that you tell him that I am faint with love.* (Song of Songs 5:8,
> WEB)

What would people say when they noticed my passion for Jesus? Would they say I'm "faint with love"? That would be powerful.
Another Bible translation even says: "Tell him I am lovesick." Such
passion, such ardor.

THE LOVE VIRUS

This is what our first love for Jesus should be like, and how our love for Him should stay. Everything in us should desire Him. When you wake up early in the morning, let your first thought, the first thing you say, be about Him. And when you go to bed at night, softly express your desire for Him as you fall asleep. In this way, you will open your heart and begin to hear His loving voice day and night. Try it.

People who are passionate about Jesus have been infected by this heavenly love virus.

People who are passionate about Jesus have been infected by this heavenly love virus injected in their hearts by the Holy Spirit.[5] They're "lovesick." They do things they didn't think were possible before they fell in love and it makes them attractive and gives them an air of eternal youth. It is this passion for Jesus that can make the church attractive, turning it into an inviting place for people out in the world, searching for love. The love virus is very contagious. It's also indestructible and equipped to annihilate every form of bitterness, indifference and laziness. This is what the church of Jesus needs now more than ever before.

THE FIRST LOVE

When the apostle John meets the risen Lord at the end of his life, Jesus speaks to him about His church in Ephesus, among other things. Jesus loves His people and knows all about them. His followers in Ephesus are hard workers, making great efforts for God's Kingdom, and He honors them for their persistence. He knows how they refuse to endure evil and how they have suffered in His name without growing weary.[6] But then He says to them, very lov-

1   THE MAN WITHOUT SIN

ingly: "But I have this against you, that you have left your first love." In other words: "You don't love me as much as you used to."

Jesus is all about passion. They might not have lost their zeal for Him, but it's not what it used to be. And that cuts right to the heart of Jesus. That's why He reprimands them: "Come on, my dear people, return to your first love. Return to your passionate love for me. Everything else I will give to you."

In the Netherlands we have a saying that goes: "First the job, then the girl," but in God's Kingdom, it is exactly the other way around. Our passion for Jesus should supersede everything else. Don't let your passion be diminished by disappointment in people, by all your hard work for His Kingdom or by painful circumstances. Don't ever let that happen. If you notice that your original love is dwindling, you need to drastically change your lifestyle. Make a radical U-turn. Who would want to be a Christian without a passion for Christ? It is this passion that will get a church moving again even if it has ground to a halt.

A LETTER OVERFLOWING WITH PASSION

I love to talk about my greatest passion: Jesus. He's the love of my life and He has convinced me that everything I do and say must be permeated with His passion for this world. The passion of Jesus in us will change people. A little while ago, I received a letter that touched me deeply. This letter shows how powerful the passion of Jesus is:

Dear Wilkin,

Some time ago we brought a friend of ours (Fred) to a meeting where you spoke about being passionate about Jesus and about His love. Fred had a terrible childhood: he was abused and spent time in special homes and foster families. He had ADHD and moved out on his own at a young age. He had no proper schooling and owing to his lack of discipline he was unable to find a job. He started using a lot of drugs and began drinking. He drove everyone crazy. He couldn't maintain relationships. He never stuck to any agreements and wherever he was, his presence was about 100% clear. Simply being in contact with Fred was a very intense business. He was a thief, and active mostly at night. He owned nothing and had huge debts because of his drug habit. He hated his father and wanted to murder him. We met Fred when he was ten; he used to come to our house. Fred loved being in our home. Wilbert, my eldest brother, stayed in touch with him as we grew up. Last year, in September, we took him to a healing crusade. It was there that he gave his heart to Jesus. He was happy, but soon backslid into his former habits. He lived alone and had no real friends (except for the wrong kind). We kept in touch.

In January we took Fred to the meeting I mentioned at the beginning of this letter. Your message on being passionate about Jesus and receiving His passion in return really touched him deeply. Fred cried his eyes out. God touched his heart there and then.

From that day forward, things moved fast. 'Coincidentally', he met a girl in his apartment building who attended a church. She and her friends encouraged him to read the Bible, pray, surrender his life to God, live a holy life and get rid of his sin. The change was complete: he asked people to forgive him and forgave those who had hurt him. He returned stolen bikes to their rightful owners and completely quit drugs, smoking and drinking. He stopped being a skinhead. He even got a job. He paid off his debts. He started witnessing to young people and shared in our prayer group. He started to call his second father 'Daddy'. He read his Bible until it nearly fell apart. He got rid of his TV. He became a calm and wise person. He told his family, friends and acquaintances about the love of Jesus.

While he was busy with all these things he died, quite suddenly. Thankfully, one of his friends from church was there, so he didn't die alone. Just the Sunday before his passing he had been so upset about the division between the churches. The previous Saturday evening, he had encouraged the teenagers and on Monday evening he had said that he really wanted to meet Jesus and speak to Him. On Thursday he had been planning to join us in street evangelism. He wanted to tell everyone about the love of Jesus for sinners like him. 'A grain of wheat that falls on the ground will never be more than one grain unless it dies. But if it dies, it will produce lots of wheat.'

We placed the following obituary:

'Praise the Lord, Fred K. has gone home.

A few weeks ago Jesus captured his heart. The result was an overwhelming passion for his Savior and Father. Everyone had to hear; he was not ashamed (Romans 1:16a). Now his greatest wish has been fulfilled: on April the 8th he went to meet his Father for the first time.

On behalf of all your brothers and sisters, one in Christ.'

This obituary was placed in both a local and a national newspaper, along with the date and location of the memorial service and the funeral. Through death, new life arose. The result was that countless people contacted the newspaper editors. A journalist came to the funeral and wrote an article about it. Journalists were interviewing the people who lived in Fred's apartment building. The Dutch Reformed church and the Pentecostal church organized the farewell service together. The church hall was packed and the meeting was full of the gospel and of Christian testimonies. Someone was saved during the funeral service and prayed that morning for the first time. A number of young people wanted to talk afterwards, and God touched many people. Basically, the death of Fred became like a seed planted in fertile soil. The results were salvation and unity, a call to a holy lifestyle and surrender to God. Praise the Lord.

Bert and Mary

Identifying with Jesus

To me, Jesus gets more intriguing all the time. I read the stories about Him again and again, each time in a different Bible translation. I want to learn more from Him. I want to know everything about Him. My hunger for Him cannot be satisfied. I want to identify with Him. I want to think as He thinks, love as He loves, feel as He feels, believe what He believes. When I read the things that have been written about Him, I try to picture how He might have looked at people, touched them, spoken to them. I want to have this picture of Him imprinted on my mind. I want to know Him, follow Him, become like Him: Jesus, the Man without Sin.

That is the heart of the gospel and it fascinates me, even though I know that none of us can fully understand His sinlessness because Jesus had a different nature from ours.

Our Sinful Nature

The word of God says that we have a sinful nature. The Bible calls this our "flesh,"[7] or our "old man."[8] It is clear what our sinful nature produces: adultery, sexual immorality, uncleanness, lustfulness, idolatry, sorcery, hatred, strife, jealousies, outbursts of anger, rivalries, divisions, heresies, envy, murder, drunkenness, orgies, and things like these.[9]

Nothing in the world is as underestimated as the destructive power of sin. Always and in every situation, sin is destructive. It ruins so many things. It spoils our relationship with God and our relationships with others. Isaiah shows us what sin does to our relationship with God:

> Don't think that the Lord is too weak to save you or too deaf to hear your call for help! It is because of your sins that he doesn't hear you. It is your sins that separate you from God when you try to worship him. (Isaiah 59:1–2, GNB)

Sin brings division; it throws up a barrier between God and humankind. The result is that we are unable to see the hand of God in our lives or to hear His voice. On the other hand, God cannot reach us either. The Bible book of Lamentations states this very clearly:

We have transgressed and have rebelled; you have not pardoned (...). You have covered yourself with a cloud, so that no prayer can pass through. (Lamentations 3:42, 44, WEB)

Because of our sins, God is hidden from us; we cannot reach Him. He has covered Himself in a cloud, so that even our prayers cannot reach Him. Many Christians do not realize this: they might complain with regard to their prayers that the heavens seem to be made of brass, but they forget that their own sin may very well be the reason why God does not hear or answer their prayers. Sin is a much bigger problem than most people think. All of human nature has been infected with the sin virus. Some people have such a gentle personality or care for others so selflessly that I might think: "That is such a beautiful person." Yet God says: "There is no one on earth who does what is right all the time and never makes a mistake."[10]

> **All of human nature has been infected with the sin virus.**

The Bible says that through Adam we all have sinned; through him sin has entered the world and death now rules as king in this world:

Sin came into the world through one man, and his sin brought death with it. As a result, death has spread to the whole human race because everyone has sinned. It is true that through the sin of one man death began to rule because of that one man. But how much greater is the result of what was done by the one man, Jesus

Christ! All who receive God's abundant grace and are freely put
right with him will rule in life through Christ. So then, as the one
sin condemned all people, in the same way the one righteous act sets
all people free and gives them life. (Romans 5:12, 17–18, GNB)

Sin has gained such power over us that our human nature has been irrevocably changed into our current sinful nature. We aren't sinners because we have sinned, but we sin because we're sinners. Through our sinful nature, all kinds of sinful passions and desires are expressed.[11]

By sinning we have become slaves to sin.[12] Because of our sinful nature, no good lives within us.[13] Our sinful nature is hostile toward God and refuses to submit to Him.[14] Our sinful nature cannot please God.[15]

I can see this sinful nature expressed in people's almost insatiable hunger for bad news, a desire of which practically all of the media eagerly take advantage. I can see it in the gap between rich and poor, maintained by the greed and selfishness of the so-called "first world," which practices a modern form of slavery by having its products produced for scandalously low wages in the so-called "third-world" countries. The only difference between this form of slavery and that of previous ages is that nowadays we don't ship the slaves from one country to another, but the products. It's a lot easier to cope with, as in this way we are not visually confronted with the unfairness and inhumanity of the practice.

I see the sinful nature in the men and women of Baghdad who plundered their "own" hospitals, museums and schools, et cetera, when the regime of Saddam Hussein fell.

I can recognize the sinful nature in statistics that say that more than forty percent of the Dutch population by their own account cannot stand being told what to do by the law. Statistics do not lie. They also tell us that 50,000 to 80,000 children are abused in our country each year. And that every year fifty to eighty children die in the Netherlands as a result of child abuse. Statistics tell us that every day about 50,000 Dutch people visit a prostitute and that every month twenty percent of Internet users visit erotic sites (each month, at least 47 million sex pages are viewed in the Netherlands). The sex industry in the Netherlands has a 1.6 billion euro turnover each year.

I also discover this same sinful nature in myself, when I come home late at night and am tempted to turn on the TV and surf through the different channels, allowing the filth of the world to invade my spirit.

JESUS' DIVINE NATURE

But Jesus had a divine nature.[16] He was the man without sin. That explains why He, and only He, could remove our sins. Sin had no power over Him. If I'm struggling with a certain sin and cannot seem to free myself from it, I will never to be able to help someone else struggling with the same sin. If, for example, I am living in impurity by watching films I shouldn't watch or looking at women in a way in which I shouldn't, how will I ever be able to help someone else to lead a pure and holy life? This is why before Jesus there was no one on earth who could solve the problem of sin for us.

> **The biggest sacrifice that Jesus made was that He gave up His sinlessness.**

Jesus, the man without sin, was sent by God into this world to set us free from the sinful nature that is cutting us off from God's presence. Jesus has come to set us free from our slavery to sin and our fear of death:

> *Since the children, as He calls them, are people of flesh and blood, Jesus himself became like them and shared their human nature. He did this so that through his death he might destroy the Devil, who has the power over death, and in this way set free those who*

were slaves all their lives because of their fear of death. (Hebrews 2:14–15, GNB)

The biggest sacrifice that Jesus made was that He gave up His sinlessness and identified with our sin.

THE BIRTH OF JESUS:
A MIRACLE OF CREATION

His coming into this world was accompanied by many supernatural events. The prophet Isaiah had prophesied 700 years earlier that the Messiah would be born of a virgin:

But the Lord will still give you proof. A virgin is pregnant; she will have a son and will name him Immanuel. (Isaiah 7:14, CEV)

The world cannot understand this. And sometimes I think that many Christians also fail to understand it. Sin has penetrated our humanity, our thinking, our feelings, our senses, our emotions and our bodies so deeply that we say, a man without sin? Impossible. Jesus, born of a virgin? Impossible. Of course, in the natural world it is impossible. But nothing is impossible for God. We need to start thinking in an entirely different way. You see, Jesus could never have been born of a natural man and a natural woman, or their sinful nature would have entered into Him. God had to work a miracle. From the moment of conception, when the Holy Spirit came upon Mary and God performed a miracle of creation in her womb, the heart of God was beating in this baby. Jesus did not inherit genetic material from Joseph, but from God. He received the characteristics and the divine nature of His Father in heaven. It was Joseph's calling to be a good adoptive father to Him, and I know from personal experience what a rich blessing this can be. The birth of Jesus is a great wonder. Nothing like this had happened on earth since Adam and Eve. A human being, without sin from the very start. An unbelievable story. But then, Jesus' entire life is a series of unbelievable wonders.

AN UNBELIEVABLE STORY

At times I think that God purposely made His plan of salvation seem so foolish. Whichever way you look at it, He certainly didn't try very hard to make it all look plausible. He chose an insignificant girl of about sixteen years old to be the mother of Jesus. A girl of no importance. She did not conceive in a natural way; she conceived because she was touched by the power of the Holy Spirit. God did not make things easy for Mary. Who would ever believe her? How was she ever going to tell Joseph? And even if he believed her, Jesus would be surrounded for his entire life by gossip and rumors: "Jesus is an illegitimate child!"

How do I see the birth of Jesus? He was born in a lowly animal shelter in a poverty-stricken village in a country oppressed by a cruel occupying force. No one would even have taken any notice of his arrival if it hadn't been for the fact that God sent a heavenly army of angels to protect the birth of His Son and to proclaim the news. But how does the Great Director go about it? He sends His angels to a group of shepherds, at that time the scum of the earth. Hardly anyone would believe their story. Men like them weren't even recognized as witnesses in the Jewish court of law. Is this how to convince the world? Is this the way to save the world? Who would believe a story like this? The "foolish" story of Jesus' birth, life, crucifixion and resurrection can only have been thought up by God. If a human had been the author, all the unbelievable elements would have been left out to make the story seem more credible. But the Bible tells us something else:

God was wise and decided not to let the people of this world use their wisdom to learn about him. Instead, God chose to save only those who believe the foolish message we preach. Jews ask for mira-

cles, and Greeks want something that sounds wise. But we preach that Christ was nailed to a cross. Most Jews have problems with this, and most Gentiles think it is foolish. Our message is God's power and wisdom for the Jews and the Greeks that he has chosen. Even when God is foolish, he is wiser than everyone else, and even when God is weak, he is stronger than everyone else. (1 Corinthians 1:21–25, CEV)

We can hardly believe that there was a person who lived on this earth without ever having sinned. We cannot imagine what it's like not to be infected by sin, because we simply do not know what it is like to live without sin. Our lives are so influenced by the power of sin. We don't have a clue how destructive it really is. Sin has so much destructive power that our entire human nature has been infected by it. That's why the life of Jesus is a big mystery to us. That's why to many people, even some Christians, Jesus has become a mythical, illusory figure.

How Others Viewed Jesus

How did the men and women who met Jesus in real life view Him?

- Peter, who spent more than three years with Jesus and who was a witness to the sufferings of Christ,[17] testified to the fact that Jesus never sinned; neither was deceit found in His mouth.[18]

- John, the apostle whom Jesus loved, writes: "You know that Christ appeared in order to take away sins, and that there is no sin in him."[19]

- Even the wife of Pilate got involved in Jesus' trial by sending her husband the following message: "Have nothing to do with that innocent man, because in a dream last night I suffered much on account of him."[20] She calls Him dikaios, which means "righteous and without blame."

- Three times Pilate goes back to the religious leaders and the crowd to ask them what Jesus has done wrong. Three times they adapt their accusation. Three times he says: "I see no evil in him; this man is innocent." Finally, he gives in to the demands of the Jewish religious leaders, because his own position is in danger, and hands Jesus over to be crucified. But not without first publicly washing his hands in a show of innocence. He says: "You brought this man to me and said that he was misleading the people. Now, I have examined him here in your presence, and I have not found him guilty of any of the crimes you accuse him of."[21]

- Even Judas, who betrayed Him and handed Him over, sees that Jesus is a man without sin. Before he hangs himself he says, in utter despair: "I have sinned by betraying an innocent man to death!"[22]

- And when the Roman centurion sees what happens at the Cross, he glorifies God and says: "Certainly this was a righteous man." He uses the same word the wife of Pilate used: a righteous man, without blame.[23]

- Jesus Himself at one point says to the religious leaders: "Which one of you can prove that I am guilty of sin?"[24]

Throughout the entire Bible, this is the message about Jesus Christ. It is the heart of the gospel. This is where the message of the Cross starts: Jesus can completely sympathize with all of our weaknesses. He has been through all the trials we go through. Only He never sinned.[25] He was holy, guiltless, undefiled.[26]

A Character Analysis

I often try to imagine how Jesus lived. What does someone who has never sinned look like? What is His character like? I once tried to make a character analysis of Jesus, until I discovered that the Bible itself already gives us a very precise one. When Paul tells the church in Galatia what our sinful nature brings forth,[27] he does not refrain from telling us what the fruit of the Spirit looks like: in other words, the character of Jesus (His divine nature). Jesus was full of love, joy, peace, patience, kindness, goodness, faithfulness, humility and self-control.[28] As I study the life of Jesus, I discover again and again that He had a pure soul, a clean spirit and an untainted body.

JESUS HAD A PURE SOUL

They say the eyes are the windows of the soul. So what would you see if you looked into the eyes of Jesus? What is it like to be a man without sin? The soul is the throne of our emotions, our will and our mind. Our emotions often do battle with our mind in order to take our will captive. My feelings sometimes say: "Just act normal and don't draw attention to yourself." And my mind says: "What will people say if you do this or that?" Sometimes there is a battle raging in my soul that paralyzes my will. Some people are more emotional, others are more rational. As for Jesus, I've discovered that He always placed all of his emotions and thoughts under the discipline of the Holy Spirit. In all of his emotions, I see a purity that transcends my imagination. Jesus could be filled with joy in the Holy Spirit,[29] but He could also be troubled or angry.[30] He was moved with compassion for the people and could be so touched by the Holy Spirit that He cried for them.[31] Fear was another emotion Jesus experienced. In the garden of Gethsemane, He was deeply troubled about what was going to happen to Him.[32] But, through all these emotional experiences, Jesus submitted His will to that of His Father:

> *Father, if you are willing, remove this cup from me. Nevertheless, not my will, but yours, be done.* (Luke 22:42, WEB)

> *My food is to do the will of him who sent me, and to accomplish his work.* (John 4:34, WEB)

Jesus did not allow Himself to be led by His emotions. His soul was subject to His spirit, which was connected to the Spirit of His Father. His mind, His wisdom and His insight surprised many. It was said about His childhood:

> *The child was growing, and was becoming strong in spirit, being filled with wisdom, and the grace of God was upon him.* (Luke 2:40, WEB)

As a twelve-year-old boy, He sat among the teachers in the temple and listened to them and asked them questions. Everyone who heard Him was amazed at His understanding and His answers.[33] Many times, the religious leaders tried to trap Him with trick questions. Each time, Jesus had an unexpected answer that amazed His listeners; the people were deeply impressed by Him.[34] Jesus was different from us, because His soul was not influenced by sin.

JESUS HAD A CLEAN SPIRIT

Not only did Jesus have a pure soul, but He also had a clean spirit, untainted by sin.

The human spirit was created to seek contact with God, who is Spirit. God's Spirit does not focus initially on my soul (my feelings and mind), but on my spirit. His Spirit wants to connect with my human spirit,[35] so that in my spirit I will react to what He wants me to do. God wants us to be sensitive in our spirits to hear His voice, to know His will and to have an intimate relationship with Him. Of course, my soul will also react to the personal voice of God when He addresses my spirit. When, for example, the Holy Spirit convicts me of sin, my soul will not be too pleased, because it means I will have to confess this sin to others[36]—an activity my soul does not enjoy at all.

I remember the day when God's Spirit told me to go to someone and ask forgiveness for the fact that I had hated him for something that had happened in the past between him and my wife, before I knew her. It was as if a bomb had just exploded in my soul. Everything in me revolted. My mind reasoned that I was not the guilty party; he was. I wasn't the one who should be asking for forgiveness; he was. I reacted emotionally; my feelings rebelled. I became confused. There was a battle raging inside me, in which my soul finally gained control: I did not contact the man in question. Weeks passed without any action on my part. But God never gives up. God spoke to me again, this time through an unknown missionary who was on furlough in the Netherlands and attended our Sunday service. In the middle of the service, he stood up from his seat and shared "a word from the Lord," in which he said there was someone to whom God had spoken, telling him to go to another person, which he had not yet done. That morning God spoke to me again: "Go!" It really scared me. The prophecy was so accurate, I was afraid my name would be called out. However, I still didn't dare to take the step and make an appointment by phone. I was afraid of the confrontation, but most of all I was afraid of facing up to the thoughts and feelings inside myself, which I knew were not very nice. I kept justifying these feelings and my behavior until finally, God, who was very patient with me, spoke to me for a third time. This time I knew I had no choice but to obey. In my spirit, I knew that obeying Him would bring healing to my soul. So I picked up the phone, praying that the other guy wouldn't be home (we really do some strange things at times), yet at the same time I knew that God had other things in mind. In the end, I made an appointment with the man and went to see him. The only thing I can recall of our conversation was that I drank coffee (which I never do) and that—to his utter astonishment—I asked him to forgive me for the hateful thoughts and feelings I'd had toward him. I can't remember anything else; I must have been very nervous. But I did it. A huge weight was lifted from my shoulders. I felt much lighter and on the inside it felt as if I had more space. A few weeks later, the man walked into a Sunday-morning service. He gave his life to the Lord and some time later I had the privilege of baptizing him myself.

My will should not be directed by my feelings or my mind, but by my spirit, which is connected to the Spirit of God. The spiritual life of many Christians is usually played out in the realm of the soul. They complain about the length of the church service, the "noise" the children make, the type of music or the speaker's clothing or choice of words. They cannot "worship" if the music is too loud or not loud enough, and when someone lovingly corrects them they mutter that "there is no more love in the church," or, even worse, they say that "the Holy Spirit is no longer present in the church." These people come to church with their soul in control; they're led by what goes on inside their soul or their mind. And if things don't go the way they want them to, their spiritual thermometer drops from "hot" to "frosty."

Jesus, on the other hand, stayed tuned to the Father in everything through His Spirit. He said:

> *God is spirit, and those who worship Him must worship in spirit and truth.* (John 4:24, WEB)

JESUS HAD A CLEAN CONSCIENCE

My conscience is embedded in my spirit. It gives me the ability to discern good from evil. The Greek word for conscience *(suneidesis)* is derived from the verb *suneido*, which means "to understand or become aware of something with another, and to be conscious or (clandestinely) informed of." My conscience is actually a "knowing with another." Now we understand how Paul can say: "God's Spirit joins himself to our spirits to declare that we are God's children,"[37] and what Jesus meant when He said:

The Son can do nothing on his own; he does only what he sees his Father doing. What the Father does, the Son also does. (John 5:19, GNB)

Our conscience has been infected, and dulled, by sin. Sin silences the voice of God in our lives. The Bible says that our conscience has been seared by sin.[38] Sin makes it numb and insensitive. The result is that our discernment becomes blurred and we call good evil and evil good. The prophet Isaiah said:

You are doomed. You call evil good and call good evil. You turn darkness into light and light into darkness. You make what is bitter sweet, and what is sweet you make bitter. (Isaiah 5:20, GNB)

Jesus' conscience, however, was completely clean. It was not influenced by sin. That's why He was able to resist Satan's temptations at the beginning of His ministry. He recognized the snares of the evil one. That's why Jesus was able to say, just a short while before He died, that "the ruler of this world is coming. He has no power over me."[39] Jesus' discernment was undamaged. He knew what really mattered and saw what others did not see. This was because His senses were tuned in to the Spirit of God. That's why the Holy Spirit could work through Him so powerfully.

JESUS HAD AN UNTAINTED BODY

All of Jesus' senses were pure and focused solely on God. Not only that, but his senses also functioned under the discipline of the Holy Spirit. He saw in the Spirit, heard, felt, tasted and smelled in the Spirit. He saw what was in the hearts of people;[40] He saw and heard the Father speak to Him in the Spirit.[41] He could sometimes feel the power of God leave His body,[42] and could sense whether or not someone's heart attitude was pure.[43] He could smell whether someone exuded the fragrance of life or the stench of death.[44]

Jesus, the man without sin, could look at a woman without desiring her. In His presence, people felt completely accepted, loved, safe and protected. He never sent anyone away with the message: "There is no healing, salvation or freedom for you." He could take a leper, whom everyone avoided, and hold him in His arms. He accepted the outcasts. Matthew, the tax collector who was despised by everybody because he collaborated with the enemy, was chosen out of hundreds of potential disciples to follow Him. Matthew, the man everyone loved to hate, was loved by the Man without Sin. Jesus also chose Simon the Zealot, a revolutionary who had taken up the sword to free Palestine from the Romans by means of violence. Not everyone was pleased about this. But Jesus said to him: "Simon, you belong to me. Learn from me, for I am gentle and humble in spirit." Jesus even chose Judas Iscariot as one of His disciples, even though He knew from the start that eventually he would betray Him.[45]

How do I see Jesus? Is He a good man, a prophet, a teacher? Or is He the Son of God, the Man without Sin, who was so pure, so flawless, that when one of His disciples asked Him to show them God the Father, Jesus said to him:

> *Have I been with you such a long time, and do you not know me, Philip? He who has seen me has seen the Father. How do you say, "Show us the Father?"* (John 14:9, WEB)

WHY DOES GOD NOT INTERVENE?

Our sinful nature cannot be changed or transformed into the divine nature of Jesus. There is just no way this could happen. God knows better than anyone else that we cannot change our sinful nature. Not by reading the Bible, nor by fasting and praying. Even the Holy Spirit cannot change our sinful nature. In God's eyes, our sinful nature is hopeless, useless and irreparable.

I have often heard people ask: "Why doesn't God just intervene?" But how should He intervene? And, more importantly, where would you want the intervention to stop? Should God have intervened the moment Adolf Hitler decided to eradicate all the Jews in his empire? After all, the death of that one man could have saved millions of lives. Should God intervene when a "father" is about to molest his daughter? Should God intervene when someone is thinking about adultery? Who decides where God should start, or stop, intervening? Maybe the answer is too confronting. Let's face it, if God were to intervene on the basis of His own values and standards, none of us would be alive.

The fact that God does not intervene—at least not in the way we want Him to—illustrates His mercy and love. In the parable of the prodigal son it becomes clear that God loves us so intensely that He would never force us to stay with Him. God gave us the freedom to live our own lives because He loved us, even though He felt the pain this would cause both Himself and us. God loves mankind so much that He would never force his love on us.

But the deeper truth is that God has intervened, in a way none of us would have expected. The wonder of the Cross is that God decided to intervene supernaturally in human affairs. In order to understand this, we must focus intently on the last eighteen hours of the life of Jesus of Nazareth.

Father in heaven,

I want to fix my eye on Jesus, who bore the pain and stigma of the Cross. Open my eyes, open my mind, so that I will see and understand what You have done for me. Open my eyes to see what happened in the last eighteen hours before Jesus died, so I will understand the message of the Cross and, above all, so that the wonder of the Cross may become reality in my life.

Amen.

THE SEVEN WONDERS OF THE CROSS

You have come ... to the sprinkled blood
that speaks a better word than the blood of Abel.

(Hebrews 12:24, NIV)

CHAPTER 2

According to historians, Jesus was crucified on the fourteenth day of the month of Nisan in the year 3793 of the Jewish calendar. In our calendar, this would be April 7th, 30 AD. The time between His visit to the garden of Gethsemane and His crucifixion on the hill called Golgotha was exactly eighteen hours. The four evangelists, Matthew, Mark, Luke and John, have accurately recorded what happened in those final eighteen hours. They wrote down the names of all those involved, the times at which everything took place and the conversations that occurred in the Sanhedrin, the Jewish Council, as well as in the Pretorium, the headquarters of the Roman prefect, Pontius Pilate.

THE DIRECTOR OF GOLGOTHA

It is important that we see how God left nothing to chance in the last eighteen hours before the death of Jesus. The Bible teaches us that God Himself was the director of all that occurred at Golgotha. Every Jewish deed and every Roman act was desired and inspired by Him. Peter makes it clear that everything that happened in the last eighteen hours before the death of Jesus was in accordance with God's will and that He had determined it would happen ahead of time:

> *People of Israel, listen! God publicly endorsed Jesus the Nazarene by doing powerful miracles, wonders, and signs through Him, as you well know. But God knew what would happen, and his pre-arranged plan was carried out when Jesus was betrayed. With the help of lawless Gentiles, you nailed him to a cross and killed him.* (Acts 2:22–23, NLT)

> *For indeed Herod and Pontius Pilate met together in this city with the Gentiles and the people of Israel against Jesus, your holy Servant, whom you made Messiah. They gathered to do everything that you by your power and will had already decided would happen.* (Acts 4:27–28, GNB)

Peter and the apostles saw God's own "power and will" in the last eighteen hours of the life of Jesus. Without realizing it, the Jewish and Roman leaders fulfilled God's plan with their verdict.

YOM KIPPUR

To understand the events that took place in the last eighteen hours before the death of Jesus, we must first understand what happened on Yom Kippur, or the Day of Atonement.[46] In the coming chapters we will discover that there are great similarities between the events on the Day of Atonement and the last eighteen hours before Jesus died on a wooden cross. On the Great Day of Atonement, there was a special ceremony. It was only on this day that the high priest was allowed to enter into the Holy of Holies. After he had been through all kinds of cleansing rituals, the high priest then filled his incense bowl with glowing coals from the altar. On these coals he was to lay two handfuls of finely ground incense. Then he would carry the incense into the Holy of Holies, so that the smoke would all but obscure the Ark of the Covenant from view. The Ark of the Covenant was a chest made of acacia wood and completely overlaid in gold. The chest contained among other things the two stone tablets with the Ten Commandments engraved on them. On the chest there was a golden lid—the Mercy Seat—with two angels made of pure gold.[47] It was the place where God would speak to Moses, as a friend, face to face.[48] Dressed in plain linen, the high priest would take the blood from the sacrificial animal into the Holy of Holies to make atonement for all the sins the people had unwittingly committed.[49] The high priest would dip his fingers in the blood and sprinkle it seven times on the Mercy Seat and then seven times on the earthen floor (Leviticus 16). The golden Mercy Seat would be sprinkled with blood as a sign or as evidence for heaven that the yearly sacrifice for atonement had been made. But why did the earth also need to be sprinkled seven times with the blood?

The answer is that the sprinkling of the earth was a prophetic act pointing to the last eighteen hours before the death of Jesus. Just as the high priest was commanded to sprinkle the earth seven times with the blood of the sacrificial animal on the Day of Atonement, in the same way the blood of Jesus drenched the earth seven times on Good Friday. The sevenfold sprinkling in the temple was a prefiguration of the seven times that Jesus would bleed for us in the last eighteen hours before His death.[50]

Adam—Adamah

In Genesis, we read that God formed Adam from the earth. There is a linguistic connection between the Hebrew words *adam* (man) and *adamah*, which means "red-brown earth." We read how God created Adam from the dust of the earth:

Yahweh God formed man (adam) from the dust of the ground (ad-amah), and breathed into his nostrils the breath of life; and man became a living soul. (Genesis 2:7, WEB)

We are all children of Adam. We too have been created from dust and will return to dust.[51] Through the fall of Adam, sin entered the world and so has completely penetrated our *adamah*—our human nature.

Sin came into the world through one man, and his sin brought death with it. As a result, death has spread to the whole human race because everyone has sinned. (Romans 5:12, GNB)

The Bible teaches us that, after the fall, sin and death became the masters of mankind. Our original God-given nature degenerated into our current sinful nature.

But they have all turned away; they are all equally bad. Not one of them does what is right, not a single one. (Psalm 53:3, GNB; see also Psalm 14:3 and Philippians 2:15)

Sin has penetrated our lives and started to rule over our thoughts, our feelings and our will. Whether we like it or not, we are addicted to and have become bound by sin. All this is the result of the fall of man. Adam and Eve could pass on natural life after the fall, but not spiritual life. All of their offspring were alive physically, but born spiritually dead. This means that God could no longer maintain a personal relationship with them. And so each of us was born as a creation of God, but not as a child of God. A miracle is needed for this: the wonder of the Cross!

JESUS BLED SEVEN TIMES

The prophets and the four writers of the Gospels tell us that Jesus bled seven times for us in total. Therefore, the seven times that He bled did not occur by accident. Each occasion was a prophetic act, which had been prophesied many hundreds of years before, wanted and inspired by God and carried out by sinful Roman soldiers. God wants to make clear to us what the wonder of the Cross means for us through these prophetic acts.

In the Bible, the number seven is connected with the person and work of the Holy Spirit. In a vision on Patmos, John saw seven torches, which are symbolic of the Holy Spirit, and the seven-pronged lamp stand in the temple points to God's presence in our midst by means of the Holy Spirit.[52] When we speak of the *wonder* of the Cross, then, we mean that the Holy Spirit wants to work out supernaturally in our lives what Jesus achieved for us in His last eighteen hours of earthly life. Based on our faith in the blood of the Lord Jesus (in what He has done for us), the Holy Spirit can work the seven wonders of the Cross in our lives.

The number seven is also, biblically speaking, the number of fullness, and always means that something is complete and perfect. The seven wonders of the Cross lead us to Jesus, who through suffering brought about the perfect sacrifice to reconcile us completely with God. That is why the Bible says that we can come to Jesus and the sprinkled blood:

> *You have come to the sprinkled blood that speaks a better word than the blood of Abel.* (Hebrews 12:24, NIV)

"The sprinkled blood" points to the seven times in which the blood of Jesus was sprinkled on the earth. The blood of Abel cried out for vengeance, but the blood of Jesus speaks of forgiveness and reconciliation. Peter describes God's overflowing mercy when he says that we are chosen by God to be sprinkled with the blood of the Lord Jesus:

> *God the Father decided to choose you as his people, and his Spirit has made you holy. You have obeyed Jesus Christ and are sprinkled with his blood. I pray that God will be kind to you and will keep on giving you peace!* (1 Peter 1:2, CEV)

God invites us to be sprinkled with the blood of the Lord Jesus! This is not a superstitious ritual; nor are we able or allowed to use "the blood of the Lord Jesus" as some kind of magical formula. Only by believing that Jesus gave His blood for us can we be forgiven, cleansed, saved, healed, set free and reconciled with God so that we may receive a whole new life in Christ. It is interesting to know that the Hebrew word for blood is *dam*. The blood *(dam)* of the Lord Jesus wants to soak our *adamah* seven times over, so that we can receive the sevenfold wonder of the Cross. Through the wonder of the Cross God changes us from children of Adam into children of God and brothers and sisters of Jesus!

The following overview shows clearly how often, where and why Jesus' blood flowed for us:

Jesus bled seven times for us:	The seven wonders of the Cross:
1. Jesus sweat drops of blood in the garden of Gethsemane: *Being in agony He prayed more earnestly. His sweat became like great drops of blood falling down on the ground.* (Luke 22:44 WEB)	The wonder of **forgiveness**
2. Jesus was abused in the house of the High Priest: *Then they spit in his face and beat Him with their fists, and some slapped Him.* (Matthew 26:67 WEB) "Fists" can also be translated as "rod." Micah said prophetically: *They will strike the judge of Israel with a rod on the cheek.* (Micah 5:1 WEB)	The wonder of **salvation**
3. Jesus was abused during the interrogation: *I gave my back to the strikers, and my cheeks to those who plucked off the hair* (Isaiah 50:6 WEB)	The wonder of **the cleansing**
4. Jesus was whipped by Pilates soldiers: *Then Pilate set Barabbas free for them; and after he had Jesus whipped, he handed Him over to be crucified.* (Matthew 27:26 GNB)	The wonder of **healing**
5. Jesus was crowned with a crown of thorns: *Then they made a crown out of thorny branches and placed it on his head (...) They spat on Him, and took the stick and hit Him over the head.* (Matthew 27:29–30 GNB)	The wonder of **deliverance**
6. The hands and feet of Jesus were pierced when He was crucified: *They nailed Jesus to a cross and gambled to see who would get his clothes.* (Mark 15:24 CEV)	The wonder of **reconciliation**
7. A soldier stuck a spear in his side: *One of the soldiers stuck his spear into Jesus' side, and blood and water came out.* (John 19:34 CEV)	The wonder of **being born again**

At each moment when the blood of Jesus flows, God is pointing to one of the seven wonders of the Cross, which can take place in our lives and together form one great wonder of God's love. Let me take you to each moment in the story of suffering. Let's try to look behind the scenes, both in the natural and in the supernatural realm, to discover what the suffering, death and resurrection of Jesus mean for us. The first time Jesus bled was in the garden of Gethsemane.

Father in heaven,

What I know is only in part and what I would like to say comes out all wrong sometimes. Thank you that You love me. Your unfailing love knows no limits. Your love will never come to an end. Thank You that You have so much love for the world that You gave your only Son. I want to believe that You sent Your Son to the world not to judge, but to save it from ruin, so that whoever believes in Him will not die but have everlasting life. I want to fully know Jesus fully, as He knows me fully. Will You reveal to me the seven wonders of the Cross, so that I might live in Your presence each day?

Amen.

Drops of Blood in Gethsemane

But we do see Jesus, who for a little while was made lower than the angels, so that through God's grace he should die for everyone. We see him now crowned with glory and honor because of the death he suffered.

(Hebrews 2:9, GNB)

Chapter 3

Every evening throughout the last week before His death, Jesus goes to the garden of Gethsemane to pray: *"Jesus spent those days teaching in the Temple, and when evening came, He would go out and spend the night on the Mount of Olives."*[53] The last night is no different: after He and His disciples have finished the Passover meal, at about 9 p.m., their small company walks eastward in the direction of the Mount of Olives. There are eleven disciples with Jesus. Judas, the man from Iscariot, has left the upper room earlier to betray his master.

It is no surprise to the disciples that they are going to the garden of Gethsemane. It is a special place. From this point one can look out over the whole city. Even in the dark one can still see the great temple of Solomon and the fort of Antonia, where the Roman governor Pontius Pilate resides. In the days of old, this Mount of Olives was a place of prayer.[54] It is also the place where Ezekiel saw the *Shekinah* of God, the visible presence of God, as it rested cloud-like on the Mount of Olives.[55]

Gethsemane is an olive orchard with an olive press. Olive trees have many branches, which provide shade during the day and shelter at night. The garden is thus an ideal place for Jesus to retreat to and pray, thereby preparing Himself for what lies ahead. Gethsemane means "olive press," a place in which olives are crushed until they burst and the red fluid flows out. It is in this place that the most dramatic struggle in world history is about to take place.

"MY SOUL IS EXCEEDINGLY SORROWFUL, EVEN TO DEATH"

On arrival in Gethsemane, Jesus becomes "greatly troubled and distressed." He says to His disciples: "My soul is exceedingly sorrowful, even to death. Stay here, and watch."[56] Luke says that Jesus "was in agony."[57]

He has experienced this before. That same week, just a few days earlier, He stood in the temple square, surrounded by people celebrating. The place was teeming with sacrificial animals. They had come from all over—even from other countries—to celebrate the Passover in Jerusalem and to sacrifice their paschal lambs. Many had brought their own lambs for slaughtering in one of the many places designated for this purpose throughout the city. During Passover Jerusalem became one big slaughterhouse. The air was rank with the smell of the blood of slaughtered animals. And, as He stood there, Jesus knew that in a few days' time He would give His own life voluntarily: the Lamb of God that was to take away the sins of the world. He knew what He was facing. While the people pressed in around Him, He said:

Now my heart is troubled—and what shall I say? Shall I say: "Father, do not let this hour come upon me?" But that is why I came— so that I might go through this hour of suffering. Father, bring glory to your name! (John 12:27–28, GNB)

The Greek verb that John uses to explain how Jesus felt ("my heart is troubled"), is *tarasso*, which means "to stir up" in the sense of "becoming agitated and fearful," but it also refers to "great trouble and disturbance." Jesus experienced the powers of hell amassing themselves to deal what they thought would be a lethal blow to the Son of God. At this crucial point a voice sounded from heaven. Some thought it was thunder; others believed an angel was speaking to Him. But it was the voice of God that spoke: "I have brought glory to it, and I will do so again" (verse 28)!

Now He is in the garden. Once again a terrible fear is flooding His senses, only this time its grip is even stronger than before. He takes Peter, James and John with Him into the garden; the others stay behind. Just a stone's throw away from the others, Jesus drops to His knees and starts to cry out to God. He begins to wrestle. The disciples do not know what is happening. They do not understand what is being played out before their eyes on this night in the garden of Gethsemane. They have no idea what Jesus is going through. For all they know, they're just spending another night with Jesus on the Mount of Olives. Like men satisfied after a good meal, they fall asleep one by one. Thus deprived of human support, Jesus becomes very troubled. The battle is so severe that "his sweat became like great drops of blood falling down on the ground."[58]

HEMATIDROSIS

Jesus' battle in the garden of Gethsemane is so intense that the blood vessels in His sweat glands rupture and blood comes out, falling to the ground in big red drops. It is a very rare condition, but this phenomenon of "sweating blood" is medically known as *hematidrosis*. There is a network of blood vessels around the sweat

What caused Jesus to suffer such extreme anxiety that He began to sweat blood?

glands, and when a person is under great emotional stress these vessels contract. As the extreme emotions subside, the blood vessels then expand to the point of bursting, allowing blood to flow into the sweat glands. If these glands then produce a lot of sweat, they propel the blood to the surface, so that drops of sweat mix with the blood. The question is not whether or not Jesus could actually have sweated blood. The real question is this: what caused Jesus to suffer such extreme anxiety that He did in fact begin to sweat blood?

THE CUP OF GOD'S WRATH

Jesus is fully aware of the horrific physical pain that awaits Him, but that is not what causes Him such distress. He is not asking His Father to spare Him from dying on the Cross. Jesus is not begging the Father to take away the Cross, but "the cup":

Father, if you are willing, remove this cup from me. Nevertheless, not my will, but yours, be done. (Luke 22:42, WEB)

What cup is Jesus talking about? What is He dreading so much that His soul is overwhelmed with deadly distress? The answer to this question can be found in the prophets of the Old Testament. Jeremiah speaks of "the cup of God's wrath," which has been filled to the brim by the sins of the nations. The people must drink this cup themselves, as it is filled with their own sins. The result of drinking this cup is that they will be abandoned, hated and accursed from that moment on. This cup, meant for the nations, was to be presented to Jesus:

The Lord, the God of Israel, said to me, "Here is a wine cup filled with my anger. Take it to all the nations to whom I send you, and make them drink from it. When they drink from it, they will stagger and go out of their minds because of the war I am sending against them." So I took the cup from the Lord's hand, gave it to all the nations to whom the Lord had sent me, and made them drink from it. Jerusalem and all the towns of Judah, together with its kings and leaders, were made to drink from it, so that they would become a desert, a terrible and shocking sight, and so that people would use their name as a curse—as they still do. (Jeremiah 25:15–18, GNB)

A priest once said to me that his sins did not require anyone's death; he was aware of his responsibility and would gladly be held accountable. He had no idea that the result of his actions would be eternal death! The cup that Jesus had to drink was filled with our sins and they are our responsibility. Jesus said to the religious leaders and the Pharisees:

How terrible for you, teachers of the Law and Pharisees! You hypocrites! You clean the outside of your cup and plate, while the inside is full of what you have gotten by violence and selfishness. Blind Pharisee! Clean what is inside the cup first, and then the outside will be clean too! (Matthew 23:25–26, GNB)

The cups of life of the Pharisees looked nice and shiny on the outside, but on the inside they were filled with deadly venom! If Jesus hadn't done it for us, we, too, would have had to drink the cup of our lives, filled to the brim with our own sins, and as a result, we would be hated, accursed and abandoned, finally facing eternal death.

Jesus knows He has come into the world specifically for the eighteen hours that lie ahead of Him. The man without sin, whose own cup of life is filled with love, joy, peace, patience, kindness, goodness, faithfulness, humility and self-control,[59] is now about to fill it with adultery, sexual immorality, uncleanness, lustfulness, idolatry, sorcery, hatred, strife, jealousies, outbursts of anger, rivalries, divisions, heresies, envy, murders, drunkenness, orgies and things like these, brought about by our sinful nature.[60]

> **Every sin of the whole world, from Adam straight through to the last one to be born, was concentrated in the one cup, which was to be drunk by Jesus.**

In the olive press of Gethsemane, all of your sins and mine and every perversity the world has ever seen are pressed into one cup: the sins of the serial rapist, of inhuman dictators such as Adolf Hitler, who sent six million Jews to the gas chambers and to death, every cruelty, lust, hatred, every instance of unforgivingness, every murder and every offence—all of these are pressed together in that one cup. All the sins of the whole world, from Adam straight through to the last one to be born, are concentrated in that one cup, which is to be drunk by Jesus.

Jesus Was Made Sin for Us

The man without sin, who is perfect and pure beyond imagining, is confronted in every aspect of His divine nature with every sin of every person who has ever been born or is yet to be born in this world. The burden of sin weighs so heavily on Him that He feels as though His soul is being crushed. The Bible says that God made "him who knew no sin... to be sin on our behalf; so that in him we might become the righteousness of God." Another translation says:

> *Christ was without sin, but for our sake God made him share our sin in order that in union with him we might share the righteousness of God.* (2 Corinthians 5:21, GNB)

In the garden of Gethsemane, Jesus endures what the scape-goat endured on the Great Day of Atonement in the Old Testament. The sins of the whole world are laid upon Him. He voluntarily takes on our sins! This is what John the Baptist prophesied would happen: *"There is the Lamb of God, who takes away the sin of the world!"* (John 1:29, GNB). Just as the high priest laid his hands and with them all the sins of the people of Israel on the goat, God lays all the sins of the whole world on Jesus, the spotless and blameless Lamb of God, who will take away the sins of the world.[61] This is how the 700-year-old prophecy of Isaiah is fulfilled:

> *But the Lord made the punishment fall on him, the punishment all of us deserved.* (Isaiah 53:6h GNB)

And at the very moment Jesus needs God most, an impassible gap opens up between Him and His Father. For sin separates God and man; sin causes God's face to be hidden from us.[62] Jesus is no exception to this rule. God can no longer personally support and encourage Him. This is what Jesus has dreaded most: to be confronted with the sins of the world and thus to be separated from His Father. He who is without sin is to be made sin! The writer of Hebrews says:

> *In his life on earth Jesus made his prayers and requests with loud cries and tears to God, who could save Him from death. Because He was humble and devoted, God heard Him.* (Hebrews 5:7, GNB)

In answer to Jesus' prayer, God sends an angel from heaven to give Him strength (Luke 22:43).

JESUS WRESTLED WITH OUR SIN

How can we ever understand what Jesus went through in those moments? None of us have known a life without sin. We cannot even imagine it. Sin has influenced every part of our humanity: our soul, spirit and body. Our whole human nature has been infected with it. But Jesus was completely holy and pure, in soul, spirit and body! Words cannot convey the battle He fought against our sin, nor can they express the fierceness of His aversion to sin. This explains why Jesus sweated blood in the garden of Gethsemane.

Once our sixteen-year-old son was approached by a peer who confessed his sexual sins to him. He had committed sexual abuse. It was the first time our son had been confronted with a confession like this, and it literally made him sick: he was nauseous, vomiting and lying sick in bed for three days. He couldn't talk to anyone about it, because the perpetrator had made him promise beforehand that he would not tell anyone. Later on it all came out and the young man in question got a professional to help him get his life back on track. How intense is our aversion to sin? Through this experience our son was able to understand a little of what Jesus went through in all His purity in the garden of Gethsemane.

The "Sting of Death"

In the Bible, sin is called the "sting of death."[63] This sting penetrates deeply into Jesus' soul, spirit and body. In all these dimensions of His sinless life, He is confronted with our sin. It goes completely against His own nature! It is as if a film is being shown and He is in the middle of it. It is as if our sins are projected onto His retina. He reacts to this with all His senses and emotions.

> **This "sting of death" penetrates deeply into Jesus' soul, spirit and body. In all these dimensions of his sinless life, He is confronted with our sin.**

Satan plays on Jesus' emotions and senses, just as he did when he tempted Him in the wilderness.[64] When Jesus was hungry, Satan tried to tempt Him into changing a stone into bread. Jesus could almost smell the aroma of freshly baked bread! When He was taken to the roof of the temple, He could hear a voice urging His spirit: "Go ahead, jump! Just show us who you are!" Jesus must have felt the adrenaline pumping through His body in those moments.

In the same way, Jesus is now confronted in all of His being with our sins. He is wrestling with our sins in His body, His soul and His spirit.

A TASTE OF HELL

Jesus' cup of life has been filled with the sins of the whole world and He begins to drink it. Mouthful by mouthful. The Bible says He tasted death![65] All His senses are involved. With each sip, He tastes our emotions. He tastes the bloodthirsty hatred of the murderer as well as the sudden panic of the victim. He smells the innocent blood that has been shed and tastes the sperm violently poured out. He hears the cries of fear and sees the results of the power of sin in all of creation. He, who is one hundred percent pure in all of His emotions, is confronted with emotions totally alien to His being: fear, hatred and a paralyzing sorrow. You could almost say His character is being assassinated.

With each sip, He tastes our emotions. He tastes the bloodthirsty hatred of the murderer as well as the sudden panic of the victim.

What Jesus is going through here is nothing less than a taste of hell. When Jesus says: "My soul is exceedingly sorrowful, even to death,"[66] Mark uses a Greek word for the phrase "even to death" *(thanatos)*, which literally means "the miserable state of the ungodly in hell." This is what Jesus is subjected to in the garden of Gethsemane. All the powers, principalities and rulers of the demonic realm come at Jesus to ridicule, accuse, judge and torture Him. Jesus was in hell before it even existed. What Jesus went through in the garden of Gethsemane will in turn be the experience of those who willfully reject the sacrifice He made.

<h2>The First Wonder of the Cross:</h2>

<h1>The Blood of Jesus Cleanses Me from All My Sins</h1>

The first wonder of the Cross is this: that Jesus drank the cup of my life filled with my sins. On the battlefield, Jesus did what God asked Him to do. He drank my cup to the dregs, so that all of my sins could truly be taken away from me. Jesus has removed the wall of sin separating God and man! God no longer has to hide Himself from us. Through the wonder of the Cross, God can look upon us once more, and He invites us to draw closer to Him. What once separated us from Him has now disappeared:

> *But now, in union with Christ Jesus you, who used to be far away, have been brought near by the blood of Christ.* (Ephesians 2:13, GNB)

There is now an open door between ourselves and God. This means, however, that I must give Him the cup of my life. It is something I must do myself; no one else can do it for me. The moment I do, the first wonder of the Cross will become a reality in my life: my sins will be taken away from me and the door to God will swing open!

The Blood of Jesus Takes Away My Sins

The blood of Jesus plays a big part in the whole story of His suffering. The blood of Jesus did something that the blood of goats and bulls could not do. The blood of Jesus has supernatural, divine power.

You see, the sacrificial blood of animals covered the sins of men, but could not take them away. That's why people had to sacrifice again and again. The Bible says:

> *But the blood of bulls and goats cannot take away sins.* (Hebrews 10:4, CEV)

In reality, the sacrifices offered up by the priests in the temple could never take away the sins of the people.[67]

The sacrifice that Jesus made was once and for all, perfect, absolute and universal. Everyone who believes in the blood of Jesus will immediately experience the fact that there is divine power in the blood of "the Lamb" that cleanses our lives from all our sins.[68] Time and again, as I witness the wonder of the Cross taking place in people's lives, I am deeply impressed by the power of God's love. Whoever has experienced God's forgiveness of sins becomes a new, free person!

THE CUP OF SALVATION

The cup of God's wrath has become the cup of salvation for us. Jesus' struggle in Gethsemane has given Passover a new meaning. He took a cup:

> *"Drink it, all of you," he said; "this is my blood, which seals God's covenant, my blood poured out for many for the forgiveness of sins."* (Matthew 26:27–28, GNB)

Jesus invites us to drink from His cup of salvation, for the forgiveness of our sins. This is the first wonder of the Cross:

> *If we confess our sins, he is faithful and righteous to forgive us the sins, and to cleanse us from all unrighteousness.* (1 John 1:9, WEB)

This is the heart of the gospel:

> *For by the blood of Christ we are set free, that is, our sins are forgiven. How great is the grace of God.* (Ephesians 1:7, GNB)

WITHOUT THE WONDER OF THE CROSS THERE IS NO FORGIVENESS

If only we knew how intensely God longs to forgive our sins. He loves us so very much that He has done everything to restore our relationship with Him. His forgiveness knows no limits! Whatever has happened, wherever we've come from, no matter how badly we've sinned, God is waiting, ready to take us into His arms as His children and to forgive our sins.

Forgiveness is supernatural. People in the world try to forgive each other. They know it is a necessary part of living together. But they will only fully experience the saving power of forgiveness through the wonder of the Cross. Without the wonder of the Cross, true forgiveness is impossible here on earth. Forgiveness must always go hand in hand with the confession of sins, and only the blood of Jesus can perform the wonder of actually removing our sins, so that the wall separating God and man can be torn down and the cloud between God and man can be lifted and forgiveness can take place! Forgiveness is divine. Hebrews 9:22 says: "*...sins are forgiven only if blood is poured out.*" If people do not admit that they have sinned against God and man, they can try to forgive each other, but they will never experience the liberating power of God's forgiveness. Broken relationships can be restored only through the forgiving power of God's love.

THE POWER OF FORGIVENESS

Herman suffered from a speech impediment. It was not easy to have a conversation with him. His stammer was so bad that he couldn't utter a single word normally. Herman had been raised in a very religious home, with a lot of do's and don'ts. He rebelled as a teenager, but it didn't do him much good. One day he visited our church, and the message of God's love touched him deeply. Herman continued to attend services and discovered that he had a very twisted view of who God is. His parents had a hard time coping with the fact that Herman was visiting a different church, and became suspicious. But Herman began to change. One day when Herman was on the road he was listening to a sermon on the power of forgiveness. Herman's eyes were opened. He suddenly saw that he had never forgiven his parents and that he still resented them. This truth touched him so deeply that he had to stop the car. He got out, knelt down beside the road and asked God to forgive him as he also expressed his forgiveness toward his parents! At that moment he felt a warmth enter his being. He remembers thinking to himself that it had to be from God. When I met him a few days later and we started a conversation, my mouth dropped open in astonishment. Without a single stammer, he shared what God had done within him by the side of the road. Forgiveness releases the power of God in our lives!

> **Forgiveness releases the power of God in our lives!**

What does the cup of our life look like? Do we dare to look inside it? Maybe we've polished it beautifully on the outside. Know this: one drop of sin will forever separate me from God the Father, but one drop of Jesus' blood will bring me back to God the Father for all eternity! Do we want to give the cup of our life to Him?

Father in heaven,

I know You know my life. I know I need forgiveness for my sins to restore my relationship with You. I believe in the

sacrifice that Jesus made for me. Thank You, Jesus, that You were willing to drink the cup of my life filled with my sins. I confess all my sins (…) and give the cup of my life to You. You have seen my sins; You have tasted them. I accept that You carried all of my sins in Your body, so that I could be saved. Thank You for this sacrifice. Thank You that You have already emptied my cup and that I may experience forgiveness of all my sins and be cleansed by Your precious blood. Thank You that in faith I may take the cup of salvation. You have delivered me from my sins. Thank You for letting me come to You freely and live with You. Thank You for the wonder of the Cross. In faith I accept this wonder.

Amen.

THE ARREST

No one takes my life away from me.
I give it up of my own free will.

(John 10:18, GNB)

CHAPTER 4

It isn't difficult for Judas, who has agreed to betray Jesus, to find Him. He knows that Jesus will probably spend the night in the garden of Gethsemane again, as he has been with Him there on previous nights.[69] Around midnight he heads for the Mount of Olives with a detachment of soldiers and temple guards. They are carrying torches, lamps and weapons.

The group of soldiers Judas has with him consists of at least twenty to thirty men, and maybe even over a hundred. John speaks of a *speira* (Greek) or a *cohort* (Latin). A cohort was a tenth of a legion, roughly six hundred soldiers. It could also be *maniple* that is meant here, a subdivision of a Roman legion. That would be either sixty or 120 men.

During the Passover celebrations, there were always a lot of visitors in Jerusalem, and the city was brimming over with religious and nationalistic sentiments. In order to be able to quell possible riots, the Romans brought extra troops into the city. The leaders of the Sanhedrin, the Jewish high court, probably convinced Governor Pilate to give them extra troops too. And Pilate no doubt agreed to this, remembering the masses of people that had converged when Jesus rode into Jerusalem.

It is not clear how many Roman soldiers Judas has with him, but the group is large enough to be called a "detachment," so there must have been at least twenty to thirty, maybe even over a hundred. And then there are the temple guards, armed with sticks, plus a few chief priests and elders. They've all come to assist in arresting Jesus![70] Both Matthew and Mark speak of a "large crowd."

JESUS KNOWS EVERYTHING THAT IS GOING TO HAPPEN TO HIM

Attempts at arresting or even killing Jesus have been frequent. The inhabitants of Nazareth,[71] the Jewish authorities,[72] the inhabitants of Jerusalem,[73] the Jewish temple guards[74] and even the crowds in Jerusalem have all tried.[75] John clarifies why they all failed:

> *Jesus said all this as he taught in the Temple, in the room where the offering boxes were placed. And no one arrested him, because his hour had not come.* (John 8:20, GNB; see also 10:39 and 11:57)

Jesus has known all along that His Father in heaven will determine the time at which He is voluntarily to turn Himself in to the Jewish religious leaders.

Jesus has known from the start that He will die outside Jerusalem on a cross, at the exact same moment when the priest in the temple within the city walls sacrifices the lamb for the sins of the people. At that precise moment, Jesus will cry out: "It is finished!"

Jesus knows what the prophets have written about Him and that these prophecies are about to be fulfilled.[76] He knows that Judas will betray Him[77] and that all of His disciples will abandon Him.[78] He knows He will be handed over to the chief priests and Pilate.[79] He knows He will be ridiculed, spat on, abused, whipped and crucified.[80] Jesus knows everything that is going to happen to

Him,[81] because His Father has told Him[82] and because the prophets have written about it in detail.[83]

PREDICTIONS CONCERNING JESUS' LAST EIGHTEEN HOURS

There are hundreds of predictions about the birth, life and death of Jesus of Nazareth in the Bible, and each and every one of them came true. All four writers of the Gospels refer to what is written about Jesus in the Old Testament. Everything that happened in the last eighteen hours before Jesus' death was predicted centuries before it happened. The twenty most important predictions about His last eighteen hours are:

- The betrayal of Judas Iscariot during the last supper (Psalm 41:9)
- The payment for his betrayal: thirty pieces of silver (Zechariah 11:12)
- How the payment for Judas' betrayal is used to purchase a piece of land from the potter (Zechariah 11:13)
- Jesus' abandonment by all His disciples (Zechariah 13:7)
- The false witnesses who testify against Jesus (Psalm 35:11)
- Jesus' silence before the judges (Isaiah 53:7)
- How Jesus is whipped (Isaiah 50:6)
- How Jesus is disfigured by the abuse (Isaiah 52:14 and 53:2)
- How Jesus is punished like a criminal among other criminals (Isaiah 53:12)
- The piercing of Jesus' hands and feet (Psalm 22:16 and Isaiah 53:5)
- How Jesus is ridiculed by the onlookers (Psalm 22:7)
- How Jesus is challenged to call on God for help (Psalm 22:8)
- How Jesus' clothes are gambled for (Psalm 22:18)

- How He is offered vinegar to drink (Psalm 69:21)
- The darkness that covers the earth at His death (Amos 8:9)
- Jesus' abandonment by God (Psalm 22:1)
- How Jesus' heart stops (Psalm 22:14)
- How Jesus' side is pierced (Zechariah 12:10)
- The fact that none of Jesus' bones are broken (Psalm 34:20)
- Jesus' burial in the grave of a wealthy man (Isaiah 53:9)

JESUS FREELY GAVE UP HIS LIFE

When Jesus died on the Cross it was not an accident or something forced on Him by others. It is not as if He was just another of history's many freedom fighters, who was finally overpowered as His own pacifist lifestyle backfired on Him! It is not as if Jesus let things get out of control and was assassinated, like many other great leaders. Jesus Himself was very clear about all this:

The Father loves me because I am willing to give up my life, in order that I may receive it back again. No one takes my life away from me. I give it up of my own free will. I have the right to give it up, and I have the right to take it back. This is what my Father has commanded me to do. (John 10:17–18, GNB)

It is not Judas but Jesus Himself, who, being the true High Priest, provides the Lamb for the altar. This becomes clear in the course of the events that follow Judas' arrival and betrayal of Jesus with a kiss. Jesus is the one taking the initiative. Jesus already knows what is going to happen, yet He asks: "Who are you looking for?" They answer: "We are looking for Jesus from Nazareth!" Jesus tells them: "I am Jesus!"[84]

What happens then shows that Jesus is Lord and Master of the situation. He exudes so much power that all the Roman soldiers, the Jewish temple guards, the chief priests and elders and their servants stagger backwards and fall on the ground. Later on Saul—and those with him—would experience something similar on the road from Jerusalem to Damascus, where Saul was heading in order to persecute and arrest the Christians.[85] What a display of power. Can you imagine all those heavily armed soldiers falling to the ground? What made that happen? The secret of Jesus' power is hidden in the reply He gives. He literally says: *ego eimi* (I am). This reminds us of the covenant name with which God revealed Himself to Moses at the burning bush: "I AM who I AM."[86] Jesus identifies Himself with His Father in heaven, who now glorifies Him by displaying His power to the rulers of this earth. Just as Moses could not get closer to the burning bush, the soldiers and temple guards cannot just walk up to Jesus. Jesus makes it clear that He is above those who have come to arrest Him. As they scramble back onto their feet, Jesus repeats the question: "Who are you looking for?" They are shocked by what has just happened to them and answer almost automatically: "Jesus of Nazareth." Jesus answers

When Jesus died on the Cross, it was not an accident or something forced on Him by others.

them: "I already told you that that is me. If it is me you are looking for, then let these people go!" The soldiers are powerless to take Jesus. The disciples are safe. And even in this hour of danger Jesus is thinking of His disciples, who, He knows, are about to abandon Him.[87] Jesus is completely in control of the situation. If God had not allowed it, it would have been impossible to arrest Him.

JESUS HEALS THE EAR OF MALCHUS

Even though Jesus gave him the chance to flee, Simon Peter stays with Him. He wants to keep his word about never leaving Jesus; He wants to give his life for his Master. Peter is carrying a sword. Now that the soldiers are threatening to arrest Jesus, he attacks the one standing closest to him, who turns out to be the personal slave of the high priest. Peter may well have meant to behead him, but the slave jumps aside and only his right ear gets sliced off. Jesus rebukes Peter and tells him to put his sword away. He says:

> *Don't you know that I could call on my Father for help, and at once he would send me more than twelve armies of angels?* (Matthew 26:53, GNB)

Then He touches Malchus' ear and miraculously heals him. All of these supernatural events surrounding the arrest of Jesus go to show that Jesus is completely in control of the situation. Then He says:

> *Do you think that I will not drink the cup of suffering which my Father has given me?* (John 18:11, GNB)

Jesus knows that the cup of suffering has not yet been completely emptied. He knows what is going to happen yet His deepest desire is to carry out the will of His Father! The Roman commander arrests Jesus and ties Him up like a criminal. Jesus is taken to the house of the high priest Caiaphas, close to where He celebrated the last supper with His followers.

JESUS IS BETRAYED AND ABANDONED

Jesus' family was worried because people were saying: "He's gone mad!"[88] The religious leaders said that He was demon-possessed[89] and thought that He would kill Himself.[90] His half-brothers, who at that point did not believe in Him, tried to get Him to work wonders.[91] People tried to discredit Him by spreading lies about Him, calling Him a blasphemer[92] and a deceiver of the people.[93] They sent the tax inspector after Him,[94] they tried to trap Him,[95] they took offense at Him,[96] they watched Him continually,[97] and some tried to crown Him king by force.[98] But no one could control Him. Many abandoned Him, leading Him in the end to ask His friends: "Do you want to leave as well?"[99] This is not what the disciples had expected. So much misunderstanding; so much hostility. On this dark night, all of His disciples do indeed abandon Him. One by one, they disappear from the scene.

Father in heaven,

You see everything about me. You know me just as I am. Everything I do is known to You. You are with me, beside me, in front of me, behind me. Your hand rests on me. It is impossible for me to understand this. It is so amazing, so beyond my comprehension. You have counted all my hairs. You know what will happen to me. Teach me to be like Jesus. Just as He gave his will to You, I also want to lay my will in Your hands by saying: Not my will but Yours be done in my life! I want to obey You. Give me strength to remain standing, so that I can walk in Your presence daily.

Amen.

THE SECOND AND THIRD WONDERS OF THE CROSS:

THE ABUSE

*He was treated harshly, but endured it humbly; he never
said a word. Like a lamb about to be slaughtered,
like a sheep about to be sheared, he never said a word.*

(Isaiah 53:7, GNB)

CHAPTER 5

The soldiers and the temple guards arrest Jesus. They tie Him up and take Him first to the house of former high priest Annas, then to the palace of the current high priest, Caiaphas, and, finally, to the palace of the Roman governor, Pontius Pilate.

Annas was high priest from 6–15 A.D., but he was removed from his position by the Roman procurator Valerius Gratus. Even so, he still wields a lot of influence. Five of his sons, one son-in-law and one grandson were high priests after him. Because the Jews believe that being high priest is something you do for life, Annas has retained his title and influence regardless of the measures taken by the Romans. This eighty-year-old is probably responsible for what are known as "the stalls of the sons of Annas" in the temple, booths at which temple visitors could purchase things for sacrificing. He certainly will not have forgotten how Jesus threw out the money-changers and the merchants selling sacrificial animals and religious items, while shouting out: "My temple will be called a house of prayer for the people of all nations. But you have turned it into a hideout for thieves!"[100]

Jesus is first brought to Annas, because the members of the Jewish high court (the Sanhedrin) officially require two hearings held on two consecutive days before the death penalty can be imposed. This fact poses a serious problem: the arrest has taken place between Thursday night and Friday morning and both the Sabbath and the annual Passover feast commence on Friday evening. Conducting a hearing either on the Sabbath or on Passover is not permitted. That is why Jesus is first taken to Annas: the idea is to hold the first hearing there, while Annas' fanatical son-in-law Caiaphas quickly calls the members of the Sanhedrin together for a so-called second hearing before the Sanhedrin. No one seems to object to the fact that this procedure is illegal.

JESUS IS DANGEROUS

Annas' questioning of Jesus focuses on two things: His disciples and His teaching.[101] The first of these is the most important to Annas: how successful is Jesus? Does He have many followers? And if He does, has He trained them to start a revolt, so that they, too, must be arrested? In short: is Jesus dangerous?

Jesus doesn't answer Annas' questions about His disciples. Will He tell His interrogators that one of His followers has just betrayed Him, that all of the others have fled and that Peter is about to deny even knowing Him? No: even now, Jesus protects His disciples, this time by remaining silent.

Jesus does comment that He has always spoken openly rather than in secret. His approach contrasts with the secretive methods of the Jewish religious leaders He is facing.[102] His night-time arrest is unlawful, as are many other things that are to take place under the cover of that dark night.

Then Jesus suddenly says: "Why are you asking me all this? Plenty of people have heard me speak." He points to several of them, probably Jewish temple guards standing by, and says: "Ask them. They can tell you exactly what I said."

This does not go down well. One of the guards that Jesus has pointed at hits Him in the face, probably with a stick, and says: "That is not how you speak to the high priest!" This is the first, but not the last, time that Jesus is struck without reason. He answers: "If I have said something wrong, then tell me. But if I am right, then why do you hit me?" The soldier remains silent. Annas, upset by the fact that his interrogation is plainly failing, has Jesus tied up again and sends Him to the high priest Caiaphas, who in the meantime has summoned the Sanhedrin.

Jesus is Falsely Accused in the Palace of Caiaphas

The high court, or Sanhedrin, consisted of seventy-two people, most of whom were members of the two most important religious groups at the time: the Sadducees and the Pharisees.

The Sadducees consisted largely of the nobles and chief priests who controlled the temple and the worship services. They were rich, well-educated men who got on well with the Roman government but were not popular with the people. They were far from pleased with this traveling carpenter, who told them that tax collectors and prostitutes would enter the kingdom of heaven before they did.[103]

The Pharisaic movement was originally a "revival movement," but had deteriorated into a hypocritical bunch of leaders who tried to attract people's attention to their piety with fancy prayer belts and tassels. It was the Pharisees who determined who was worthy enough to enter the synagogue. But Jesus compared them to white-washed graves: clean on the outside but filled with dead bones on the inside.[104]

Normally the Sanhedrin gathered in the so-called *liskat ha-chasid,* that is "the room of the pious," in one of the temple buildings. Because this room cannot be accessed at night, Jesus is brought to the palace of the reigning high priest, Caiaphas.

This hearing is a farce. Jesus' death has been prearranged. The Sanhedrin met and decided to arrest and kill Him a few days earlier.[105] However, they have not yet formulated a proper charge, so they quickly round up some accusers. A legal accusation must be confirmed by at least two witnesses, who cannot contradict each other, otherwise their charge is considered invalid. The many witnesses the Sanhedrin brings in are all false and contradict each other. There is no investigation to find out whether or not their accusations are true and no defense is allowed. Finally, the Sanhedrin finds two men willing to issue a statement concerning Jesus' "blasphemy": He allegedly attacked the temple, the house of God. Jesus remains silent, which drives Caiaphas crazy. He commands Jesus to speak the truth by the living God. He wants an answer under oath to the following question: "Tell us, are you the Messiah, the Son of God?" Jesus answers:

> *So you say. But I tell all of you: from this time on you will see the Son of Man sitting at the right side of the Almighty and coming on the clouds of heaven!* (Matthew 26:64, GNB)

Caiaphas is enraged. He tears his clothes and screams: "He is blaspheming God! Do we still need witnesses? You have all heard what he said! What shall we do with him?" The men of the Council all cry out: "He must be executed!"

JESUS IS ABUSED

Jesus must have been exhausted after a sleepless night and a huge spiritual battle against sin. The suffering is about to get worse. In line with Isaiah's prophecy:

> *I bared my back to those who beat me. I did not stop them when they insulted me, when they pulled out the hairs of my beard and spit in my face.* (Isaiah 50:6, GNB)

The Sanhedrin allows the servants to beat Jesus with their fists and to spit in His face.[106] In the Middle East, spitting is the worst expression of contempt. Others ridicule Jesus. They tie a cloth over His face, pummel Him with their fists and then ask Him to tell who hit Him. The servants of the Sanhedrin mock Jesus as a prophet, and later the Roman soldiers deride the idea of Him as a king.

> **They pummel Jesus with their fists and sticks, until He bleeds.**

Translators have noted that the Greek word *rhaapizo* probably does not mean "hit in the face," but "hit with sticks." This coincides with the prophecy in Micah:

> *They will strike the judge of Israel with a rod on the cheek.* (Micah 5:1, WEB)

They beat Jesus with their fists and with sticks until He bleeds. He is ridiculed, made fun of and slandered. Centuries before, Isaiah had prophesied this:

> *He was treated harshly, but endured it humbly; He never said a word. Like a lamb about to be slaughtered, like a sheep about to be sheared, He never said a word.* (Isaiah 53:7, GNB)

THE SECOND WONDER OF THE CROSS:
THE BLOOD OF JESUS FREES US
FROM THE ACCUSATION OF THE EVIL ONE

Throughout the interrogation and the false accusations, Jesus is abused until His body is bleeding. During this cruel abuse, the Man without sin bleeds twice: the temple guards not only hit Him, they also pull the hair of His beard out of His cheeks (Isaiah 50:6). This brings us to the second and third wonders of the Cross.

So many people are burdened by feelings of guilt. They are haunted by the mistakes and sins of the past and feel guilty, even though they know in their mind that their sins are forgiven. They only partially experience the wonder of forgiveness, because they keep being accused daily. They cannot break free from their past. They wrestle and do their very best to survive rather than truly living. How can this be? How can they remain under accusation? It is vital that we know exactly what Jesus did for us. The answer to these questions is that Jesus not only washed away our sins

It is not our sins that are nailed to the Cross, but the evidence against us, our "criminal record" that proves us guilty and condemns us.

with His blood, but He also took away every bit of blame and all accusations. These are two different things. Our sins are not left hanging on the Cross. They have been taken away from us, washed away by the blood of the Lamb! It is not our sins that are nailed to the Cross, but the evidence against us, our "criminal record" that proves us guilty and condemns us:

> *You were dead, because you were sinful and were not God's people. But God let Christ make you alive, when he forgave all our sins. God wiped out the charges that were against us for disobeying the Law of Moses. He took them away and nailed them to the cross. There Christ defeated all powers and forces. He let the whole world see them being led away as prisoners when he celebrated his victory.* (Colossians 2:13–15, CEV)

God has taken the record that accused us and nailed it to the Cross! The Greek word that Paul uses for "charges" is *cheirographon*, which means "handwriting." It reminds me of how God wrote the Ten Commandments, which we are to obey, on the stone tablets with His finger.[107] It was His handwriting that has made us realize ever since that time that we cannot possibly keep God's law. None of us can say that we haven't sinned. And we all know how guilt can plague us. But it is not God who is accusing us.

THE DEVIL IS ACCUSING US

Jesus was innocent, but He did not defend Himself when He was falsely accused, and allowed Himself to be beaten until He bled, so that we could be freed from every accusation that the devil fires at us. The evil one's tactic is that he first tempts us to sin and then accuses us when we do so: "You brought it on yourself"; "What you have done is unforgivable"; "Think God is going to *forgive* you if you come to Him again for forgiveness? You knew very well that what you were doing was wrong." If we allow ourselves to be accused by the evil one then we will continue to feel guilty. Some Christians come to the incorrect conclusion that they have committed the "unforgivable sin," because they allow themselves to be accused and feel guilty about it![108]

The Bible teaches us that the devil accuses us day and night before God:

> *Then I heard a loud voice in heaven saying, "Now God's salvation has come! Now God has shown his power as King! Now his Messiah has shown his authority! For the one who stood before our God and accused believers day and night has been thrown out of heaven. They won the victory over him by the blood of the Lamb and by the truth which they proclaimed; and they were willing to give up their lives and die."* (Revelation 12:10–11, GNB)

Jesus took each of these accusations, and every feeling of guilt that is attached to them, upon Himself during the abuse that He endured. The blood of the Lamb frees us from every accusation of the evil one. When Jesus was nailed to the Cross, our record was nailed to the Cross as well. This is how the devil and every power in hell were conquered and disarmed. It means that he can no longer accuse us because Jesus took our punishment and we have been acquitted of all guilt:

> But he was pierced for our transgressions, he was crushed for our iniquities; the punishment that brought our peace was on him; and by his wounds we are healed. All we like sheep have gone astray; everyone has turned to his own way; and Yahweh has laid on him the iniquity of us all. He was oppressed, yet when he was afflicted he didn't open his mouth; as a lamb that is led to the slaughter, and as a sheep that before its shearers is mute, so he didn't open his mouth. (Isaiah 53:5–7, WEB)

THE ACCUSER HAS BEEN CONQUERED

God has cleaned the slate of our record from the stain of the past that witnessed against us, with the blood of His Son, Jesus, so that the devil, or accuser, has no more power over us. Now that is real freedom! In the legal world, if there is no evidence against a person, then the suspect is immediately freed. This is what Jesus has done for us: by His taking our sins upon Himself and taking the punishment in our place, we are one hundred percent freed from every accusation, so that we can stand before God free of guilt.

Through the wonder of the Cross Jesus has completely freed us from the power of the accuser! The voice of the accuser will be silenced in our lives through the blood of Jesus and the truth that we proclaim, for there is no condemnation for those who are in Christ Jesus.[109] Jesus takes us with Him in His victory and gives us the authority to silence the devil in His name when he accuses us.[110] Let us use the authority that Jesus has given us to silence the devil in Jesus' name!

Father in heaven,

Thank You that the blood of Jesus Christ has purified my heart from all sins. Thank You that You have taken all my sins from me and thrown them away, as far as the east is from the west. My desire is that every wonder of the Cross may take place in my life. I believe that Jesus Christ has nailed every accusation against me to the Cross. The devil no longer has the right to accuse me, because Jesus has taken my punishment!
I no longer want to be burdened by the yoke of incriminations, (false) accusations and feelings of guilt.
Thank You, Jesus, that You have given me the authority to say to the devil: "By the blood of the Lamb and the truth that I proclaim, you have been conquered. God has forgiven all my sins. I will no longer allow myself to be incriminated and accused by you. I am cleansed, made holy and justified by the blood of the Lord Jesus. There is no condemnation for those who are in Christ Jesus! Therefore, I command you to be silent in the name of Jesus: hold your tongue and be silent!"
Thank You, Father, that I too have been freed from the accusations of the evil one through the wonder of the Cross, and that You accept me as Your beloved child.

Amen.

The Third Wonder of the Cross:
The Blood of Jesus
Cleanses our Conscience

Throughout the years, we have seen that genuine Christians who know that God has forgiven their sins, and that the accusations of the evil one should be silent, still struggle with feelings of guilt. How is this possible? Well, the blood of Jesus not only cleanses our hearts from sin, it not only takes away every accusation, but it also cleanses our conscience, which accuses us on the inside:

> *His blood will purify our consciences from useless rituals, so that we may serve the living God.* (Hebrews 9:14, GNB)

But what is our conscience? The Greek word *suneidesis* means "to know something with someone else." It is an innate perception that warns us not to do that which is wrong, and therefore to sin. You could call it our God-given built-in alarm system.

The biblical definition of my conscience is that I have a "consciousness of sin"[111] and that I am "conscious of His will."[112] That all sounds very nice, but we have one problem: because of sin, our conscience has become infected, so that we no longer naturally feel what is right or wrong.

Paul says to Timothy that people who persist in their sin are seared in their conscience, that their conscience becomes silent:

> *The Spirit says clearly that some people will abandon the faith in later times; they will obey lying spirits and follow the teachings of demons. Such teachings are spread by deceitful liars, whose consciences are dead, as if burnt with a hot iron.* (1 Timothy 4:1–2, GNB)

Our conscience becomes numbed by sin; it grows dull and less sensitive to discerning good from evil. This has negatively influenced our consciousness of God and what sin does in our lives.[113] It is a process in which we slowly but surely slide down away from God.

"TO SEE IN YOUR MIND'S EYE"

Our conscience is also our consciousness. The Greek word for conscience, *suneidesis*, is derived from the verb *suneido*, which can be translated as "to see in your mind's eye." King David says in one of his psalms that he is continually conscious of his sins:

I know about my sins, and I cannot forget my terrible guilt. (Psalm 51:3, CEV)

David's past haunts him. Without wanting to, he sees in his mind's eye how he committed adultery with Bathsheba and sent Uriah, her husband, to his death. Another translation puts it like this:

I recognize my faults; I am always conscious of my sins. (GNB)

We are not looking at an accusation of the evil one here. It is David's tainted conscience that accuses him. He is worn out. David cries out to God:

Close your eyes to my sins and wipe out all my evil. Create a pure heart in me, O God, and put a new and loyal spirit in me. Do not banish me from your presence; do not take your Holy Spirit away from me. Give me again the joy that comes from your salvation, and make me willing to obey you. (Psalm 51:9–12, GNB)

We are often not conscious of the fact that memories are saved as pictures in our mind. We do not realize, for example, how seeing sexually charged photos and/or films will influence our lives. These pictures and/or experiences from the past will be stored in our consciousness whether or not we want this to happen. They can haunt us, as Sean found out.

SEAN AND THE GALLERY OF PICTURES

As a seven-year-old boy, Sean found some *Playboy* and *Hustler* magazines. He found them in the shed, where his father had hidden them. His sensitive young eyes were drawn to the pictures of sexual activity and they awakened feelings in him and aroused his senses. He was still so young and no one knew what he was doing. His body reacted to what he saw and it wanted more. One thing led to another. As a teenager he was exposed to pornographic magazines. At first it was soft porn but later it became hard-core. Sean started dating a nice girl. She became pregnant with his child and an abortion soon followed. They married at a young age, but Sean still wanted more. He had become addicted to sex. As a result of alcohol abuse and the wrong kind of friends he got into the world of prostitution. Short-lived affairs became part of his life. Sean was unfaithful to his wife several times but she did not know about it. If his secret life had become known, it would have meant the end of everything. Sean and his wife came into contact with a Christian couple in our church. They became friends. Slowly but surely they gained Sean's trust. One day he could no longer keep silent and shared his problem with his friend. This was the beginning of a long process, in which Sean got to know God the Father, who loves him deeply and whose forgiveness knows no boundaries. Sean and his wife both decided to lay their lives in God's hands: the past, present and future. It was the beginning of a difficult period for Sean's wife. She found out for the first time about her husband's secret life, and it cut her to the core. Their marriage nearly ended. But God is faithful and did not let go of either of them as He worked out His plan in both of their lives. Sean and his wife chose the path of forgiveness and reconciliation. God healed the wounds that had been made. Sean was still struggling with what he called his "gallery of pictures." It was as if the unclean images had been burned on his retina. They had been saved in his subconscious and popped up at the most inopportune moments, making him feel dirty and unclean. One day Sean heard a sermon on the wonder of the Cross: God not only takes away our sins, but also wants to cleanse our conscience! Sean took an important step in faith: he asked for prayer and asked that the blood of Jesus cleanse the "gallery of pictures" in his subconscious mind, so that he could "come near to God with a sincere heart and a sure faith, with a heart that has been purified from a guilty conscience and with a body washed with clean water!"[114] God worked a wonder in Sean's life, and he is now learning step by step what it means to live a holy and pure life.

Sean was able to experience the wonder of the Cross in his life. He did not let shame hold him back, but broke the silence about the secrets in his life. He asked God to do a wonder in his life: "Father, cleanse my conscience with the blood of the Lord Jesus, so that all the impure images that have been saved in my subconscious mind are erased so that they can no longer weigh down my soul, spirit or body. I am washed, made holy and justified by the blood of Jesus. Thank you for the wonder of the Cross!"

GOD DOES NOT REMEMBER MY SINS

God says to everyone who is standing at the foot of the Cross and has their eyes fixed on Jesus:

I will forgive their sins and I will no longer remember their wrongs. (Jeremiah 31:34, GNB)

Let these words penetrate deeply. Isn't it wonderful that God does not remember our sins? But has He actually forgotten them? No, thankfully not. Can you imagine that God would be absent-minded and that He would forget one of His promises to us? No; the word that God uses (*zakar*) means that He is capable of no longer thinking of it, no longer recalling it. It is no longer in His thoughts! This is what happens when we allow our conscience to be cleansed by the blood of Jesus. Then a wonder occurs: we too receive the ability to no longer think of it.

THE ROLL OF FILM

My wife's story reflects that of many other men and women. As a teenager, before she met God, Ann had a boyfriend. As is the case for many other boys and girls at that age, it was considered normal that after a period of dating she would sleep with him. Even though Ann's conscience told her it wasn't right, it still happened. In this relationship Ann was forced to commit certain sexual acts. It damaged her on the inside more than she realized at the time. She did not feel safe or cherished, but dirty and condemned. Her conscience accused her and she didn't know what to do. She started searching and heard the gospel explained one day. Ann gave her life to Jesus, knew that her sins were forgiven, and got baptized. She broke off her relationship with her boyfriend. Even though she knew her sins were forgiven, she was haunted by all kinds of bad memories in her dreams. She carried a burden just as King David did:

> *I know about my sins, and I cannot forget my terrible guilt.* (Psalm 51:3, CEV)

Even though she knew her sins were forgiven, she was being accused time and again in dreams and thoughts. When Ann shared her story with someone, they prayed with her not only that the blood of Jesus would cleanse her heart from sin, but also that her conscience would be cleansed so that it would no longer accuse her. Shortly afterward she had a dream, in which she saw her life on a roll of film. But the negative had turned black; all the pictures of the past were no longer visible. She saw how a hand picked up the roll of film and threw it into a bottomless trashcan. God cleansed not only her sins but also all the impurities of her conscience. In this way Ann received a pure heart and a clean conscience from God through the wonder of the Cross! The bad dreams never came back.

God Heals the Pain in the Memories

The painful memories of sin are stored in our consciousness (*suneidesis*). Professional counselors and pastoral workers cannot easily access this pain, if at all, because such memories have usually been repressed in order for us to survive. Yet through the wonder of the Cross, God can do the impossible and cleanse our conscience of dead works:

> *How much more will the blood of Christ, who through the eternal Spirit offered himself without blemish to God, cleanse your conscience from dead works to serve the living God?* (Hebrews 9:14, WEB)

God can touch the pain that is stored in our consciousness through the memory of the sin.

This means that God can touch the pain—which is stored in our consciousness through the memory of the sin—and we can receive inner healing. Only then can we forget what lies behind us and reach for what lies ahead of us (in Jesus).[115] In this way is fulfilled in our lives Isaiah's prophecy that Jesus will bear our suffering too.

> *Surely he has borne our sickness, and carried our suffering; yet we considered him plagued, struck by God, and afflicted.* (Isaiah 53:4, WEB)

Because Jesus was abused, rejected and condemned in our place, we in turn have been fully accepted by God in His place, and can receive inner healing for our wounded souls in His presence. Of all the seven wonders of the Cross, for me this one is the most impressive wonder that God has prepared for us through Jesus Christ.

A HORRIFIC DRAMA

On the night of the 7th of September 1978 a tragedy takes place in the home of the Bioch family in Dordrecht. A fire breaks out and the flames spread quickly. Hans and Nelleke wake their children on the first floor so they can leave the building as quickly as possible. The fire has set ablaze the stairs that lead to the second floor, where Job (seven) and Harro (four) are sleeping. Hans uses a ladder to climb onto the roof to rescue the boys through the attic window. But the flames spread so quickly that the firefighters have to get Hans off the roof. Job and Harro cannot be reached and are burned alive.

This horrific event leaves Hans with incurable trauma. Five years after the fire, he can barely sleep and has serious physical problems. Hans is treated by Professor Bastiaans, a Dutch psychiatrist who is internationally known as a trauma specialist. His approach is controversial because he treats heavily traumatized adults with LSD, hoping to force an opening and offer some form of relief. This treatment is so dangerous that he is the only one who was allowed to administer the drug.

Hans is diagnosed with concentration camp syndrome (also known as survivor syndrome). Before each treatment session Hans and Nelleke pray for God's help and protection, seeing re-experiencing the fire as their last chance for healing.

On October 4th 1992 a Boeing 747 cargo plane owned by the Israeli airline El Al crashes into two high-rise apartment buildings in the Bijlmermeer area of Amsterdam. This disaster causes Hans to relive all the memories. He is continually tortured by the terror of the nightmares that exhaust him physically and mentally. The pain, the sorrow and the anger flare up again and again. It is a hopeless battle. Hans becomes ill and cannot work. For years, he has to deal with the tension that the nightmares bring, nightmares that keep flaring up like an inextinguishable forest fire. Throughout this difficult period, Hans and Nelleke witness to how they have experienced God being near to them in the battle. Nearly thirty years later, Hans and Nelleke visit our two-day conference in Maastricht. On the last day, there is a lot of time for teaching and prayer so that people can receive the wonders of the Cross. Among other things, people are invited to have their conscience and their consciousness cleansed by the blood of the Lord Jesus. Many people come forward, but Hans and Nelleke remain at the back of the hall. They don't dare to approach. While they watch how people are being prayed for at the front of the church, the Holy Spirit reveals to me that He is also at work at the back of the hall. At the same moment, Hans experiences God's Spirit touching the pain that lies stored in the memory of the trauma, and God's love healing his wounded heart in an instant. After having lived with the terror of the nightmares for thirty years, he now receives rest, peace and quietness. The nightmares have never returned.

God is the God of wonders. I am deeply impressed every time I see how the Holy Spirit, based on what Jesus has done for us, heals people of inner pain, wounds and traumas when He pours out the supernatural love of the Father in their hearts. Thank You, Jesus, for the wonder of the Cross: the amazing gift of Your love!

Father in heaven,

Thank You that the blood of Jesus Christ has purified my heart from all sins. Thank You that You have cleansed my heart from all sin. Thank You that You have freed me from the accusations of the evil one and that with You I am more than a conqueror and I no longer need to feel accused by the enemy. The blood of the Lord Jesus has cleansed me, made me holy and justified me. I ask You to cleanse my conscience in the name of Jesus, to remove every impure image that has been burned onto my retina or has been saved in my memory, to wash it clean through the blood of the Lord Jesus. Thank You that Jesus carried my suffering too. I believe that the blood of Jesus can also cleanse my subconscious and that

at this moment You can touch the pain that is stored in the memory of sin so that I may receive inner healing for my wounded soul. Thank You that I can be Your child and that I can receive Your healing love in Your presence.

Amen.

TRADING PLACES

Don't you realize that it is better for you
to have one man die for the people,
instead of having the whole nation destroyed?

(John 11:50, GNB)

CHAPTER 6

Early in the morning, the members of the Sanhedrin are discussing how they can convince the Roman prefect, Pilate, to have Jesus executed. They themselves are not authorized to have someone executed (the so-called *potestas gladii*). That's why Jesus, who has not slept all night and has been beaten and abused, is turned over to Pilate, chained like a criminal.

PONTIUS PILATE

Pontius Pilate was the Roman prefect in Judea for ten years, from 26 to 36 A.D. He answered to the proconsul of Syria, who in turn answered to the Emperor Tiberius. Pilate was the highest Roman authority in Judea. "Pontius" was probably a nickname he acquired in the battle at Pontus (near the Black Sea). His headquarters were in Cesarea, but during the holidays he stayed in Jerusalem to prevent disruptions.

According to the historians Philo and Flavius Josephus, Pilate was a cruel and corrupt man and a harsh ruler, who provoked the

Jewish people. He brought the standards bearing the likeness of the Roman emperor to Jerusalem, despite the revulsion the Jews felt for the use of images. He also used money from the temple treasury to build an aqueduct from Solomon's pool in Bethlehem to Jerusalem. Pilate did not hesitate to use his soldiers to violently suppress uprisings among the people.

Luke mentions one of the horrific deeds of Pilate.[116] He writes that Pilate had some pilgrims from Galilee killed during the Passover feast, while they were sacrificing at the temple. It was probably the kind of harsh countermeasure Pilate often took when he suspected people of an uprising against his leadership. While they were slaughtering their sacrificial animals and the blood was being collected by the priests to be poured out at the base of the sacrificial altar, the Roman soldiers came into the outer court of the temple (where soldiers, being pagans, were not allowed), and killed the men from Galilee, so that their blood was mingled with that of the sacrificial animals. Their sacrifice was made unclean and could no longer make atonement. And because Pilate's soldiers killed these men, they were incapable of sacrificing again for the atonement of their sins. The Jews were really upset about this. The whole city was talking about it and many were convinced that these men must have been greater sinners than all other men in Galilee, because they had not been able to make atonement with God. When they confronted Jesus about this event, He said:

> *Because those Galileans were killed in that way, do you think it proves that they were worse sinners than all other Galileans? No indeed! And I tell you that if you do not turn from your sins, you will all die as they did.* (Luke 13:2–3, GNB)

In the year 36 A.D., after several complaints, Pontius Pilate was summoned to Rome to give an account of his policy. He was interrogated, and put in prison and probably committed suicide to prevent being executed by Emperor Caligula.

JESUS IS TURNED OVER TO PILATE

Together, the Jewish leaders take Jesus to the Pretorium, the former palace of King Herod in the western part of the city, where Pilate resides during the festivities in Jerusalem. There are also some barracks with an estimated six hundred Roman soldiers there.

It is normal for Pilate to start his work early, at about six a.m. The Jewish leaders, however, are in a rush. They want to deal with Jesus before the seven-day Passover feast starts.

Pilate's guards take Jesus into the courtyard, but the members of the Sanhedrin do not go into the Pretorium; they wait until Pilate comes outside, not wanting to defile themselves by entering the home of a heathen. Pilate, who is aware of this Jewish taboo, comes outside. He acts according to the Roman law *ne quis indicta causa condemnetur*: no one is to be convicted without a hearing. Now that the detainee has been brought in for a preliminary hearing, he must find out what the accusation is. That is why he asks what crime Jesus is being accused of. Now the members of the Sanhedrin have a problem. They do not have a legal accusation that will be recognized by the Roman prefect. The fact that Jesus says He is the Son of God is no reason to have Him crucified. So instead they try to overwhelm Pilate. They are impudent, proud and arrogant.

> **Every single event on this day is unfolding just as God has foretold through the prophets.**

Without a shred of evidence, they try to pass Jesus off as an "evildoer," a criminal. They think this should be enough and that Pilate should impose the death penalty without conducting any kind of investigation. Surely he must understand that the highest Jewish court would not call for a crucifixion without serious grounds! They hope the prefect will not be too concerned about the life of a Jew, preferring to keep the peace in the city, as there are many visitors there for the Passover feast.

Pilate is not eager to conduct a lengthy investigation. Maybe he thinks this is about some trivial Jewish religious issue. The detainee does not seem dangerous to him, so he says: "You have your own laws. You be the judge of him!" That way, he will be rid of Jesus. But the Sanhedrin answers: "We are not allowed to execute someone!" The Jewish leaders do not dare take the law into their own hands this time (as they would later do with Stephen[117]). They know that Jesus is popular with the people; how will they react if He is executed? They also want to avoid performing an execution on a Jewish holiday. They don't want to get their hands dirty. Also, if Pilate calls for an execution and there is resistance from the people, he will be able to manage it.

In reality, neither the Jews nor Pilate are in control. Every single event on this day is unfolding just as God has foretold through the prophets. Jesus is to be crucified as a cursed man, just as He Himself prophesied, and therefore Pilate must judge Him.

THE FIRST HEARING

When Pilate makes his first suggestion to the Sanhedrin, he does not think they are out to have Jesus executed. The Jewish leaders now start to falsely accuse Jesus: "This man is turning the people against the Roman occupiers. He says we do not need to pay taxes to the emperor. He claims he is the Messiah, the king!" This last charge should be enough for Pilate to set up a thorough investigation into whether the Roman government is in danger. Jesus would indeed be a political threat if He really thought He was king of the Jews. Pilate retreats to the court hall and has Jesus brought to him. "Are you the king of the Jews?" he asks.

Jesus answers: "Are you asking this for yourself or have others been talking to you about me?" Of course, Pilate is thinking about an earthly kingdom. If Jesus answers "yes," He will be guilty of high treason to the emperor and the death penalty would be justified. That is why Jesus repeats three times that His Kingdom is not of this world: "My Kingdom is not of this world. If that were the case then my bodyguards would have used violence to stop me from falling into the hands of the Jews. No, my Kingdom is not of this world."

Pilate asks Jesus: "Are you a king then?"

"You yourself use the word king," Jesus answers. "Indeed, I am a king. I was born and came into the world to make the truth known. Everyone who loves truth will listen to what I say."

Pilate does not react to this invitation from Jesus, who has said earlier that He is the truth. This cynical reply is as far as he gets: "What is the truth?" He does not discover that the truth that sets a man free is standing right in front of him.[118]

Pilate goes outside without waiting for an answer. He is now certain that Jesus is not a political rebel. This is no case of high treason against the emperor or the government. Jesus is innocent; there is no case against Him.

Once outside, Pilate sees that a large crowd has gathered in front of his palace. He says to them: "I find no guilt in this man." It is the first time that he declares that Jesus is innocent; later on he will do this a second time.

The Jewish leaders do not give up; they say: "He has incited revolt with his teachings; first in Galilee, later in Judea and now even in Jerusalem!"

"Is He from Galilee, then?" asks Pilate. This gives him the opportunity to rid himself of the case and to leave it to Herod, who rules in Galilee. When Pilate hears that Jesus does indeed come from Galilee, he sends Him to Herod, who has just arrived in Jerusalem.

HEROD ANTIPAS

Herod Antipas was the ruler of Galilee and Perea.[119] He was one of the sons of Herod the Great, who was king over all of Judea at the time of Jesus' birth. He divorced his first wife, the daughter of the king of Nabatea, and married his cousin Herodias, who was the wife of his half-brother Philip, whom he met during a visit to Rome. John the Baptist spoke to him about this, and it cost John his life. Jesus called him "the fox"[120] because he was cunning. Herod Antipas was later charged with treason by his cousin Agrippa and was banished in 39 A.D.

JESUS APPEARS BEFORE HEROD

Luke is the only Gospel writer who writes about the hearing in front of Herod. It is likely that he heard of this event from Joanna, the wife of Herod's court officer, who had been healed by Jesus and who served Him by providing materially for Him and the disciples.[121] It is also possible that he learned about it via Manaen, who had been raised with Herod and later became a believer.[122]

Herod is probably staying in the family palace in the center of the city. He is very happy to see Jesus. He has heard many things about Him and hopes that He will work a miracle in his presence. Herod takes a lot of time questioning Jesus, but does not get any answers. The members of the Sanhedrin have accompanied Jesus and the guards from Pilate's palace to that of Herod and they start to shout all kinds of accusations. They're fanatical. Herod does not pay any attention to them. He knows that the accusations are not true and have no proof whatsoever. Jesus remains silent. This is no true hearing; Herod only wants to be amused by Jesus. He and the soldiers who are present start to make fun of Him and laugh at Him. As a joke the soldiers clothe Jesus in a beautiful garment, like a royal robe. Jesus endures all this without reacting even once. Despite the horrendous accusations of the Jewish leaders, Herod does not convict Jesus of the charges. He sends Him back to Pilate.

Herod and Pilate have always been each other's enemy, but on this day they become the best of friends.[123]

THE SECOND ROMAN HEARING BEFORE PILATE

Pilate summons the Jewish leaders, but he gathers the people together as well, and says: "You have brought this man to me based on the charge that he has been inciting rebellion against the government. I have questioned him closely about this and have reached the conclusion that he is innocent. Herod seems to agree and has sent him back to me. No, this man has done nothing that deserves the death penalty. I will have him whipped and then he is to go free." Pilate does not wish to have Jesus killed at all; he would much rather set Him free. He emphasizes that Herod has reached the same conclusion!

JESUS OR BARABBAS?

It is a custom for the Roman prefect in Judea to free a prisoner during the Passover feast. Pilate thinks he can use this tradition to deliver Jesus by letting the people choose between Him and a no- torious criminal already in prison, whose name is Barabbas. Pilate asks the people who are crowded in front of his palace: "Whom shall I free? Barabbas or Jesus, who is also called the Messiah? What do you want?" He is aware now that the Jewish leaders have had Jesus arrested because they are jealous.

While he is conducting the court case, something unusual happens. Pilate's wife tells him that Jesus is innocent. Obviously, she must have accompanied him to Jerusalem, which was unusual in those days. The message, which she sends to her husband, reach- es him while he is still in the judge's seat, on the so-called *gabbatha*, an elevated mosaic floor from which he will pass judgment. The wife of Pilate sends him this message: "Let that good man go. He is not at all guilty. I was greatly troubled in a dream about him." She does not say what her dream was about. How amazing that this woman has a dream about Jesus on the night He is arrested, and that she sees this as a sign. It is not clear whether she is defending Jesus or warning her husband for fear that bad things might other- wise happen to them.

Meanwhile, the men of the high court have riled the crowd so that they demand that Barabbas is freed and Jesus executed. When

Pilate asks again: "Whom of these two men shall I free?", the people cry: "Barabbas!" Pilate is shocked.

"But what shall I do with Jesus, the one they call the Messiah?" he asks. They shout: "Crucify him!"

"But why?" Pilate asks for a third time. "What evil has he done? I do not see why he should be executed. I will have him whipped and then set free." But they keep shouting that Jesus must die. They just will not stop. Not because Barabbas is so popular with the people (he was jailed for rioting and manslaughter), but because the members of the Sanhedrin have incited the many visitors to Jerusalem to ask for Barabbas to be freed instead of Jesus.

Jesus in the Place of Barabbas

There were probably three executions planned for that Friday, including that of Barabbas. He was arrested because he had killed at least one man during an uprising.[124] Barabbas had chosen the path of violence to realize his political goals. They had imprisoned him and now he was waiting in his cell to be brought out and crucified. Barabbas had probably not slept much that night, as, just like Jesus, he knew he was going to die. He was not aware of the unrest in Jerusalem that had kept many people awake.

The name "Barabbas" was a common one and means "son of the father." I think we can see Barabbas as a symbolic representation of the human race. His life of rebellion, violence and death represents our sinful and rebellious nature. God showed Barabbas and us His great love by sending Jesus and letting Him die for us while we were still guilty sinners.[125] Just like Barabbas, I am a son of the Father, destined to live in the presence of the Father:

In the end, Jesus died on the Cross originally intended for Barabbas.

You used to be far from God. Your thoughts made you his enemies, and you did evil things. But his Son became a human and died. So God made peace with you, and now he lets you stand in his presence as people who are holy and faultless and innocent. (Colossians 1:21–22, CEV)

The Son of God took the place of all the condemned sons and daughters of the Father. In the end, Jesus died on the Cross that was originally intended for Barabbas. We do not know whether Barabbas understood what happened that day at Golgotha, just outside the city of Jerusalem. The question, though, is whether *we* understand that Jesus took the punishment that we deserved, so that we can freely go to God the Father.

THE LAST PROPHECY

It was the high priest Caiaphas who had told the Sanhedrin a few days before all this:

Don't you realize that it is better for you to have one man die for the people, instead of having the whole nation destroyed? (John 11:50, GNB)

Caiaphas was in fact not speaking of his own accord. John tells us that there is more going on in this situation than we initially might think. He explains:

Actually, he did not say this of his own accord; rather, as he was High Priest that year, he was prophesying that Jesus was going to die for the Jewish people, and not only for them, but also to bring together into one body all the scattered people of God. (John 11:51–52, GNB)

Without realizing it, Caiaphas utters the last prophecy about the Messiah. As the high priest and therefore the head of Israel's sacrificial services, Caiaphas points to Jesus as the sacrificial Lamb.

WHY DID JESUS WANT TO SWITCH PLACES AND DIE FOR ME?

Keeping Barabbas and Jesus in mind, we can understand that Jesus died on the Cross so that an exchange could take place. In his book *Bought with Blood: The Divine Exchange at the Cross*, Derek Prince shares how the wonder of the Cross at Golgotha was a sevenfold exchange:

1. Jesus took our sins upon Himself, so that we could receive forgiveness. (1 Peter 2:24)
2. Jesus was beaten, so that we could receive healing. (1 Peter 2:24)
3. Jesus was made sin for our sins, so that we could be justified by His righteousness. (2 Corinthians 5:21)
4. Jesus died our death, so that we could receive His life. (Hebrews 2:9)
5. Jesus became poor with our poverty, so that we might be made rich with His wealth. (2 Corinthians 8:9 and 9:8)
6. Jesus endured our rejection, so that we could be accepted as children of God. (Matthew 27:46, 50 and Ephesians 1:5–6)
7. Jesus became a curse, so that we could receive the blessing. (Galatians 3:13–14)

Father in heaven,

What can I give to You, who gave all? You gave Jesus for me. Thank You, Jesus, that You took my place, while I was guilty. Thank You for switching places with me at the Cross, so that I can stand spotless and blameless before God! I do not want anything to prevent me from loving and serving You.

Amen.

THE WHIPPING

But because of our sins He was wounded, beaten because of the evil we did. We are healed by the punishment He suffered, made whole by the blows He received.

(Isaiah 53:5, GNB)

CHAPTER 7

Both Pontius Pilate and King Herod have judged that Jesus is innocent.[126] They find no guilt in Him. Both of these authorities testify to Jesus' innocence. This means that Jesus should have been acquitted, according to Deuteronomy 19:15: "One witness is not enough to convict someone of a crime; at least two witnesses are necessary to prove that someone is guilty." After a second attempt to prove Jesus' innocence, Pilate makes a statement about what he will do with Jesus: he wants to free Him, but not before he has had Him whipped. The word that Luke uses for whipping (*paideuo*) literally means "to train, chastise." Pilate wants to teach Jesus a lesson by having Him whipped. The measure is completely illegal, because he has just pronounced Him innocent! Maybe Pilate hopes to appease the people, thinking they will allow Jesus to go free after a severe beating. So Pilate takes Jesus inside and has Him whipped.

THE WHIPPING

The whippings given by the Roman soldiers are known to have been very bloody. They left stripes on the entire body. The Romans had especially designed their whips to rip bits of flesh out of the body of the victim. Jesus is bound by ropes, completely naked, to a stone pillar. His arms are stretched upward, His face toward the pillar. There were usually two soldiers to carry out the whipping and they took turns at hitting with the so-called *flagrum* or *flagellum*, a Roman whip. This had a short handle with two leather strips attached to it. Lead bullets about the size of hazelnuts, or the small foot bones of a sheep, were attached to the ends of these strips. Jesus' skin was literally ripped to shreds with this terrible instrument. The blows were administered systematically from the shoulders to the calves. The Romans did not set a limit to the amount of blows dealt; they just waited to see how much the prisoner could handle. Sometimes as many as a hundred blows might be dealt. By that time, the victim would most likely hang unconscious in the ropes, surrounded by a large pool of blood, with little left of his skin. The Romans often applied a whipping prior to a convict's execution. The damage done to so much skin and the bruising of the muscle tissue are comparable to third-degree burns to half of the body. Without medical help, a victim might die within hours or days. That is why the Jewish law had determined that the maximum amount of blows was to be thirty-nine.

The blows from the whip were designed to make the pain excruciating. They also caused fluid to collect around the lungs. In the state Jesus is in, the whipping alone is enough to kill Him. His body is destroyed, beaten to a pulp and disfigured. He has not eaten for hours and owing to heavy perspiration and bleeding, He has lost a lot of fluid.

JESUS, THE MAN WITHOUT SICKNESS

Jesus was born of a virgin, which means that His conception was a supernatural miracle of creation. This fact lies at the heart of the Christian faith. Jesus had His heavenly Father's DNA. As the Man without sin, He was never subjected to the curse of sin in His body. His body was therefore immune to sickness or death (like Adam and Eve, who also did not know sickness or death before they sinned). Because Jesus had a divine nature and had never sinned, His life was not subject to the power of death. Every sickness is, in fact, a form of death in our lives. Neither sickness nor death had any power over the life of Jesus—no matter how many times His enemies tried to kill Him! It is very important to keep this in mind, so that we can understand what the exchange at the Cross meant for our health! Roman soldiers whipped the body that had never known disease, until the muscles and tendons were exposed and Jesus was so badly mutilated that He could no longer be recognized. The blows dealt by the whips had such a devastating effect on the body of Jesus that people could no longer bear to look at Him and turned their heads away, just as Isaiah prophesied:

> **Jesus had his heavenly Father's DNA. As the Man without sin, He was never subjected to the curse of sin in his body. His body was therefore immune to sickness or death.**

> *Just as there were many who were appalled at him—his appearance was so disfigured beyond that of any human being and his form marred beyond human likeness—so he will sprinkle many nations, and kings will shut their mouths because of him. For what they were not told, they will see, and what they have not heard, they will understand. (...) He had no beauty or majesty to attract us to him, nothing in his appearance that we should desire him. He was despised and rejected by mankind, a man of suffering, and familiar with pain. Like one from whom people hide their faces he was despised, and we held him in low esteem.*

*Surely he took up our pain and bore our suffering, yet we consid-
ered him punished by God, stricken by him, and afflicted. But he
was pierced for our transgressions, he was crushed for our iniquities; the punishment that brought us peace was on him, and by his
wounds we are healed.* (Isaiah 52:14 and 53:2–5, NIV)

Why did the body of Jesus, which had never known sickness,
have to be mutilated so terribly that people could no longer bear
to look at Him? Why did Jesus have to suffer so much that people could no longer recognize Him? Just as the Man without sin
identified Himself with our sins and drank the cup filled with the
sins of the world to the very last drop, in the same way the Man
who knew no sickness let His perfect body be destroyed. Through
the whipping, which wrecked His body, all of our sicknesses were
laid on Him. Every destructive and incurable disease known to
man was laid on Jesus. Jesus became "acquainted" with all our
illness and pain.[127] There is no disease that Jesus did not bear in
His body during this destructive whipping. Therefore, we must not
look away from the destroyed and deformed body of Jesus. In His
inhumane mutilation lies our supernatural healing!

The Fourth Wonder of the Cross:
By His Stripes We Are Healed

The wonder of the Cross does not just result in the forgiveness
of our sins, delivery from accusations and (feelings of) guilt and the
cleansing of our consciences, but also in the healing of our bodies!
Just as Jesus drank the cup that was filled to the brim with our sins
in Gethsemane, He also, with every blow of the whip, took our
sicknesses upon Himself. "By his stripes you are healed!" Isaiah
cries out to us. It is finished! Peter quoted Isaiah:

*... who his own self bore our sins in his body on the tree, that we,
having died to sins, might live to righteousness; by whose stripes you
were healed.* (1 Peter 2:24, WEB)

The evangelist Matthew also quoted the well-known prophecy of Isaiah, when he informed us that all the sick who came to Jesus were healed:

> When evening came, they brought to him many possessed with demons. He cast out the spirits with a word, and healed all who were sick; that it might be fulfilled which was spoken through Isaiah the prophet, saying: "He took our infirmities, and bore our diseases." (Matthew 8:16–17, WEB)

Matthew declares that Jesus healed all the sick who came to him, so that the words of Isaiah would be fulfilled that He would bear all our sicknesses and diseases. How could Matthew declare that the sick were healed through His stripes even before Jesus had suffered and died? Was Matthew getting ahead of himself, or did he want to open our eyes to see something we had not yet perceived?

There are a lot of people who think along these lines and wonder how the death of Jesus, which occurred two thousand years ago, can still be effective now. How can Jesus' suffering be accepted by God as atonement for our sins and as a means of healing for our bodies? The answer is that Jesus' death was not just a historical event that took place long ago, but that He is the Lamb who was "slain from the foundation of the world."[128]

When God created man, Jesus already knew the price He would pay for our salvation. The suffering that Jesus endured on this earth was a manifestation of the pain that He suffered throughout eternity for mankind. The Cross was already in His heart from the start of eternity! From a human perspective, the believers who lived before Jesus appeared on earth looked ahead to the Cross, while those who lived after His coming look back to the Cross. In actual fact, the wonder of the Cross is an eternal reality and cannot be contained in time! That is why the Bible speaks of "eternal salvation."[129]

We were born long after Jesus' death and had not yet done anything good or evil when He was whipped and crucified. Nonetheless, by believing in what Jesus has done for us, we too will receive forgiveness for our sins and healing for our sicknesses—just like the people who lived at the time of Jesus. "He offered one sacrifice, once and for all, when he offered himself."[130] The wonder of the Cross is an eternal reality!

God knew how quickly the Cross would become "normal" in our lives. He knew that understanding the wonder of the Cross would be something that does not come naturally to us. That is why He commanded us to celebrate the Lord's Supper regularly, so that the meaning of the Cross, the wonder of it all, would remain vivid for us. Each time we eat the bread and drink the cup, we "proclaim the Lord's death until he comes."[131] God wants us to continually remember Jesus' suffering and death, so that we will not become indifferent or discouraged and give up on our faith.[132] As we stop viewing the wonder of the Cross as a past historic event and accept it as an eternal fact, the death and resurrection of Jesus become an intimate daily reality and source of strength in our personal lives.

> **In actual fact, the wonder of the Cross is an eternal reality and cannot be contained in time!**

Throughout church history, Christians have believed the words of Isaiah and many sick people have been healed. We have been privileged to witness many times in our own lives and ministry that Jesus is still the Lord of Healing today. Every time someone is healed through the power of the Holy Spirit and in the name of Jesus it is a testimony to the fact that Jesus is alive! I myself have been personally healed of infertility (we have four sons) and of epilepsy. Both healings have been confirmed by doctors and are evident in my day-to-day life! We have seen kneecaps moved, backs healed, tumors disappear, ears opened, rheumatism disappear and all kinds of asthmatic conditions healed. Several people we know were on disability pay but are now working full-time, much to the amazement of the social services. This is what Jesus is doing today! We are happy that in many churches praying for the sick has become a regular part of worship. Jesus commanded us to do this:

> *Believers will be given the power to perform wonders: they will drive out demons in my name; they will speak in strange tongues; if they pick up snakes or drink any poison, they will not be harmed; they will place their hands on sick people, and these will get well.* (Mark 16:17–18, GNB)

To pray for the sick is a command. But just as Jesus Himself said that "I can do nothing on my own authority,"[133] we also must know that we are incapable of healing the sick in our own strength. It is our job to (continue to) pray for the sick: we pray; Jesus heals. When we do pray for those who are ill, it is important that those praying and those being prayed for stay focused on Jesus.[134] He is the Lord of healing through us!

THE ROAD TO HEALING

The Bible teaches us that God wants to give us healing, but that there is a route to follow. Exodus 15:26 is the first verse in the Bible that states that God is our healer:

> *He said, "If you will obey me completely by doing what I consider right and by keeping my commands, I will not punish you with any of the diseases that I brought on the Egyptians. I am the Lord, the one who heals you."* (Exodus 15:26, GNB)

God shows us here that the road to healing involves a) listening to His voice and b) obeying Him by doing what He asks! That is why it is important that nothing should come between God and me. Every sin in my life forms a barrier, hindering me from clearly hearing God's voice. Hebrews 12:14 says that we will not see the Lord unless we live a holy life. Without living a holy life, in which we turn from sin and focus wholly on Him, we will not hear His voice! Sin hardens our heart, so that we are no longer sensitive to the Spirit of Jesus, who lives in us and wants to speak to us.

It is no coincidence that there is a clear order in the wonders of the Cross.

It is no coincidence that there is a clear order in the wonders of the Cross. This order confirms that there is a route to healing. God wants to a) heal our sins, b) free us from all guilt and accusation, c) cleanse our consciences, and d) let us receive healing. Jesus warns us with the following words:

> *But if you do not forgive others, then your Father will not forgive the wrongs you have done.* (Matthew 6:15, GNB)

If God cannot forgive our sins because we have not forgiven others, then our decision not to forgive blocks the road to healing! I have discovered that the inability to forgive is one of the greatest barriers to receiving healing. Jesus asks us to forgive seventy times seven.[135] The unlimited vengeance of Lamech[136] must be replaced by unlimited forgiveness! Then the power of healing can be released in our lives. Then we will see the words of Jesus become a growing reality in and through us:

> *If you remain in me and my words remain in you, then you will ask for anything you wish, and you shall have it.* (John 15:7, GNB)

The second part of this verse ("then you will ask for anything you wish, and you shall have it") cannot be separated from the first part ("If you remain in me and my words remain in you"). Again, Jesus is teaching us here that there is a route to healing. The route of a) being in Him and b) believing His words and doing them! But what if we do all this and still are not (yet) healed?

MY OTHER LIST

Although I'm excited about the list of healing wonders we've been allowed to experience, honesty compels me to mention my other list as well. It is a list of the names of men, women and children who have not (yet) been healed by God and who, medically speaking, cannot be healed. Men and women who are walking on the road to healing with great care, who love Jesus and who have a pure relationship with Him. The list even includes the names of children who have died of their illnesses. Each name is etched on our hearts. We don't want to hide this second list, or pretend it isn't there. The Bible teaches us to rejoice with those who rejoice and weep with those who weep.[137] In many churches, there is little or no attention paid to those who are, or remain, sick. Many times, this is because of the leadership's fear of failure. The healing of the sick is often (subconsciously) connected with the success of a leader's "own" ministry. The absence of healing can be experienced as a personal failure on the part of the minister, who may then respond by neglecting those who are, or remain, ill. To my shame, I must admit that I, too, have been guilty of this. I discovered that I wasn't dealing with this issue because of an identity problem. If I am sure of the Father's love for me, I no longer have to focus on the visible results of "my" ministry; my first and foremost desire is to share God's love with all those who (still) need healing and support. In a healthy Christian community, preaching about healing goes together with caring for those who, despite our prayers, remain sick. They are a reality we cannot ignore. The writer of Hebrews puts it like this:

> *You have put all things in subjection under his feet. For in that he subjected all things to him, he left nothing that is not subject to him. But now we don't see all things subjected to him, yet. But we see him who has been made a little lower than the angels, Jesus, because of the suffering of death crowned with glory and honor, that by the grace of God he should taste of death for everyone.* (Hebrews 2:8–9, WEB)

Years ago, this passage in the Bible answered many questions I had (and still have) about healing. We see here that "everything" (including all sickness) is under the power of Jesus, but that we don't see "everything" (including all sickness) subjected to Him yet! In other words: the truth of the wonder of the Cross is that we have been healed by Jesus' stripes. The fact is that we cannot yet see that all sickness has been subjected to Him. Faith does not mean we deny the facts through our faith in the wonder of the Cross, but that we subject the facts to the truth that we have received healing by the stripes of Jesus! This is a thin line to balance on. No

In a healthy Christian community, preaching about healing goes together with caring for those who, despite our prayers, remain sick.

wonder the writer of Hebrews urges us to hang on to the following four words in all circumstances: "But we see him!" This is the testimony of the apostle Paul, too. God performed many unusual wonders through Paul.[138] But even he knew periods of disease and hardship in his personal life:

> You remember why I preached the gospel to you the first time; it was because I was sick. But even though my physical condition was a great trial to you, you did not despise or reject me. Instead, you received me as you would an angel from heaven; you received me as you would Christ Jesus. (Galatians 4:13–14, GNB)

In spite of his illness, the Galatians saw Jesus Christ in Paul. What a testimony of God's love! Let us not "despise" or "reject" those who are ill. Of all people, they are the ones who need our support and encouragement! Let us see Jesus Christ in them, just as Paul says:

To whom God was pleased to make known what are the riches of the glory of this mystery among the Gentiles, which is Christ in you, the hope of glory. (Colossians 1:27, WEB)

Let us keep our eyes on Jesus, who lives in us, and not on the disease!

A CHALLENGING TESTIMONY

My thoughts go back to Peter and Sue. Peter was a fanatical hockey player. Hockey was his life. Hockey came first in his life—and his relationship with Sue suffered as a result. But Peter was not quite aware of this. Not until he met Jesus and his life was changed drastically. Peter decided to give up hockey so that he would have more time for his family and his relationship with Jesus. He and Sue both loved the Lord and were enjoying the new life they had received. Children were born, three boys and a girl. But something went wrong when the fourth was born. It was a very difficult birth and the little boy died when he was just one week old, while Sue was partially paralyzed by a stroke. This was the beginning of a difficult time. Peter and Sue were mourning the loss of Pieter-Bas and the whole family was under tremendous pressure because of Sue's disability. Despite professional therapy, Sue could hardly walk and ended up in a wheelchair. Miraculously, though, Peter and Sue remained firm in their faith. While crying out to God, they discovered what the Bible says about healing. They wanted to trust the God who raised Jesus from the dead. They ended up in our church. How important it is for people to be touched by God's love in our churches! Peter and Sue experienced the tender loving care of the Father. They opened their hearts and began to believe that God could heal Sue. During a Sunday service, God spoke to my heart, saying He would heal Sue in three waves. And that is just how it happened. The first time Sue encountered the power of Jesus, she could lift her knees and walk up the stairs! This boosted the faith of all of us. A short time later God touched her a second time, and

Sue gained more strength in her body. I will never forget the third time. God's power was so strong that Sue fell to the ground and I knelt beside her to bless the work of the Holy Spirit in her. At that moment I heard the same Holy Spirit speak to me: "Go away; this is a work of God and not of man!" I moved several feet away and sat down on a chair, quite shaken. God taught me in that defining moment that healing is His work and not mine or anyone else's!

The healing of Sue made a deep impression on all of us. She no longer needed the wheelchair! Peter and Sue shared how the love and power of Jesus had healed her with everyone, everywhere they went.

Two years later Peter, Sue and their children moved to another town. God had called them

> **It seems to me that God reacts more to "what" questions than to "why" questions.**

to help set up the first evangelical high school in Holland. Shortly after their move, Sue was unexpectedly confronted with a new disease: breast cancer. Their first reaction was: this can't be happening! Surely, God did not heal her body from the results of the stroke just to let her die of cancer? Both the new congregation they had just joined and our church prayed for Sue. Peter and Sue experienced the intensity of death threatening to destroy her life. Once again, there was a huge spiritual battle raging in and around their family. They knew how important it was to stay close to Jesus. But this time, despite all the prayers sent up to the throne of God, Sue was not healed. She went through an operation and chemotherapy. The lymph nodes were removed from her armpit, with the result that the fluid balance in that arm no longer worked properly and her painful arm needed to be bandaged daily. At the time of writing, she still has to wear an elastic stocking on her arm.

Peter and Sue are an example to us of faith, patience and endurance. Many times I have laid my questions before God, without receiving an answer. Has God changed? No. Everyone who commits their life to praying for the sick will be met with disappointment. Some will not be healed. People in this world cling to a lie they themselves have created: as long as you are healthy, things will be fine. I have discovered that in God's Kingdom a different truth applies: as long as you are in God's presence! Peter, Sue and others have taught me that, despite the situation we are in, it is possible to live continually in His presence. This is the power of the wonder of the Cross! Whoever experiences this ceases to depend on circumstances, even physical circumstances. Just like King David, we may know and experience peace amid trials:

> *Even if I go through the deepest darkness, I will not be afraid, Lord, for you are with me.* (Psalm 23:4, GNB)

This is why we have stopped asking the old "why" questions. Instead, we have learned to ask the "what" question: "What do we do now?" It seems to me that God reacts more to "what" questions than to "why" questions. By asking "what" questions, our spirits tune in to God's solution for our lives. "What" questions bring hope through the realization that our lives are in His hands. To belong to Him and to be with Him, that's what we're alive for!

POWERS OF THE AGE TO COME

Paul knew like no other that we can experience and taste the "powers of the age to come,"[139] even though not everyone he prayed for was healed:

> *Erastus stayed in Corinth, and I left Trophimus in Miletus, because he was sick.* (2 Timothy 4:20, GNB)

In his book *Heal The Sick!*, my friend the author Dr. Willem J. Ouweneel observes that a great many of those who were or are "effective ministers of healing" suffer from ongoing diseases themselves. The fathers of the Pentecostal movement, William Seymour and Charles Parham, both died of heart disease. They lived to be only fifty-two and fifty-six years old, respectively (dying in 1922 and 1929). John G. Lake died of a stroke at the age of sixty-five (1935). Kathryn Kuhlman suffered from heart disease for twenty years and died after open heart surgery in 1976. John Wimber from the USA suffered from cancer and underwent chemotherapy, but died at sixty-three years of age owing to hemorrhaging caused by a tumor (1997).

Yonggi Cho in Korea, the pastor of what may be the largest church on earth, has been very ill at times, but has had himself brought to the services in his bed—while many have been healed through his ministry.

These and many other examples teach us that Hebrews 2:8 and 9 are a daily reality: we know that all things are subjected to Jesus, but we also see that there is a spiritual battle raging. Throughout this battle we want to keep our eyes fixed on Jesus! To receive healing, we not only need faith but persistence and patience to receive what God has promised:

You need to be patient, in order to do the will of God and receive what he promises. (Hebrews 10:36, GNB)

God is not unfair. He will not forget the work you did or the love you showed for him in the help you gave and are still giving to other Christians. Our great desire is that each of you keep up your eagerness to the end, so that the things you hope for will come true. We do not want you to become lazy, but to be like those who believe and are patient, and so receive what God has promised. (Hebrews 6:10–12, GNB)

How important it is that we keep on "doing the will of God," despite hardships and disappointments. This means we must continue to pray for the sick, persevering in faith. God wants us to "keep up our eagerness to the end, so that the things we hope for will come true!" In other words: have faith, keep doing God's will, and persevere!

How important it is that we keep on "doing the will of God," despite hardships and disappointments. This means we must continue to pray for the sick, persevering in faith.

IF HEALING HASN'T (YET) TAKEN PLACE

Our job is to keep on preaching God's word while at the same time caring for all (!) people. It is possible that people do not have faith that they will be healed; however, this is rare. Nowhere in the Bible do we find a person who is not healed owing to lack of faith. If you're praying for healing and it has not (yet) occurred, the following points may help you strengthen your relationship with Jesus, the Healer:

- The Bible teaches us that there is not one prayer that gets lost. Our prayers are of eternal value! In Revelation 8:3–5, we read that the prayers of the saints are kept on a golden altar before God on His throne, until God gives the sign to throw the fire from the altar to earth, as an answer to those prayers. Our times are in God's hand, including the time of our healing! We prayed for many years that a couple in our church would become pregnant. Several servants of God gave them a word from the Lord saying they would have a child. After ten (!) years of praying, they were with us in a healing service, at the end of which the pastor called forward those who were barren. Dick and Ellen went forward and within a month they were expecting a child, and Ellen later gave birth to a healthy daughter. It wasn't just that one prayer by the pastor that was answered by God, but all the other prayers that had been sent up to God throughout those ten years. Those prayers had been kept in front of His throne, until the moment God answered with fire from heaven! Let us not forget that as we persevere in prayer.

- Remind each other that we are to fix our hope and attention on Jesus, our Healer, and not on the healing itself. Healing is not our greatest hope. Only Jesus can realize the hope of this world.

- Make sure no one feels guilty because healing has not (yet) taken place. Encourage the sick to study God's word on healing and apply it to their own situation.

- If the person you are praying for is a Christian, encourage him/her to join you in prayer for others who are sick. Seeing God use them to heal others will strengthen their own faith! Prayer for others also prevents the sick from becoming obsessed with their own illness. This Scripture applies to the sick as well as to the healthy: rejoice with those who rejoice and weep with those who weep.

- Remind each other that we are fighting a spiritual battle and the enemy does not want us healed, but that the enemy has been defeated and conquered by Jesus Christ on the Cross at Golgotha!

- Speak about and pray through your own personal situation with others who have more experience in the healing ministry, and be open to suggestions.

- Ask yourself this question: have I been obedient in everything that the Holy Spirit has said to me? Pray and fast for God's direction and thank God for the wonder of the Cross in your life. Know that *Yahweh Rapha* ("I am the Lord, the one who heals you")[140] is with us and will hold us in his hand.

Father in heaven,

How can I ever thank You for what Jesus did for me? Thank You that Jesus took my sickness in His body and bore my pain. I believe that by His stripes I am healed. Jesus is my healer,

too! I believe that every sickness is subject to Him and that I therefore may come to You for healing in my body. I know that my sins have been forgiven by You and I also forgive those who have sinned against me, so that no barrier can stop Your healing power. By the power of the blood of Jesus, the power of sin, sickness and death has been broken in my life. Help me to persevere in doing Your will by also praying for the healing for others who are sick. Thank You that I may continually live in Your presence through the wonder of the Cross.
Thank You for so much love!

Amen.

THE FIFTH WONDER OF THE CROSS:
THE CROWN OF THORNS

But by becoming a curse for us Christ has redeemed us from the curse that the Law brings; for the scripture says, Anyone who is hanged on a tree is under God's curse.

(Galatians 3:13, GNB)

CHAPTER 8

After the cruel whipping, the soldiers take Jesus into the inner court of the Pretorium. There they call in the whole battalion, about 600 soldiers. These soldiers ridicule Jesus, who by now is semi-conscious. Without Pilate's permission they rip off His clothing and think it is a great joke to drape a red Roman soldier's cape over the shoulders of this man, who in their eyes is a mere Jew from the country. His countrymen had hailed Jesus as king when He came into Jerusalem, so they make fun of Him by giving Him a reed stick to hold as a scepter and they weave a "crown" of thorns and jam it roughly on His head.

This crown of thorns was probably made out of dried branches of the *Zizyphus spina*, a tree which has razor-sharp thorns about 2.5 cm long, which can easily pierce the skin over the skull.

The soldiers mockingly drop to their knees and "hail Him as king." They spit in His face, rip the reed stick from His hands and hit Him on the head with it, so that the thorns penetrate His skin and He starts to bleed for a fifth time.

THE FIFTH WONDER OF THE CROSS:
JESUS FREES US FROM
EVERY CURSE IN OUR LIVES

The "coronation" of Jesus by the Roman soldiers in the inner court of the Pretorium is not just circumstantial. It becomes clear later on that this event was completely directed by the Father to give us the fifth wonder of the Cross and its meaning for our lives: that the blood of Jesus frees us from every curse.

The crown of thorns that was placed on Jesus' head by the Roman soldiers is symbolic of the curse, or, in other words, the result of sin in our lives. In Genesis 3:17–19 we read: "Cursed is the ground because of you; in pain you shall eat of it all the days of your life; thorns and thistles it shall bring forth for you." The thorns are symbolic of the cursed ground (the result of sin). Jesus died on the Cross not only to take away our sins but also to destroy the consequences of those sins.

> **Jesus died on the Cross not only to take away our sins but also to destroy the consequences of those sins.**

THE SPIRITUAL MEANING OF A CURSE

The Bible teaches us that the results of a curse are like a *spiritual power* that can come on us and pursue, overtake and destroy us. God warned the people of Israel with the following words:

All these curses shall come on you, and shall pursue you, and over-take you, until you are destroyed; because you didn't listen to the voice of Yahweh your God, to keep his commandments and his statutes which he commanded you. (Deuteronomy 28:45, WEB)

A curse cannot hurt you unless there is a cause (sin).

Like a flitting sparrow, like a flying swallow, so a curse without cause shall not alight. (Proverbs 26:2, NKJV)

A curse can come over someone only if there is a valid reason. This is a spiritual law that still applies even after the death and resurrection of Jesus, if we persist in our sin. If we do not stop sinning, then we are called *children of cursing*.[141] In the same way the sons of Eli brought down a curse on themselves because they were sleeping with the women at the tent of meeting.[142] Didn't Peter say that the devil still walks around like a roaring lion, seeking people to devour?[143] Only if there are hidden sins in our lives, or perhaps the ongoing effects of the unconfessed sins of our ancestors, will the devil be able to lay a demonic claim on our lives, aiming to keep us away from God and eventually to destroy us. God made it clear to Joshua that a curse had come over him and the army because they had sinned in secret. They were continually exposed to the torment of the enemy and God could no longer protect them:

The Bible teaches us that the results of a curse are like a spiritual power that can come on us and pursue, overtake and destroy us.

Get up! Why have you fallen on your face like that? Israel has sinned, Yes, they have even transgressed my covenant which I commanded them. Yes, they have even taken some of the devoted things, and have also stolen, and also deceived. They have even put it among their own stuff. Therefore the children of Israel can't stand before their enemies. They turn their backs before their enemies, because they have become devoted for destruction. I will not be with you any more, unless you destroy the devoted things from among you. Get up! Sanctify the people, and say, Sanctify yourselves for tomorrow, for Yahweh, the God of Israel, says, There is a devoted thing among you, Israel. You cannot stand before your enemies until you take away the devoted thing from among you. (Joshua 7:10–13, WEB)

In the same way, there can be powers at work in our lives that have their origins in previous generations. God spoke to the people of Israel and said that if they did not obey the Ten Commandments, He would bring down punishment on the children to the third and fourth generation for the sins of the fathers.[144] This can lead to a weak spot and a tendency in the family to sin in a specific area. The Bible says:

Our ancestors sinned, but they are dead, and we are left to pay for their sins. (Lamentations 5:7, CEV)

The few of you who survive in the land of your enemies will waste away because of your own sin and the sin of your ancestors. (Leviticus 26:39, GNB)

In the same way, we read in the Bible how Judah slept with his daughter-in-law Tamar, which led to a tendency in his family line to sin in this area. According to the Bible, a curse will come over those who commit incest. A curse will be passed down through the family line:

A bastard shall not enter into the congregation of the LORD; even to his tenth generation shall he not enter into the congregation of the LORD. (Deuteronomy 23:2, KJV)

King David was born ten generations after Judah.[145] It is striking to see how King David also falls into the sin of impurity. It is even more shocking to see that Amnon, a son of David, has an incestuous relationship with his half-sister, another Tamar.[146] In the royal family of David, the pattern of immorality repeated itself generation upon generation.

A Fierce Example

A fierce example of how a curse can influence several generations is to be found in the story of a friend of ours. One day he and his wife discovered that the man's son from a previous marriage had sexually abused two of their children. This happened when the two victims were eight years old. The discovery caused a complete upheaval in the lives of the family members. In the weeks and months that followed, the family went through an traumatic time, especially the two children who had suffered the abuse. After a while, it became clear that our friend, their father, was having all kinds of problems in his life. We talked and prayed together several times and eventually the story came out. It turned out that the father, too, had been abused as a child of eight years old! When he told his own mother what had happened to him and his children, she burst into tears. It turned out that she and her father had also both been sexually abused at the age of eight!

So you see how a curse can affect generation after generation until the sins (including those of the forefathers) have been confessed, the curse has been broken and restoration can take place in the name of Jesus Christ.

Confessing Someone Else's Sin

The Bible tells four times how Pontius Pilate saw no sin in Jesus. He did his best to have Jesus released.[147] Eventually he would come under so much pressure from the Jewish leaders that he would hand Jesus over to be crucified. He then washed his hands of blame and declared: "I am innocent of the blood of this righteous person. You see to it."[148] Pilate would not take responsibility for the possible consequences. The people reacted and all cried out: "May his blood be on us, and on our children!" In this way they brought down a curse on themselves and their children. A curse that would come over them, pursue them, overtake them and destroy them. This verse has been wrongly interpreted by many Christians who called the Jews "Murderers of Christ" and believed that the Holocaust was a direct result of this curse, which they called down on themselves. They forget that Jesus Himself broke this self-imposed curse by asking His Father to forgive their sins:

> *Jesus said, Father, forgive these people! They don't know what they're doing.* (Luke 23:34, CEV)

If we want to be free from the curse on our lives, then it is good to confess the sins of our "ancestors" just as Jesus did—after we have turned away from the sinful lifestyle of those ancestors.[149] Then we will personally begin to experience the truth that God's blessing is stronger than any curse. Because Jesus Christ bought our freedom from the curse on the Cross, the blessing of Abraham can come over us! Jesus purchased our freedom from the curse by becoming a curse for us Himself:

> *Christ redeemed us from the curse of the law, having become a curse for us. For it is written, "Cursed is everyone who hangs on a tree," that the blessing of Abraham might come on the Gentiles through Christ Jesus; that we might receive the promise of the Spirit through faith.* (Galatians 3:13–14, WEB).

Sin and the curse have a spiritual power that can only be broken in a spiritual way, through the Cross! That is why Jesus identified Himself not only with our sins but also with the results of our sins, which He bore in His body. He did not just become sin for us, but also became a curse for us! If we now confess our sins and ask

God for forgiveness and turn from our sinful ways, then we may recant and break every curse in our lives through the name of Jesus. God's blessing will come to us through the wonder of the Cross and heal us. The wonder of the Cross shows us that God will give us back sevenfold what the devil has stolen from us.[150]

My Crushed Pinky

In the days when we were taking our first steps in the deliverance ministry, we were confronted with a few terrifying events in our family. Every time our team prayed for someone's deliverance, we were attacked in our own home by all kinds of spooky happenings. Nowadays we're pretty straightforward and don't get easily upset, but after a few of these experiences, it became clear that whenever we prayed for someone to be delivered, we could expect something to happen in our house. On several occasions, for instance, one of our children was attacked in his dreams the night we prayed for someone. One of our boys would have "nightmares" about the horrible sins that had been confessed by the person who had confided in us. We have experienced situations that I don't even dare to write down on paper. One night, after yet another "nightmare," our son was so scared and out of control that he didn't know how to get out of his bedroom any more. He slammed his entire body into his bedroom door several times. When I ran to help him, my left little finger got caught between the bedroom door and the doorpost and was crushed. It was fractured in several places. Weeks later (after an operation and much prayer), it became clear to us that we did not have to tolerate "all this" in our own home. My wife and I asked our colleagues to pray with us about what was going on. One of them experienced an inner prompting while praying and asked if we had family in Barneveld, a town in Holland. I said we didn't and she left it at that. It wasn't until the following day that I realized that maybe she was referring to my mother's maiden name, "van Barneveld." When I shared this with her, she said she had had a vision of an older man with a hat on and a pick-ax in his hands. "That is my grandfather van Barneveld," I exclaimed. "He worked in the mines for a while!" We decided to pray about this the following night. To this day, we have never quite understood what exactly opened the door for these things to happen in our house. But we stood in the place of our forefathers and asked God to forgive their sins, so that every entrance they might have created for the devil would be closed in the name of Jesus. Since then we have had the privilege of praying for countless people. But never again have any of us been harassed by these nasty events. We live under God's protection, and on most nights we enjoy a good night's sleep.

Jesus Became the "Victim" in Our Place

Many Christians are caught up in the injustices of their past. They are stuck in the role of victim, while deliverance and freedom are within their reach. They think they have the right to act in a certain way because of what has been done to them. By justifying this attitude (on the grounds of the past), they miss out on a large part of the wonder of the Cross. They believe that their present lives are determined by their past. But that's a lie. The truth is that my present life is determined by the choices I make as I go along. The (good or bad) choices I made yesterday will determine the quality of my life today. If I believe in what Jesus did for me, my life will no longer be determined by what people may have done to me in the past, but by what Christ did for me on the Cross!

On the Cross, Jesus became an offering and a sacrifice to God, but also the "victim" of the curse in my place. He does not want me to hold on to my role as a victim for one more minute, but rather encourages me to completely embrace the wonder of the Cross, so that His love will heal me.

Walk in love, even as Christ also loved you, and gave himself up for us, an offering and a sacrifice to God for a sweet-smelling fragrance. (Ephesians 5:2, WEB)

Jesus let Himself be falsely accused and ridiculed like a lamb being led to the slaughter. He was rejected, disowned and beaten until He bled, because He loved us! He wants nothing more than for us to accept His sacrifice.

This is the choice we must make, the choice that has the potential to change the quality of our life completely. Jesus wants us to give the crown of thorns resting on our life to Him: our past, our memories, our pain, our anger, our sadness, our rejection, our insecurities, our right to revenge, our role as victim.

> **However, the truth is that my life is determined by the choices that I make!**

How do we see what took place in the inner court of the Pretorium? Do we recognize that the Roman soldiers crowned Jesus with a crown of thorns on your and my behalf? Jesus came to this world to be crowned by us with the curse of our lives—the curse of the painful consequences of sin.

See how the King of kings bows down before us and says: "Come, it is finished. I have fought the battle. When the soldiers hit my head with a stick and the thorns penetrated deep into my skin, I took all the consequences of the sin in your life upon me. Do not be afraid. Place your crown of thorns on my head."

HOLDING THE CROWN OF THORNS

We have a Cross in our church, with a crown of thorns on it. The crown of thorns—a symbol of the curse, the result of sin in my life—is hanging on the Cross. I remember that after a sermon on this part of the wonder of the Cross a woman came forward to give the curse of her life to God. One of our colleagues gave her the crown of thorns to hold and said: will you give Him the pain and the injustices done to you? I could see at a distance how difficult it was for this woman to let go of the crown of thorns of her life.

Through the wonder of the Cross we can be freed from the consequences of the past: the guilt, the shame and our role as a victim.

She was holding on so tightly that the thorns were sticking into her hands!

Why is letting go so very difficult for so many of us? Often the lie that our present depends on our past is so intertwined with our thoughts and actions that it must first be exposed. That is why a counselor's first task is always to help people expose the lies in which they have been entangled and to replace them with the truth of the wonder of the Cross. Through the wonder of the Cross we can be freed from the consequences of the past: the guilt, the shame and our role as a victim.

TRAPPED IN THE ROLE OF A VICTIM

How do you know whether you've taken on the role of a victim? Maybe you'll recognize one or more of the following characteristics. If you do, make a choice today to turn your life around. Embrace the fact that it is not your past but the choices you make today that will determine your future.

- Victims tend to dwell on the wrongs of the past, because their conscience or consciousness (chapter 5) has not been cleansed. The film of Psalm 51:3: "*I know about my sins, and I cannot forget my terrible guilt...*" is constantly playing in their mind, entangling them in a web of self-pity. But God has said: "*Through the eternal Spirit he offered himself as a perfect sacrifice to God. His blood will purify our consciences from useless rituals, so that we may serve the living God.*" (Hebrews 9:14, GNB).

- Victims do not ask for mercy. They are too busy demanding compensation for what has been done to them—or expecting others to judge them for their own wrongdoing. They insist on justice and on punishment—either for themselves or for someone else. But God says: "Vengeance belongs to me!"[151] He wants the miracle of reconciliation to take place in our lives: reconciliation with God, with ourselves and with the people around us.

• Victims live in frustration and anger and that is often the reason why they do not step out of their role as a victim. The Bible says: "God's plan is to make known his secret to his people, this rich and glorious secret, which he has for all peoples. And the secret is that Christ is in you, which means that you will share in the glory of God."[152] Forget the things that are behind, and stretch toward the things that lie ahead![153]

EXPLOSION OF JOY

When I was invited to Kyrgyzstan to train a group of some four hundred pastors and cell group leaders in the ministry of deliverance, I was told that no less than eighty percent of Kyrgyz people have experienced sexual abuse and that each firstborn child is customarily given to its grandparents. These kids are raised with the lie that their father and mother are their brother and sister. I have seldom seen such deep pain and rejection in a people. After we had given some solid teaching on these issues and set aside a lot of time for the confession of sins, we broke the curse of sexual abuse and rejection in Jesus' name. It was as if all hell had broken loose. God freed hundreds of men and women at the same time from the curse that had tormented their lives for such a long time. I will not easily forget the explosion of joy that broke out that day among the Kyrgyz people. I will carry those memories with me as a tribute to Jesus, who, through the wonder of the Cross, makes this possible time and again.

Father in heaven,

Thank You that Jesus carried the curse for me. Thank You that Jesus surrendered Himself as a sacrifice for me so that I could be freed from every curse in my life. I decide now to give Jesus the crown of thorns of my life, because He has completed the work for me. I give Him my past, my pain, my anger and sadness, my rejection and feelings of inferiority, and my right to vengeance. Forgive me, Father, that I have allowed myself to be held captive in the role of a victim. I thank You that Jesus became a curse on the Cross so that I can be freed from the consequences of sin in my life and can receive Your full blessing. Through what You did on the Cross I now set myself free from every curse, every evil influence and every dark shadow over me and my family in the name of Jesus. I now choose to obey You and to walk in Your blessing every day. I can never thank You enough for the wonder of the Cross in my life. Thank you!

Amen.

THE JUDGMENT

You have authority over me
only because it was given to you by God.

(John 19:11, GNB)

CHAPTER 9

Pilate was not present during the whipping and mocking of Jesus by the soldiers, but he now comes back outside. He announces that he will take Jesus outside and show Him to the people. He will show them that the sentence he passed has been fulfilled and that Jesus is completely harmless and can be released. So he takes Jesus out to the public, with a crown of thorns on His head and a red Roman soldier's cape on His shoulders, and presents Him to the public with the now-famous words *ecce homo:* "Behold the man!"

It must have been a horrible sight. Blood is streaming over His face. His clothing is soaked with it. It is possible that He could hardly stand on His feet.

Maybe Pilate hopes to arouse the compassion of the people by showing Jesus publicly, so that they will not demand further action. But this does not happen. As soon as the high priests and their servants see Jesus, they start to shout: "Crucify him! Crucify him!" They want Jesus to be condemned to the Cross this very day. There isn't much time. Once again, Pilate tries to pass on the case to someone else. With a loud voice, he calls out for the third time that he cannot find any guilt in Jesus. He insists that the Jewish leaders should judge Jesus themselves and carry out the punishment: "Do it yourselves! I say he is innocent!"

A SON OF THE GODS?

For a moment, it seems as if the Jewish leaders will not get their way. So they change their charge. This time, they say that Jesus is a blasphemer, because He has claimed to be the Son of God. The law says He must die for this![154] When Pilate hears this charge, it scares him. As a Roman, he believes that the gods can appear on earth in human form. These "sons of god" have supernatural powers. Pilate knows very well that Jesus has performed many miracles. He needs to tread carefully. Perhaps this man standing before him really is a "son of the gods." If he condemns Him to death, he will be in terrible trouble. Add to this the message his wife sent concerning her dream about Jesus and her warning that he should not harm this man because He is innocent, a "righteous man,"[155] and you can imagine why Pilate decided to give Jesus a second hearing before calling down the wrath of the gods on himself.

> His silence is that of the King who, despite all the abuse He has gone through, is still the One who will determine the outcome of the court case. The whole thing is His initiative.

So Pilate and Jesus go back into the court for a second hearing. The first thing he wants to know is whether Jesus is a normal human being like everyone else. "Where are you from?" he asks. For the fourth time, Jesus remains silent. The first time was when He was led before the high priest,[156] then when He appeared before Herod,[157] and again when He faced Pilate and the Jews who were accusing Him.[158] Now, as Pilate questions Him himself, He is silent again.[159] His silence is that of the King who, despite all the abuse He has gone through, is still the One who will determine the outcome of the court case. The whole thing is His initiative.

Pilate doesn't mind that Jesus will not speak to the Jews, but His refusal to speak to *him* is a different story. Twice he threatens Him: "I have the power! I have power! The power to free you and the power to crucify you!" Now Jesus does answer: "You have authority over me only because it was given to you by God."[160] Jesus makes it clear that this entire trial is in the hands (and therefore the power) of God, His Father. Pilate must submit himself to the plan of God, which is for Jesus to lay down His life as an innocent lamb, so that many might be saved from the power of sin and death by the wonder of the Cross.

AMICUS CAESARIS

On the basis of Jesus' words, Pilate decides He must be set free. His words have given Pilate the impression that Jesus is indeed a son of the gods, and this has only increased his fear. Pilate tries to release Jesus in several different ways that are not described in detail. But all these attempts fail. When Pilate informs the Jews of his decision, they return to their initial charge. They start to threaten Pilate: "If you set him free, that means you are not the Emperor's friend! Anyone who claims to be a king is a rebel against the Emperor!"[161] The term *amicus caesaris* ("friend of the emperor") was an honorary title for high officials in the Roman Empire. If the Jews were to file a complaint against Pilate, he would lose his position of privilege and fall from grace with the Emperor Tiberius (14–37 A.D.) His very life might be at stake. Pilate, the mighty governor, is at the mercy of the Jewish leaders. He is not willing to give up his earthly position for this heavenly King. If it is going to cost him everything, he will no longer try to stop the crucifixion.

THE VERDICT

Once again Pilate has Jesus brought outside and takes his place in the judge's seat. "Here is your king!" he cries out to the crowds in front of him. This comment riles the crowds, provoking fierce resistance. They shout: "Away with him! Away with him! Crucify him!" Pilate challenges them by asking whether they really want their king to be crucified. Then the high priests answer: "He is not our king! We have only one king and that is the Emperor!"

It is interesting that it is the high priests who say this. The high priests were mostly Sadducees who recognized only the books of Moses and rejected every prophecy about the coming Messiah. They were focused on Israel's earthly situation and had accepted Roman rule. They were willing to do anything as long as Jesus was crucified.

Pilate sees that the crowd can no longer be controlled. Riots are likely to break out at any moment. At his wit's end, he decides to let them have their way. But before he utters the final verdict, he has a bowl of water brought to him. He washes his hands in front of the people and says: "I am innocent of the blood of this righteous person. You see to it." (Matthew 27:24, WEB) He is in effect saying: "I am not responsible for the death of this man!" The washing of hands was a Jewish ritual intended to convey one's innocence (Deuteronomy 21:6–7). The people now support their religious leaders and cry as one: "May his blood be on us, and on our children!" Then Pilate releases Barabbas, the murderer. And even though he knows that the Jews are not allowed to carry out an execution on the Passover feast, he still hands Jesus over to them and gives the order to have Him crucified.

DEALING WITH FEELINGS OF INFERIORITY

Jesus is innocent, yet He is rejected, disowned and condemned. It is unbelievable how many people, even among Christians, suffer from feelings of rejection and inferiority. In the years in which I have been privileged to be a pastor, I have discovered this: every person suffers from rejection and feelings of inferiority in some way or another. The power of sin destroys more than we realize: it destroys our identity. In the parable of the prodigal son, the son says to his father after he has returned to him:

"Father," the son said, "I have sinned against God and against you. I am no longer fit to be called your son." (Luke 15:21, GNB)

I believe that each person, as a result of sin, suffers from feelings of inferiority in his or her life. The power of sin has a deeper influence on our lives than we are aware. How important it is that this power of sin is broken.

A few years ago, when we were abroad, a much-respected pastor asked us to pray for him. Despite the fact that he had been blessed richly by God in that he led a growing church and regularly preached to over ten thousand people, he felt as if he had slammed into a wall in the ministry given to

We can exchange our feelings of inferiority for the certain knowledge that we are God's beloved son or daughter.

him. In one of our exploratory conversations, I was deeply moved as he told me that unless something changed, he would be unable to continue. He told me about his feelings of inferiority, and the doubts and fears that assailed him every time he walked out to the pulpit. No one knew about this. It cost him so much to fight these feelings off every time that he was running out of energy. We talked about this and prayed for him and his wife. It was not until later that I realized that these feelings of rejection and inferiority are a direct result of the power of sin in our lives, which tells us: you have

> **Through our intimacy with Jesus, we discover our identity in Jesus and receive the authority of Jesus.**

been condemned to powerlessness, rejection and inferiority. But it is a lie; nothing is farther from the truth. Jesus broke the power of sin on the Cross! We can exchange our feelings of inferiority for the certain knowledge that we are God's beloved son or daughter. The power of sin makes us feel rejected, but God has accepted us as His own children through Jesus (John 1:12). Through Him, He has given us the power to become children of God.

It is vital to know who we are in Jesus Christ. Through our intimacy with Jesus, we discover our identity in Jesus and receive the authority of Jesus!

Father in heaven,

Thank You that Your judgment passes me by because I have been made righteous through the blood of Jesus Christ. He has broken the power of sin in my life! Thank You that Jesus wishes to reveal every lie in my life and that I may exchange all my feelings of inferiority for the certain knowledge that I am God's beloved son/daughter. Thank You that You have accepted me as Your child and that I may discover who I am in Jesus Christ.

Amen.

THE CRUCIFIXION

Many people were shocked when they saw him;
he was so disfigured that he hardly looked human.
But because of our sins he was wounded.

(Isaiah 52:14 and 53:5, GNB)

CHAPTER 10

The soldier's robe, now soaked with blood, is torn from Jesus' shoulders, causing Him tremendous pain as it rips open the wounds inflicted on Him with the whip. Jesus starts to bleed again. On His way to be executed, He is allowed to keep His own clothing on. This is a concession to the Jewish law, which prohibits nudity. Under Roman law, convicts were forced to stumble to their death naked.

Jesus is told to carry His own Cross, or at least one part of it, the crossbeam, called the *patibulum*. Made of cypress wood, this piece probably weighed somewhere between thirty and fifty kilos. His arms are stretched out and tied to the crossbeam, so that the weight presses down on the bones protrud-

As a carpenter, Jesus was used to carrying heavy beams on His shoulders, but this time He is unable to carry the load.

ing from His upper spinal column. Jesus is brought to the place of execution, along with two criminals.

As a carpenter Jesus was used to carrying heavy beams on His shoulders, but this time He is unable to carry the load. The road from the Pretorium to Golgotha, later named the *Via Dolorosa*, is about six hundred meters long and if you walk slowly you can cover that distance in about twelve minutes. But it is a narrow and uphill road, badly paved, and bustling with traffic pushing its way through. It is along this road that Jesus must carry the heavy crossbeam on His bleeding shoulders. He probably falls a few times until He cannot get up any more.

Golgotha

A random passer-by named Simon of Cyrene, just coming in from the fields with his two sons, is forced by the Roman commander to carry the crossbeam for Jesus. There is a huge crowd of people following Jesus. The women are crying and wailing. Jesus turns around and says to them:

> *Daughters of Jerusalem, don't weep for me, but weep for yourselves and for your children. For behold, the days are coming in which they will say, "Blessed are the barren, the wombs that never bore, and the breasts that never nursed." Then they will begin to tell the mountains, "Fall on us!" and tell the hills, "Cover us." For if they do these things in the green tree, what will be done in the dry?* (Luke 23:28–31, WEB)

It is about nine in the morning when the group reaches *Golgotha*, "the place of the skull." The soldiers give Jesus wine containing a sedative before they hammer in the nails. But when Jesus tastes it, He refuses to drink it. He refuses to be sedated and chooses to bear His suffering in a fully conscious state.

At that moment, the clothes are stripped off His body. He is undressed in front of His own mother and loved ones. Shamed in front of His family, He is made to lie down on the wooden cross-beam, His shoulders still raw from the whipping.

THE CRUCIFIXION

While one or two soldiers hold Jesus' arm at His hand and elbow, another places a nail point-down to His wrist, exactly at the spot where the lower arm is connected to the hand, under the ball of the thumb and right in the middle. With a strong blow of the hammer, the nail, about fifteen to twenty centimeters in length and square in profile, is driven through the wrist. With a few more blows it is attached to the wood. Then the other wrist is pierced. The whole procedure takes just a few minutes.

The late Prof. Dr. Bob Smalhout indicated that the nails did not go through the palms of His hands: "It has been proved that that part of the body could not carry the body weight. The hands would have just torn straight through. The nail was placed in a crevice between the so-called carpus bones, as described by the French anatomist Destot. This caused them to dislocate and move, but they were not crushed. If someone has ever dislocated, sprained or broken their wrist, they will have an idea of how that feels."

But that isn't all. There is an important nerve running through the wrist, the *nervus medianus*. This has a dual function. It not only helps the thumb to move, it also gives a part of the hand the ability to feel. This *nervus medianus* was nearly always touched by the nail. Touching and damaging a nerve causes one of the most acute forms of pain possible. The nerve would be stretched over the sharp edge of the nail as a string is stretched taught over the bridge of a stringed instrument. The thumb cramps up owing to the nerve damage, causing the thumbnail to push hard into the palm of the hand.

After both wrists are attached to the crossbeam, the soldiers lift it up. Jesus must first sit up and then stand with His back against the vertical pole, the *stipes*, which was usually permanently anchored in the ground. The *patibulum*, with Jesus hanging on it, is then lifted up at both ends and placed on the *stipes*. The *stipes* was not usually very high, around two meters or so. Additional height was unnecessary and would have made things very difficult for the soldiers. The resulting low, T-shaped cross was called a *crux humulis*, literally a low cross. In special circumstances the Romans sometimes used a high cross, called a *crux sublimis*. However, this was rare, as it was difficult to hang the condemned person on a high cross and they would have had to use ladders. Golgotha had low crosses. They had already been there for many years and for the Roman legionaries the crucifixion on Friday 7th April, 30 A.D. was a routine job.

Jesus' knees are bent so that one of His feet can be placed flat against the *stipes*. Then a eight-inches-long nail is driven straight through the top of the foot, right between the second and third metatarsal bones. As the nail exits the sole of the foot, the other leg is bent so that the nail can be driven through the second foot into the wood of the *stipes*. Thus Jesus is hung on three nails (possibly with additional ropes to prevent Him from falling forward). Blood loss is minimal, but the pain is unbearable and the death throes start.

A MEDICAL–HISTORICAL RECONSTRUCTION

What did Jesus die of? Medically speaking, what was the actual cause of death? According to Professor Dr. Smalhout, His death can be reconstructed with great accuracy: The sweat drips down Jesus' body, causing His temperature to rise to a high level. In medical terms this condition is known as *hyperthermia*. The muscles are continually cramped. The dislocated wrists and feet hurt unbearably. Through blood loss, extreme perspiration, thirst and *oedema* caused by the whipping, the amount of blood circulating in the body has diminished substantially. The blood pressure drops, the pulse rises. The biochemical makeup of the blood has become acidic owing to a huge loss of salt, and is hardly able to sustain life. The heartbeat starts to fail. A so-called *decompensatio cordis* (Congestive heart failure) takes place, causing fluid to enter the lungs. This is called *pulmonary oedema*. The breathing becomes rattly. The heart beats irregularly. Jesus suffers unbearable thirst.

The wounds in the wrists and feet are not lethal, nor is the blood loss. Death on a cross is caused by an entirely different process. If someone is hung by their wrists, the body is pulled downward by the force of gravity. This causes the muscles in the arms, shoulders and chest to tighten. The ribs are pulled upward so that the maximum amount of air can be inhaled. However, exhalation becomes difficult and Jesus starts to have difficulty with this after about ten minutes. His breathing might be compared to an asthma patient having a severe attack. The heavily tensed arm, shoulder and chest muscles become severely cramped. The muscle metabolism is increased, while there is less oxygen available owing to obstructed blood circulation. The result is that large quantities of lactic acid are produced, finally causing the entire body to turn acidic, a condition known in medical terms as *metabole acidose*. This condition is experienced by athletes who have pushed their body to its limits, causing it to cramp up. The situation is made worse by the fact that Jesus cannot exhale properly and therefore His body cannot rid itself of carbon dioxide. This causes *respiratoire acidose* to occur (acidity due to lack of ventilation), which worsens the aforementioned *metabole acidose*. Jesus begins to perspire extremely, causing the sweat of death to stream down His body. His lips become greyish-blue, while slowly but surely all the muscles, including the ones in His torso and legs tense into terrible cramps. Eventually every person who is crucified suffocates.

THE BATTLE OF DEATH

The Romans did not intend those who were crucified to die quickly. That is why they nailed the feet to the cross as well. This ena-bled the condemned person temporarily to postpone suffocation by pushing himself up on the nail in his feet, straightening his legs and thus relieving the pressure on the arm and chest muscles. Then he could breathe reasonably well for a short time. The acidity of his body would lessen and the skin would regain some color for a brief moment. However, standing with your full body weight on a square nail that has been driven between the bones of your feet, causes excruciating pain. The condemned person would thus be quickly forced to bend his knees and lower his body back down until he was hanging by his wrists on the nails once again. The nerve in the wrists, the *nervus medianus*, is stretched over the nail again, the burning pain rushes through both arms, while the suffocation and cramping starts all over again. Thus the crucified person stretches out what is left of his miserable life. Again and again he will try to raise himself and then lower himself, forced to do so by the pain. Up and down. Ten times, one hundred times, until exhaustion makes all movement impossible and he dies of suffocation.

JESUS THE NAZARENE, KING OF THE JEWS

A sign is hung on the Cross, the so-called *titulus*, on which the crime of the condemned man normally is written. However, Pilate has ordered the words "Jesus, the king of the Jews" to be written on His *titulus*. It was common practice for the condemned to wear this sign around their neck on their way to the cross. It is not known whether this also happened with Jesus. At any rate, Pilate succeeds in riling the Jewish people and the religious leaders. Golgotha lies along a busy road near Jerusalem and many pilgrims, both national and international, who have come to Jerusalem to offer a sacrificial lamb for the Passover, pass by the Cross. Jesus is hanging there publicly for all to see and ridicule; everyone can see why He is hanging there. The Jews read it in their own language, because part of the script is in Hebrew. The foreigners can read it in Latin, the official language of the Roman government, or in Greek, the language of trade at the time. Soon the people start to react to what they have read. The Sadducee high priests may have given up their hopes for a Messiah, but the Jewish people have most definitely not. The high priests go to Pilate and try to get him to change the sign. They say: You shouldn't have written: "King of the Jews," but rather: "*He said* he was King of the Jews"! Even though Jesus never claimed to be King of the Jews, Pilate insists on keeping the sign: "What I have written must stay!" Unwittingly, Pilate thus becomes an instrument in God's hands, proclaiming to all people that Jesus, who is crucified, is the King of the world, despite all the mockery and humiliation He has had to undergo.

JESUS LOOKED HORRENDOUS

Jesus' body is one bloody mess. The skin of His back has been ripped to shreds; the razor-sharp thorns have penetrated the skin of His skull so that His already-mutilated face is now covered in blood. Jesus is bleeding from His head, back, hands and feet and is so terribly wounded that many can no longer stand the sight and turn their heads away. Had she not been there to witness it, His own mother would not have recognized Him:

Many people were shocked when they saw him; he was so disfigured that he hardly looked human. We despised him and rejected him; he endured suffering and pain. No one would even look at him—we ignored him as if he were nothing. But he endured the suffering that should have been ours, the pain that we should have borne. All the while we thought that his suffering was punishment sent by God. But because of our sins he was wounded, beaten because of the evil we did. We are healed by the punishment he suffered, made whole by the blows he received. (Isaiah 52:14 and 53:3–5, GNB)

Jesus knew these prophecies. He knew in advance how He was going to die. He knew the plan of God and willingly and obediently yielded to it. The Son of God was born to die. I sometimes wonder which parts of the Bible Jesus read the week before He

Jesus is bleeding from His head, back, hands and feet and is so terribly wounded that many can no longer stand the sight and turn their heads away. Had she not been there to witness it, His own mother would not have recognized Him.

died. How did He view the prophecies that speak of the last eighteen hours before His death? What did He think as He read these words? For instance, what did this Scripture mean to Him?

The Lord says, "It was my will that he should suffer; his death was a sacrifice to bring forgiveness. And so he will see his descendants; he will live a long life, and through Him my purpose will succeed. After a life of suffering, he will again have joy; he will know that he did not suffer in vain. My devoted servant, with whom I am pleased, will bear the punishment of many and for his sake I will forgive them." (Isaiah 53:10–11, GNB)

Maybe Jesus clung to these words in the darkest and most difficult moments of His life here on earth—hanging between heaven and earth, abandoned by God and man. Who knows? The Good News translation says that "He will see his descendants!" I believe Jesus could endure the suffering because He was thinking of us on the Cross, because He loved us more than anything. Who will ever comprehend that?

IT IS GOD'S LOVE

On the Cross Jesus lives up to His own words: "The greatest love you can have for your friends is to give your life for them."

(John 15:13, GNB) There is no greater power in the universe than the love of God. Look at Jesus and see God's love for us. Words cannot convey this love. God's love knows no limits, always protects, does not hurt, is not selfish and does not feel insulted. God's love does not blame anyone; it never fails and it never ends. God's love protects, trusts, is full of expectation and is steadfast. It is God's indescribable love that Jesus hung on the Cross. John, who is standing next to Mary, the mother of Jesus, at the Cross, later writes about this moment:

> *And God showed his love for us by sending his only Son into the world, so that we might have life through him. This is what love is: it is not that we have loved God, but that he loved us and sent his Son to be the means by which our sins are forgiven.* (1 John 4:9–10, GNB)

JESUS IS MOCKED FIVE TIMES

Looking down from the Cross, Jesus sees His mother and senses that a sword is piercing her soul.[162] Her son is hanging there, dying! John is standing next to her. He is the only disciple who has followed Jesus to the Cross; the others are keeping their distance. There are a few other women with them: John's mother (Salome, Mary's sister), Mary the wife of Clopas, and Mary Magdalene, whom Jesus had delivered from seven evil spirits.[163] What are they thinking? Do they understand what is happening at this moment?

Jesus' eyes look at the people present. He sees clenched fists and hardened faces, filled with shameless mockery and cruel rejection. He sees eyes full of hatred, looks that could kill.

Five times, Jesus is ridiculed mercilessly: by the passers-by, the inhabitants of the city, the religious leaders, the soldiers and the criminals. Yet they are the very ones He is hanging there for. How true the words of Psalm 22 are:

But I am no longer a human being; I am a worm, despised and scorned by everyone! All who see me make fun of me; they stick out their tongues and shake their heads. (Psalm 22:6–7, GNB)

The people who pass by call Him names and shake their heads: "You were going to destroy the temple and rebuild it in three days, weren't you?" they mock. "If you are the Son of God, save yourself! Come down from that Cross!"

The members of the Sanhedrin have their say too: "He saved others," they laugh. "But he cannot even save himself! You are the king of Israel aren't you? Come on down from that Cross. Then we will believe you. He trusted in God, didn't he? If God really cares about him, let him come down and save him. Isn't he God's Son?"

Jesus' unbelievable love for humanity keeps Him on the Cross.

The soldiers laugh at Him too and give Him acidic wine to drink. They say: "Hey, you! King of the Jews! Save yourself!"

One of the two criminals hanging on crosses next to Jesus joins in mocking Him and says: "So, you are the Messiah? Prove it. Save yourself and us!" But the criminal on the other side of Jesus silences him: "Do you still not fear God, so close to dying? We get what we deserve, but this man has done nothing wrong!" He says to Jesus: "Jesus, remember me when you enter your Kingdom." Jesus answers him: "Today you will be with me in paradise. You can be sure of that!"

What powerful love Jesus must have had to hang on that Cross and to hear them scorning Him as He labored to open the way for them to salvation and eternal life. Jesus' unbelievable love for humanity keeps Him on the Cross. It becomes clear to me once again that the wonder of the Cross centers first and foremost on the miraculous fact that God loves us beyond measure!

DARKNESS COVERS THE LAND

The four soldiers who hung Jesus on the Cross divide His clothes among themselves. According to Roman law, the clothing of Jesus now belongs to the soldiers. Given up for dead, He no longer needs His clothes. The headscarf, belt, cloak and sandals are divided among the four soldiers. His undergarment is laid aside. It has no seams and to tear it in four would be a shame. Therefore the soldiers decide to gamble for it by throwing the dice—as was prophesied in Psalm 22:18. Down to the smallest detail, Jesus' suffering is determined by God.

At around twelve o'clock, our time, a deep darkness covers the land. Until three in the afternoon the sun will not be visible.

The moment this unexpected darkness descends, it becomes quiet on the hill just outside Jerusalem. From nine in the morning until noon the people have screamed until they were hoarse, mocking and making fun of Jesus. But when darkness falls, they stop scoffing, pushing and shouting. Even the religious leaders and the soldiers at the foot of the Cross are silent. It is this very silence, the total absence of sound, that makes the following three hours of Jesus' complete abandonment somewhat understandable to us. The total eclipse of the sun becomes a poignant illustration of what Jesus is going through in these six hours. The dark night covering the land mirrors the darkness enveloping in the soul of Jesus.

THE STORY OF JOANNA

Joanna was what the Bible would call broken-hearted.[164] Owing to traumatic events in her childhood, her personality had split itself into many different partial personalities, a condition known as Dissociative Identity Disorder (DID). She felt as if she was made up of many parts. These different parts (also known as alters) had developed separately from childhood on. Each experienced life in its own way. This made things very confusing for Joanna and used up a lot of her energy. Her different personalities were not connected, which caused many problems: she had trouble concentrating and was extremely forgetful. She suffered mood swings owing to switching back and forth between the different personalities. She had a confusing life.

At a certain point, she decided to look for help. Every week for eleven years a therapist treated her. Joanna yearned for restoration; she longed to become one integrated person again, the way God intended her to be. But despite the intensive professional treatment as well as many counseling sessions with pastors and endless prayer, restoration in the sense of integration did not occur. After years of struggling, Joanna was beginning to give up on life.

Then she was invited to a conference. She cried out to God: "Father, I have been fighting for so long. I know You are my only hope for recovery. I really want to leave this conference whole, as one person!" She shared her desire with the friends who had invited her along.

The following days were very difficult for her. She felt like crying a lot, but didn't want to give in to the feeling. After all those hours of therapy and all the tears she had already shed, Joanna was sick of crying. However, after three days she finally decided to give in anyway. She cried so intensely that her whole body hurt. She cried out to God from deep inside. In her intense anguish, Joanna had a vision. When she first told me about it, I was deeply moved and very impressed by what God in His mercy had shown her.

In her vision, Joanna saw Jesus hanging on the Cross; she saw herself standing right in front of Him. What happened next can hardly be explained. Jesus leaned forward, while remaining on the Cross, picked her up and pulled her to His chest. She experienced the depths of the darkness inside Him. It was not a darkness caused by the absence of light; no, this darkness was more like a tangible substance. Joanna did not really know what was happening. It was as if she could taste a small portion of what was in the cup Jesus had drunk in the garden of Gethsemane. The sins of the whole world, concentrated and pressed into that one cup, had penetrated

His soul deeply. Jesus was made sin by God. Joanna tasted a small part of the result of this in the soul of Jesus: a profound darkness and a sense of abandonment. Joanna heard Jesus say to her in that vision that she should stay with Him as long as necessary. There, deep "in the heart of Jesus" on the Cross, an amazing miracle took place.

To this day, Joanna is unable to say how long the vision lasted. But after some time she "returned" and found a place where she could take it all in. She felt strange but was unable to explain why. The following three weeks were very difficult and emotional. She couldn't figure out what was happening to her, until the moment God let her "look inside" herself and she discovered what God had done in her life through the wonder of the Cross. Since that amazing experience at the conference, she had not switched personalities again. The voices she had heard deep inside her for so long were now silent. What eleven years of therapy had been unable to achieve was done in that one moment when Joanna was drawn to Jesus' bosom![165]

Today, it is as if all the different flowers of her personality have been put together as a bouquet. A bouquet that has the lovely fragrance of Jesus, who took her pain and brokenness on the Cross so that Joanna might now experience life as one big miracle. This is the divine power of the Cross. It reveals itself in our weaknesses when we cry out to Him. It is only through the wonder of the Cross that God can take a person who is so broken and make them whole and give them hope and a future.

THE SEVEN WORDS OF THE CROSS

The six hours of Jesus' crucifixion are a torturous symphony of pain that gets worse with each movement, with each breath. Even a soft breeze brushing His skin can

For six long hours, He hangs on that Cross like a lump of raw meat.

cause agonizing pain. His lips are chapped. His mouth and throat are so dry that He cannot swallow. His voice is so hoarse that He can barely speak. His last drink was during the Passover meal in the upper room. Since then He hasn't slept, He has wrestled with our sins, He has been beaten, spat on, whipped and crucified. And all that time not a drop of fluid has moistened His throat. For six long hours, He hangs on that Cross like a lump of raw meat. Barely capable of speaking, Jesus utters the seven words of the Cross that have become famous:

1. *"Father, forgive them, for they don't know what they are doing."* (Luke 23:34, WEB)
2. *"Woman, behold your son!"* and *"Behold, your mother!"* (John 19:26–27, WEB)
3. *"I promise you that today you will be in Paradise with me."* (Luke 23:43, GNB)
4. *"My God, my God, why did you abandon me?"* (Matthew 27:46 and Mark 15:34, GNB)
5. *"I am thirsty."* (John 19:28 GNB)
6. *"It is finished!"* (John 19:30 GNB)
7. *"Father! In your hands I place my spirit!"* (Luke 23:46, GNB)

1. "Father, forgive them, for they don't know what they are doing."

Who knows what has been done to Jesus? Pain grips His body. It is so intense He wants to scream, but maybe He is too exhausted for that. But the pain does not stop Him from defending His enemies before the Father. "They don't know what they are doing!" He cries out.

Is there really no one there who knows why Jesus, abused and hated yet innocent, is hanging on the Cross? Is there truly no one who knows that from this point forward, history will be changed forever? Indeed, there is no one. But do they not also know the many prophecies about the suffering of the "Lord's Servant?" How is it possible that no one understands what is happening here? The only explanation can be that there is a huge spiritual battle raging around the death of Jesus. Satan, the god of this world, has blinded all of those present, without exception, so that they "do not know what they are doing."[166] The deep darkness that has fallen

> **Is there truly no one who knows that from this point forward, history will forever be changed?**

upon the land is a reflection of what has happened in their hearts. Darkness has filled their hearts and they are unable to see the Light of the World hanging on the Cross to take away their sins. Paul later says that "none of the rulers of this world knew this wisdom. If they had known it, they would not have crucified the Lord of glory."[167] But if we keep our eyes on Jesus, we shall see that He pleads with His Father for those who curse Him, while He is in the worst of circumstances Himself. Once again, it is the prophet Isaiah who prophesied all of this so accurately:

> *And so I will give him a place of honor, a place among the great and powerful. He willingly gave his life and shared the fate of evil men. He took the place of many sinners and prayed that they might be forgiven.* (Isaiah 53:12, GNB)

The curse that the people called down upon themselves ("May his blood be on us, and on our children!"[168]) is nullified through this word of Jesus. They did not know what they were shouting. They did not know what they were doing.

2. "WOMAN, BEHOLD YOUR SON!" AND "BEHOLD, YOUR MOTHER!"

Jesus' heart goes out to His mother, as His concern for her grief supersedes even His own pain. It must be unbearable for Mary to see her son suffer like that. She must be feeling abandoned. It seems that Joseph has already died, and her other children do not believe in Jesus![169] They haven't known how to deal with things Jesus has said, such as: "You belong to this world here below, but I come from above. You are from this world, but I am not from this world."[170] And yet they agreed that Jesus is not of this world, even declaring at one point that He was crazy.[171] How difficult all of this must have been for Mary. And now she is standing in front of Him, with so much anguish and so many "whys" in her heart.

Thankfully John, and his mother, Salome, are standing next to her. John, the disciple whom Jesus loved. Jesus speaks to His mother. He calls her "woman." He has done this before.[172] The natural bond between Him and His mother has changed. He is no longer the son of His mother, but the Son of Man, the Son of God. Mary must learn to see Jesus differently, something that her other children could not do at first. She must learn to see her son as Lord.

I sometimes wonder what Mary must have thought when she heard these words of Jesus: "My Father and I will come to them and live with them."[173] Maybe this was just as confusing for her as it had been for Nicodemus when he heard that he had to be born again. His reaction was: "How can a grown man be born again? He certainly cannot enter his mother's womb and be born a second time!"[174] When Jesus said: "My Father and I will come to them and live with them," maybe Mary shook her head.

She has carried Him for nine months in her womb; how can He be born again in her? It is not until later that Mary understands the meaning of these words, when she and 119 others are in the upper room and the Spirit of Jesus is poured out on her and them!

On the Cross, Jesus reminds her once again that there has been a change in their relationship, in the bond they share. Jesus is not just her son; He is also her Savior. This knowledge may ease the pain she is feeling. Thankfully, John is standing close to her. As Mary is on her own at this point (though later James, the half-brother of Jesus, becomes a believer—see 1 Corinthians 15:7), Jesus asks John to take care of His mother.

3. "I PROMISE YOU THAT TODAY YOU WILL BE IN PARADISE WITH ME"

The prophecy of Isaiah, that Jesus would share the fate of evil men,[175] has come true. Jesus and the two criminals have all received the same verdict. Initially, the two criminals go along with the hysteria of the masses and ridicule Jesus as He hangs between them.[176]

One of them just will not stop, and mocks: "So you are the Messiah? Prove it. Save yourself and us!" But the other criminal silences him: "Do you not fear God, even now when you are so close to death? We are getting what we deserve, but this man has done nothing wrong!" This one criminal realizes that Jesus is indeed the King and that His Kingdom stretches beyond the boundaries of death. Jesus has been called an "evildoer," a criminal, by the Sanhedrin. "But this man has done nothing wrong," the criminal says. His confession is similar to the words of Peter later on. Jesus was no "evildoer," but a doer of good:

> You know about Jesus of Nazareth and how God poured out on him the Holy Spirit and power. He went everywhere, doing good and healing all who were under the power of the Devil, for God was with him. We are witnesses of everything that he did in the land of Israel and in Jerusalem. Then they put him to death by nailing him to a cross. But God raised him from death three days later and caused him to appear, not to everyone, but only to the witnesses that God had already chosen. (Acts 10:38–41, GNB)

Then he says to Jesus: "Jesus, remember me when you enter your kingdom."

Jesus answers him: "I promise you that today you will be in Paradise with me." Within several hours, this man will witness the "greatest exodus of all time," when Jesus, between the Cross and the resurrection, preaches the gospel in the realm of death, and takes countless souls with Him to heaven.[177] This man's faith in Jesus, there on the verge of death, has saved him for all eternity.

4. "MY GOD, MY GOD,
WHY DID YOU ABANDON ME?"

By the time the darkness has lifted, at about 3 p.m., Jesus cries out with a loud voice in Aramaic: *Eloi, Eloi, lama sabachthani*, which means: "My God, my God, why have you abandoned me?"

This citation from Psalm 22 may well be the only sentence in the Old Testament that can express what is happening inside Jesus, invisible to human eyes. This psalm, written more than seven hundred years before the crucifixion of Jesus Christ, paints an accurate prophetic picture of what is to happen on Golgotha:

Verses 11–13 (GNB) describe the spiritual situation:

Do not stay away from me! Trouble is near, and there is no one to help. Many enemies surround me like bulls; they are all around me, like fierce bulls from the land of Bashan. They open their mouths like lions, roaring and tearing at me.

Verses 14–15 (GNB) describe the physical situation:

My strength is gone, gone like water spilled on the ground. All my bones are out of joint; my heart is like melted wax. My throat is as dry as dust, and my tongue sticks to the roof of my mouth. You have left me for dead in the dust.

Verses 16–19 (WEB) describe the human situation:

For dogs have surrounded me. A company of evildoers have enclosed me. They have pierced my hands and feet. I can count all of my bones. They look and stare at me. They divide my garments among them. They cast lots for my clothing. But don't be far off, Yahweh. You are my help: hurry to help me.

If the devil fought for the body of Moses,[178] can you imagine what must be happening at the Cross, in the invisible, spiritual world? How do you think Satan and his demons react? The Bible does not speak about this directly, but it does offer a few indirect references. The devil is known as the accuser, and he will not have changed roles in this situation. Invisible to the onlookers, Jesus is in a battle with the devil. The first round, in the desert,[179] led to the defeat of God's adversary. But now he thinks he can win. Bloodthirsty demons screech as they encircle the Cross. They shout their accusations and ridicule Him. The mockery hurled at Jesus by humans pales in comparison. With their mouths wide open they intimidate Jesus on the Cross like roaring lions threatening to rip their prey to shreds. Jesus has fallen into their hands; He can no longer escape them. This is what Psalm 22 shows us.

Jesus knows why God has abandoned Him. He knows that by taking the sins of the world upon Himself He will be separated from His Father. His Father abandons Jesus. In this deep spiritual battle, Jesus hangs alone on the Cross between heaven and earth, abandoned by God and man.

It is interesting, but no coincidence, that Jesus' first and last utterances on the Cross begin with the Father's name for God, whereas the one in the middle omits the Father's name, as Jesus says twice: "My God, my God!" So we see the following pattern: Father—God—Father. This shows us something of God's historic relationship with the world. In paradise, God revealed Himself as the Father of Adam and Eve (Adam is called a "son of God" in Luke 3). They walk in the cool of the evening with their God and Father. Because Adam and Eve sinned, a change came about in their intimate relationship with their heavenly Father. He is no longer called "Father," but "God" (*Elohim* = powerful creator). In the whole of the Old Testament, God reveals Himself through different names, all of which express something of His character. But hardly anywhere in the Old Testament is He referred to as "Father."

Sin influences relationships in a negative way. The first to suffer is our relationship with God. As a result of our sin, God's role "changes" to that of a judge. He sentences us to drink the cup filled with our sins ourselves:

> *You hold in your hand a cup filled with wine, strong and foaming. You will pour out some for every sinful person on this earth, and they will have to drink until it is gone.* (Psalm 75:8, CEV)

As a result of our sin, God's role "changes" to that of a judge. He sentences us to drink the cup filled with our sins ourselves.

The death of Jesus brings reconciliation, so that God no longer needs to be the Judge. Now we can get to know God again as a Father.

Jesus allowed Himself to be sentenced and to take upon Himself the punishment we deserved, although He was innocent. Out of love for us, He allowed God's punishment for the world to be placed on Him by taking the cup of God's wrath, filled with the sins of the whole world, and drinking it to the last drop. In taking our punishment upon Himself, the intimate Father—Son relationship is changed into a distant Judge—Condemned relationship. This is what Jesus expresses in quoting the verse from Psalm 22: "My God, my God, why have you abandoned me?" This is what He has feared most, even though He knows it will only be temporary. While Jesus is hanging on the Cross and being tortured in every aspect of His soul, spirit and body, He is still completely conscious of the fact that He is bringing reconciliation for the world with God:

> *What we mean is that God was in Christ, offering peace and for-giveness to the people of this world. And he has given us the work of sharing his message about peace.* (2 Corinthians 5:19, CEV)

> *But when the right time finally came, God sent his own Son. He came as the son of a human mother and lived under the Jewish Law, to redeem those who were under the Law, so that we might become God's children. To show that you are his children, God sent the Spirit of his Son into our hearts, the Spirit who cries out, "Father, my Father." So then, you are no longer a slave but a child. And since you are his child, God will give you all that he has for his children.* (Galatians 4:4–7, GNB)

Throughout this intense battle, Jesus hangs alone on the Cross. All His friends stand at a distance. On the one hand they are afraid of being arrested too; on the other hand they sympathize deeply with Him. But they have no understanding at all of what is happening. Not until a few days have passed will their eyes be opened and God's light will shine on them.

5. "I AM THIRSTY."

In His physical suffering, Jesus endures terrible thirst. He knows the ordeal is almost at an end. That is why He cries out: "I am thirsty!" This is a fulfillment of yet another prophecy.[180] At the execution site there is a jug of "acidic wine." The Romans call it *posca*, and it is a soldiers' brew, made up of wine, water, vinegar and beaten eggs (not to be confused with the painkiller *edik*, which is mixed with gall, and which Jesus has refused to drink earlier). One of the legionaries gives Jesus a sponge soaked in this *posca*. But apart from the fact that Jesus' body is screaming out for fluids, His thirst also reminds us of His own words spoken earlier, that He hungered and thirsted to do the will of his Father.[181] Jesus drinks the cup filled with sin down to the last drop. That is why He, who is Himself the living water, must suffer thirst. Now that all is finished, Jesus can drink the wine offered to Him.

6. "IT IS FINISHED!"

Around three in the afternoon, the time of day when the sacrificial lamb is slaughtered in the temple, Jesus cries out with a loud voice: "It is finished!" At this time the priestly ram's horn is probably blown to announce that the priests have finished the sacrifice for the sins of Israel. The great work of salvation brought about by suffering has come to an end. This is what Jesus means when He cries out that one short word: *tetelestai*: Finished! Achieved! Done! We must never forget that the death of Jesus was perfect. His death offers us restoration in every sense. Now He can go to the Father.

7. "FATHER! INTO YOUR HANDS I PLACE MY SPIRIT!"

Jesus utters a cry, bows His head and gives up His spirit. No one can take away Jesus' spirit of life; He Himself hands it over to His Father. At that moment, something happens to the heavy curtain that hides the Most Holy Place from the people. It tears from top to bottom.[182] The tearing of the curtain is a sign that the way into God's presence is now open to everyone who believes in the wonder of the Cross.

GOD CHOOSES TO BE POWERLESS

How does heaven see these moments on the Cross? What is the Father thinking when He sees Jesus beaten, mocked, tortured and crucified? Heaven must have held its breath. God watches, but does not intervene. God is neither powerless nor at a loss as to what to do. The wonder of the Cross is so great and God loves us so very much that He chooses not to intervene in this most crucial moment in history. He chooses not to use His almighty power. Only the God who has all power in heaven and earth is able to lay down this power for a certain amount of time, and not to intervene, as proof of His inconceivably great love for us! He does this because He knows it is the only way to restore the relationship with His children here on earth. But what a price to pay. As King David once poetically wrote: "How great is your constant love for me! You have saved me from the grave itself."[183] The wonder of the Cross is the miracle of God's neverending, unfailing love for us!

> **The wonder of the Cross is so great and God loves us so very much that He chooses not to intervene in this most crucial moment in history.**

POWERLESS TO HELP

Three years ago, my wife discovered a lump in her left breast. Tests in the hospital showed it was not malignant. We were so relieved. We had a small celebration and told our boys. A week later we had an unexpected phone call: we were to be in the hospital within an hour. There we were told a "mistake" had been made. The new diagnosis was that a very aggressive form of cancer had been found. We drove home, numb with shock. How could this have happened? Ann would have to be operated on within a week. We had to tell the boys the bad news that same evening. Until that moment we had been able to deal with it. But the shocked and defeated reactions of our children broke our hearts in two. "Is Mom going to die?" What can you say? We believed that God could heal Ann, but we could not guarantee it. We knew that God could do a miracle. If Sue had miraculously got up out of her wheelchair, it was just as possible for God to heal Ann.

But God spoke in a different way. "Do not ask me if I will heal you with the snap of a finger; just ask me to go with you on this road!" To be honest, we were more focused on healing. But God spoke again: "Do not ask me to heal you just like that. Ask me to join you on this road!" God was asking us to trust Him.

We made the decision to trust Him, even though we did not know what would happen. Or maybe I should say we trusted Him *because* we did not know what would happen. A lot happened in that first week. Ann was admitted to hospital for an operation. The surgeon told us that he did not know what he would find during the operation. They might be able to save the breast and remove the cancer, but they weren't sure. I gave him my cell phone number. I wanted to be near my wife that morning. He promised to call straight after the operation to tell me how it had gone. A few friends and I stayed in and near the hospital all morning. We prayed for Ann. But the phone call didn't come. I walked to the recovery room a few times, but there was no news. The operation took longer than expected. The last hour I spent waiting alone in the room to which they were to bring Ann for recovery. There was no one who could tell me how she was doing. The phone remained silent. I felt awful.

Then I heard footsteps in the hallway. I saw a nurse wheeling in a bed with my wife in it. She was heading for the recovery room.

"Well?" I asked her.

She looked at me, puzzled. "Didn't they call you?" she asked me in surprise. I felt anger rise up within me. She left me alone with Ann and all I could do was carefully peer through the tubes and bandages to see whether or not she still had her breast. I cried, not because of what I saw (it turned out they *were* able to save her breast), but because I was so powerless to help.

The following hours were awful. Ann was in such pain. She had to vomit, which only made the situation worse. I felt so helpless. If only I could do something for her. But there was nothing I could do. As the tears ran down my cheeks, I heard a voice deep inside me whispering: "I voluntarily chose to be powerless!" This cut me to the core. At that moment I realized what God meant. God voluntarily chose to be powerless when Jesus was on the Cross. How could such a thing be possible? There in that little hospital room I discovered more than ever before how great God is and how intense His love must be for us. Only someone who possesses all power on heaven and earth can choose not to use it. All that power! Because Jesus chose to be abandoned by God and His Father chose to lay down His power, I knew that He understood my helplessness, and I felt His intense love for my wife and me enwrap us like a warm blanket. I felt my helplessness turn into a complete trust in Him, who had said He would go with us. This trust remained with us right through the chemotherapy and the radiation treatment. Because of this experience, we learned about God's faithfulness to us in a whole new way.

Today, my wife is doing very well physically. The operation was a success; the cancer was caught at a very early stage. Her shoulder was severely damaged by the radiation treatment, though; she couldn't stretch her right arm upward, despite all the physiotherapy and medical treatment. Her arm caused her permanent pain. Then one day God healed her arm quite unexpectedly within half an hour. Psalm 68:19 says: "Praise the Lord, who carries our burdens day after day; he is the God who saves us." It became a precious truth for us.

> **As the tears ran down my cheeks, I heard a voice deep inside me whispering: "I voluntarily chose to be powerless!"**

THE SIXTH WONDER OF THE CROSS:
THE MIRACLE OF RECONCILIATION WITH GOD THE FATHER

The Hebrew word for reconciliation means that you give something to a person to whom you're indebted, to compensate for whatever you owe him. Through this exchange, reconciliation takes place. God has accepted the blood of Jesus as compensation for our own lives, so that our lives can be purified and saved. By being made sin for us and dying in our place, Jesus paid the price required for us to be freed from sin! This transaction took place at the Cross. It did not occur outside of God, but was wanted and guided by Him:

> *For when we were still helpless, Christ died for the wicked at the time that God chose. It is a difficult thing for someone to die for a righteous person. It may even be that someone might dare to die for a good person. But God has shown us how much He loves us—it was while we were still sinners that Christ died for us! By his blood we are now put right with God; how much more, then, will we be saved by him from God's anger! We were God's enemies, but he made us his friends through the death of his Son. Now that we are God's friends, how much more will we be saved by Christ's life! But that is not all; we rejoice because of what God has done through our Lord Jesus Christ, who has now made us God's friends. (Romans 5:6–11, GNB)*

Many people still struggle with questions like these:

- Why is reconciliation necessary?
- Why did Jesus have to die to bring about reconciliation?
- Did God need to see blood?

- Couldn't He think of some other way to bring about reconciliation?

- How can the death of someone in times long past bring blessing and salvation to me, many centuries later?

We cannot escape the fact that reconciliation is necessary in the relationship between God and man. Man's sin caused a breach in the relationship between the Creator and His creation. Sin left a void between a holy God and sinful man, as a result of which man could no longer reside in God's presence. The prophet Isaiah speaks of this quite clearly:

> *But your iniquities have separated between you and your God, and your sins have hidden his face from you, so that he will not hear.* (Isaiah 59:2, WEB)

Isaiah goes on to describe the results of sin for each person in their day-to-day life:

> *The people say, "Now we know why God does not save us from those who oppress us. We hope for light to walk by, but there is only darkness, and we grope about like blind people. We stumble at noon, as if it were night, as if we were in the dark world of the dead. We are frightened and distressed. We long for God to save us from oppression and wrong, but nothing happens. Lord, our crimes against you are many. Our sins accuse us. We are well aware of them all. We have rebelled against you, rejected you, and refused to follow you. We have oppressed others and turned away from you. Our thoughts are false; our words are lies. Justice is driven away, and right cannot come near. Truth stumbles in the public square, and honesty finds no place there. There is so little honesty that those who stop doing evil find themselves the victims of crime. The Lord has seen this, and he is displeased that there is no justice. He is astonished to see that there is no one to help the oppressed."* (Isaiah 59:9–16, GNB)

No one on earth could change this situation, for the simple reason that everyone has fallen under the power of sin. Through sin, sickness, decay, deterioration, pain, injustice and death have gained power over those who live on earth. Jesus Himself said that we were slaves to sin.[184]

But God's love for us is so unbelievably great that He Himself took measures to save us from our dangerous and hopeless situation.

He is astonished to see that there is no one to help the oppressed. So he will use his own power to rescue them and to win the victory. (Isaiah 59:16, GNB)

Since the children, as he calls them, are people of flesh and blood, Jesus himself became like them and shared their human nature. He did this so that through his death he might destroy the Devil, who has the power over death, and in this way set free those who were slaves all their lives because of their fear of death. (Hebrews 2:14–15, GNB)

Jesus came to earth as a sinless man to take our sins, which separated us from God, upon Himself. By solving the problem of sin for us, Jesus made it possible for us to enter into God's presence once again. That is why He allowed Himself to be humiliated under the power of sin. Jesus knew that by taking our sins upon Himself, by identifying with them, He would also have to die in our place.

The death of Jesus turned out to be a "smart move," as through it, He beat the devil at his own game.

The wages of sin is death.[185] This is an irreversible spiritual law! But God used this spiritual law in His master plan. The death of Jesus turned out to be a "smart move," as through it, He beat the devil, who had power over death, at his own game, rendering him utterly powerless. In chapter thirteen, we will go into this in more depth.

God did not need to see blood as some way of getting back at us for our sins.[186] That is not what the Cross was about for Him. The only way He could free us from the slavery of sin, sickness and death was to let Jesus die so that He could conquer death for us once and for all.

For the wages of sin is death, but the free gift of God is eternal life in Christ Jesus our Lord. (Romans 6:23, WEB)

JESUS WASHED AWAY THE DEBT OF BLOOD

Without insight into the spiritual world, we cannot understand the sacrifice Jesus made. You see, sin gives the devil the right to influence the life of any person who has sinned. The Bible teaches us that any sin deserving the death penalty leaves a blood debt on the life of the perpetrator, and that as long as this blood debt is not paid off, its effect will be felt for generations.

There is a good example of this in 2 Samuel 21:3. Saul has broken the covenant that Joshua made with the Gibeonites by having some of them killed. As a result, there is a blood debt on the household of Saul, causing the people to suffer a three-year famine, long after Saul's death. King David, Saul's successor, asks the Gibeonites: "How can I bring about atonement to repay the debt of blood and restore the balance?" He then turns over to them seven of Saul's descendants 'as atonement' (in place of, or as compensation for). They are the price, and through their deaths, the deaths of the Gibeonites are atoned for and the famine ceases.

Another example is to be found in Exodus 32:30. Israel has sinned by worshiping the golden calf as its god. Moses promises the people, who are afraid of dying, that he will climb up to God. "Maybe I will be able to make atonement for your sin," he says. He means that he will offer God his own life in exchange for the lives of the Israelites; if Moses dies, then the Israelites will be able to live.

In the same way King David knows there is a double blood debt on his life after he has committed adultery with Bathsheba and had her husband Uriah murdered. Even though he is able to hide his sins from the people (the law requires the people to have the king executed), he still experiences their effects in his own life. In Psalms 18 and 116 you can read how his life has come to be ruled by the effects of his misdeeds. In Psalm 51, a well-known prayer for forgiveness, David cries out to God:

> *Purify me with hyssop, and I will be clean. Wash me, and I will be whiter than snow...Create in me a clean heart, O God. Renew a right spirit within me....Deliver me from the guilt of bloodshed, O God, the God of my salvation.* (Psalm 51:7, 10, 14 WEB)

In Psalm 32, David describes how God, in answer to his change of heart, has answered his prayers:

> *I acknowledged my sin to you. I didn't hide my iniquity. I said, I will confess my transgressions to Yahweh, and you forgave the iniquity of my sin.... You will surround me with songs of deliverance.* (Psalm 32:5, 7, WEB)

In the Old Testament, a blood debt could be paid off only with the blood, that is the death, of the perpetrator:

> *So you shall not pollute the land in which you are: for blood pollutes the land. No atonement can be made for the land for the blood that is shed in it, but by the blood of him who shed it.* (Numbers 35:33, WEB)

Because in many cases the death penalty was not carried out—either because the sin remained hidden or because of God's grace—the blood debt continued to have an impact on the life of the person involved and sometimes his or her entire family. The reason is that in the spiritual world there was a rightful claim that had not yet been fulfilled.

Isaiah, again, prophesied that one day the Messiah would wash away all blood debts through the Spirit of justice. By dying on the Cross, Jesus brought about reconciliation. He took our death penalty and our debt of blood upon Himself, so that we can be at peace with God:

> It will happen, that he who is left in Zion, and he who remains in Jerusalem, shall be called holy, even everyone who is written among the living in Jerusalem; when the Lord shall have washed away the filth of the daughters of Zion, and shall have purged the blood of Jerusalem from within it, by the spirit of justice, and by the spirit of burning. (Isaiah 4:3–4, WEB)

On the Cross, Jesus washed away every blood debt on our lives with His blood. By His blood, He brought reconciliation, so that our relationship with God could be fully restored.

In this way, the wonder of reconciliation encompasses all the other wonders of the Cross: the wonders of forgiveness, salvation, cleansing, healing, freedom and being born again.

> Anyone who is joined to Christ is a new being; the old is gone, the new has come. All this is done by God, who through Christ changed us from enemies into his friends and gave us the task of making others his friends also. Our message is that God was making all human beings his friends through Christ. God did not keep an account of their sins, and he has given us the message, which tells how He makes them his friends. Here we are, then, speaking for Christ, as though God himself were making his appeal through us. We plead on Christ's behalf: let God change you from enemies into his friends! Christ was without sin, but for our sake God made him share our sin in order that in union with him we might share the righteousness of God. (2 Corinthians 5:17–21, GNB)

Father in heaven,

Thank You for the miracle of reconciliation. Thank You that Jesus Christ has reconciled me with You through the wonder of the Cross. I thank You that Jesus took the animosity and the judgment upon Himself so that I can come freely to You and be called Your child. Help me to understand what Jesus went through for me, so that I will never grow indifferent or weak. Thank You for so much mercy.

Amen.

THE SEVENTH WONDER OF THE CROSS:
A SPEAR IN HIS SIDE

They will look at the one whom they stabbed to death,
and they will mourn for him like those who mourn
for an only child. They will mourn bitterly,
like those who have lost their first-born son.

(Zechariah 12:10, GNB)

CHAPTER 11

Jesus died on a cross on Friday 7th April, 30 A.D., at around 3:00 p.m. The Friday has almost come to an end and the Sabbath is drawing near, which this year coincides with the start of the Passover. At 6:00 p.m., the great Sabbath celebration of the Passover will start, and before that time, the bodies need to be removed from the crosses. A few members of the Sanhedrin have already gone to Pilate to ask him to speed up the crucifixions by breaking the legs of the condemned men just under the knee with an iron bar, a practice known as *crurifragium*. Usually the victim of this final measure would die within fifteen minutes, unable to push his body up to gain relief for his arms and thus no longer able to breathe properly.

The soldiers break the legs of the two criminals, who thus die of suffocation. However, they do not need to break Jesus' legs. He has already died. One of the soldiers pierces Jesus' side with his spear. Blood and water come out immediately. At this point occurs the fulfillment of two prophesies made many years before:

He protects all of his bones. Not one of them is broken. (Psalm 34:20, WEB)

And they will look to me whom they have pierced. (Zechariah 12:10, WEB)

Why Did They Pierce His Side with a Spear?

I don't know if you have ever thought about this. Why did the Roman soldier pierce Jesus' side with his spear? Everyone at Golgotha could see that He was dead! What use was there in piercing Him again if He had already died? What on earth for?

> **God wanted Jesus to be pierced after He died for our sins so that we would understand that at that point, the reign of our sinful nature was brought to an end.**

Just as the whipping and the "coronation" with the crown of thorns were no accident, so the piercing of Jesus' side was meant to happen. Each of these are prophetic actions, foretold many years before, wanted and inspired by God and performed by sinful, heathen Roman soldiers. With this prophetic action the Great Director wanted to make it clear to us what the wonder of the Cross means for us. Jesus hung on the Cross in our place. God wanted Jesus to be pierced after He died for our sins so that we would understand that at that point the reign of our sinful nature was brought to an end. The moment the spear hit the rib of Jesus, our sinful nature, our old man, our flesh, died! The blood of Jesus frees us from our sins. The Cross frees us from our sinful nature. Jesus did not only deal with our sins, but also with our sinful nature. And that is a supernatural, incomprehensible, miracle!

Dealing with Our Sinful Nature

In chapter one, we discovered how big the difference is between our sinful nature and the divine nature of Jesus. Sin has gained so much power over us that our deepest being, though originally good, has irrevocably been changed into our current sinful nature. This is why Adam and Eve could no longer stay in God's presence. They experienced shame toward each other and toward God. They felt guilty about each other and about God. Through their rebellion the power of sin entered the world. People belonging to the first generations of mankind lived for about 800 years, but after the flood, we read that the average age dropped to around 250 and then down to the current eighty-year average in the so-called "first-world" countries (and less still in the so-called "third-world" countries). The power of sin has strongly influenced our thoughts, our actions and our relationships.

That is why God does not trust our sinful nature. It is hostile to Him and does not submit itself to Him.[187] Our sinful nature tries to please God, but cannot possibly do this.[188] It is useless to God! In His eyes, our sinful nature is hopeless and unchangeable. He knows better than anyone else that we cannot change our sinful nature, no matter how hard we try. We cannot change it by reading the Bible, praying or fasting.

Even the Holy Spirit cannot change our sinful nature, because it simply cannot be changed or transformed!

Even the Holy Spirit cannot change our sinful nature, because it simply cannot be changed or transformed! Our sinful nature is irreparable and therefore totally useless. It must disappear entirely. In Jesus, God shows us the truth. Our sinful nature is good for one thing only: crucifixion. Our sinful nature must die. What we need is another life! And that calls for a supernatural miracle: the wonder of the Cross! It is for this reason that we were included in the crucifixion of Jesus.

GOD HAS CRUCIFIED US WITH CHRIST

The Cross tells us what God thinks of us: we deserve to die. We cannot change our sinful nature. It must be laid aside and ripped out; it must die. It is either this or the following:

> *That was not what you learned about Christ! You certainly heard about him, and as his followers you were taught the truth that is in Jesus. So get rid of your old self, which made you live as you used to—the old self that was being destroyed by its deceitful desires. Your hearts and minds must be made completely new, and you must put on the new self, which is created in God's likeness and reveals itself in the true life that is upright and holy.* (Ephesians 4:20–24, GNB)

We don't need an adapted nature, but a whole new nature, a new life from God. In order to receive this new life from God the creator we must first deal with the old man, our sinful nature. And because we cannot even do that, God provided a way for us when Jesus was nailed to that Cross in our place. Everyone who believes in the wonder of the Cross has been crucified with Him two thousand years ago! Through this event our life in sin has come to an end.

> *And we know that our old being has been put to death with Christ on his cross, in order that the power of the sinful self might be destroyed, so that we should no longer be the slaves of sin.* (Romans 6:6, GNB)

> *I have been crucified with Christ.* (Galatians 2:20, WEB)

What Does it Mean
to be Crucified with Christ?

In his beautiful book *The Overcoming Life*, Watchman Nee (1903–1972) describes what it means to be crucified with Christ. He is seen as one of the most important church leaders within the Chinese Christian community. He laid the foundations for house churches in China, which managed to survive the waves of persecution by the communist regime. In 1952, Watchman Nee was arrested and falsely accused of various crimes, and was imprisoned until his death in 1972. He died exactly one day before his release.

This man of God says that to be crucified with Christ, I must give up all hope in my old nature. It means that I say to God: "You have given up all hope for me. And I too have given up all hope in myself. You see me as hopeless and I too see myself as hopeless. You think I deserve to die, and I too think I deserve to die. You see me as powerless and I too see myself as powerless. You see me as useless and I too see myself as useless."

Being crucified with Christ means that I admit and confess that I am giving up my old lifestyle, because I am nothing and can do nothing without Him. It means that I allow my thoughts to be radically renewed, and that everything I have learned and been taught is held up to the light of what Jesus teaches. I want to live like He lives, think like He thinks, speak like He speaks, love like He loves, act like He acts. I don't even want to have my own opinions any more (almost unthinkable for Dutch people!). The Man who identified completely with our sins, our diseases, the curse of our lives and our death wants us to identify with Him! And the Cross makes this possible. For it is here that our rebirth takes place. By becoming one with Jesus in His death, through faith, our sinful nature dies and we receive part of the divine nature of Jesus:

So then, just as sin ruled by means of death, so also God's grace rules by means of righteousness, leading us to eternal life through Jesus Christ our Lord. What shall we say, then? Should we continue to live in sin so that God's grace will increase? Certainly not! We have died to sin—how then can we go on living in it? For surely you know that when we were baptized into union with Christ Jesus, we were baptized into union with his death. By our baptism, then, we were buried with him and shared his death, in order that, just as Christ was raised from death by the glorious power of the Father, so also we might live a new life. For since we have become one with Him in dying as he did, in the same way we shall be one with Him by being raised to life as he was. And we know that our old being has been put to death with Christ on his cross, in order that the power of the sinful self might be destroyed, so that we should no longer be the slaves of sin. For when we die, we are set free from the power of sin. Since we have died with Christ, we believe that we will also live with him. (Romans 5:21–6:8, GNB)

Through baptism we identify with the death, burial and resurrection of Jesus, which is verified for both the natural and the supernatural. Our submersion in water is a symbol of this burial, the result of dying to ourselves, the death of our sinful nature. Baptism is our request to God to be dealt with and buried. A burial is final! It is God's declaration and our acknowledgment that our old man, our sinful nature, has died. Being raised from this watery grave shows us that we may be raised with Jesus to new life. Many Christians do not realize the powerful meaning of water baptism. We have been born again through Him and therefore have a share in His divine nature:

In this way he has given us the very great and precious gifts he promised, so that by means of these gifts you may escape from the destructive lust that is in the world, and may come to share the divine nature. (2 Peter 1:4, GNB)

As soon as someone is born again, everything that belongs to and is part of Jesus becomes theirs and part of them! Everything that is in Jesus is now also available to us. Jesus' life reveals itself in us, now! We cannot do anything to deserve this; it is God's gift, which comes to us through the wonder of the Cross.

WATER AND BLOOD: SIGNS OF A NEW BIRTH

The moment one of the soldiers sticks his spear into Jesus' side, water and blood flow out.[189] The beginning of a birth always starts with the release of water and blood. The water and blood flowing out of the body of Jesus mark the beginning of our rebirth. On the Cross, Jesus begins to bring forth a new generation of children of God. He is not just the Lamb of God that takes away the sins of the world. He is like a mother, giving birth to a new man, a man who—through the wonder of the Cross—no longer is doomed to live in slavery to sin.

Just as God formed Eve from Adam's rib, so He also formed a new person from Jesus! We are born again, brought forth from a place in His side, where Jesus was pierced; a kind of womb.

The Greek word for "side" is *pleura* and it also means "rib." This event in which Jesus bled for the seventh time reminds me of Genesis 2:21, where we read how God created a new person (Eve) out of Adam's rib. Just as God formed Eve from Adam's rib, so He also formed a new person from Jesus! We are born again, brought forth from a place in His side, where Jesus was pierced; a kind of womb. It is interesting to note that Jesus spoke about the birth pangs of a woman before He was crucified:

> *When a woman is about to give birth, she is sad because her hour of suffering has come; but when the baby is born, she forgets her*

suffering, because she is happy that a baby has been born into the world. (John 16:21, GNB)

Through the wonder of the Cross, a whole new humanity is born from Jesus, just as Isaiah prophesied:

The Lord says, "It was my will that he should suffer; his death was a sacrifice to bring forgiveness. And so he will see his descendants; he will live a long life, and through him my purpose will succeed." (Isaiah 53:10, GNB)

Without the Cross, the miracle of rebirth could never take place in our lives. The wonder of the Cross brings forth a whole new creation:

Therefore if anyone is in Christ, he is a new creation. The old things have passed away. Behold, all things have become new. (2 Corinthians 5:17, WEB)

WHAT DOES IT MEAN TO BE BORN AGAIN?

Being born again means "it is no longer I that live, but Christ living in me!"[190] This means that Jesus' life becomes mine. From now on, the love of Jesus becomes my love. His joy becomes my joy. His wisdom becomes my wisdom. His patience becomes my patience. His kindness becomes my kindness. His strength becomes my strength. His victory becomes my victory. His nature becomes my nature, and so on. I am permanently and continually connected to a source that will never run dry: Jesus Christ. The apostle Paul summarizes this as follows:

For to me to live is Christ! (Philippians 1:21, WEB)

Being born again is comparable to modern heart transplantation. The sick heart (hardened by sin) is replaced with a new warm heart: the heart of Jesus. And because the Holy Spirit, who is called the Spirit of Jesus,[191] comes to live in us, we are enabled to do what He asks of us. Isn't that wonderful? Once we are born again, we receive the heart and Spirit of Jesus. The heart of Jesus beats within us. And the Spirit of Jesus lives in us.

> *I will give you a new heart and a new mind. I will take away your stubborn heart of stone and give you an obedient heart. I will put my spirit in you and will see to it that you follow my laws and keep all the commands I have given you.* (Ezekiel 36:26–27, GNB)

When we are born again, the Holy Spirit plants the life of Jesus Christ in us. Then this new life grows and reveals itself in us with increasing strength, until the likeness of Jesus becomes visible in our lives. That is what Paul means when he speaks of the birth contractions he went through for the church's sake, until Christ was formed in her.[192] From now on there is no sin too great to conquer, there is no temptation too great to resist. Could there be some sin that Jesus cannot conquer? Some temptation too strong for Him to resist?

When we are born again, the Holy Spirit plants the life of Jesus Christ in us.

> *But thanks be to God who gives us the victory through our Lord Jesus Christ!* (1 Corinthians 15:57, GNB)

> *Because every child of God is able to defeat the world. And we win the victory over the world by means of our faith.* (1 John 5:4, GNB)

THE CONFLICT BETWEEN THE TWO NATURES

We know that Jesus, when He died on the Cross, dealt not only with our sins, but also with our sinful nature. This brings us to another truth: even though our sinful nature has been crucified, our "self" is still intact. All we have to do is look inside ourselves to see that we are still very alive to sin. This sounds contradictory, but Paul establishes that the desire of the sinful nature (though crucified) is the opposite of what the Holy Spirit in us wants:

> *For what our human nature wants is opposed to what the Spirit wants, and what the Spirit wants is opposed to what our human nature wants. These two are enemies, and this means that you cannot do what you want to do.* (Galatians 5:17, GNB)

> **Even though we may in fact now live in Jesus, our sinful nature reveals itself in us when we relapse into our own strength and live according to our own insights.**

Even though we may in fact now live in Jesus, our sinful nature reveals itself in us when we relapse into our own strength and live according to our own insights. If we want to experience the life of Jesus in us, we must learn to obey the Holy Spirit. Only then will the power of sin stop influencing our lives.

What I say is this: let the Spirit direct your lives, and you will not satisfy the desires of the human nature. (Galatians 5:16, GNB)

Living in obedience to the Holy Spirit means we must trust that He will achieve what we cannot. This is an entirely different life from the one we naturally tend to live. When the Holy Spirit takes control, there is no effort on our part.

Thus the Cross has been given to us to gain salvation *for us*, and the Holy Spirit has been given to us to work out that salvation *in us*.

> *You, however, are controlled not by the sinful nature, but by the Spirit, if the Spirit of God lives in you.* (Romans 8:9, NIV)

THE BATTLE BETWEEN THE TWO LAWS

Just as there is a conflict in me between my sinful nature and the divine nature of Jesus, there is also a battle in me between the law of sin (which leads to death) and the law of the Spirit (which brings life).

So it is not just sin that is present in me, but the law of sin as well. Not just death, but the law of death. This law of sin and death resists everything that is good and paralyzes our will to do good. As a result of this law, present in our bodies, we naturally incline toward sin. The apostle Paul describes in a very recognizable way how the law of sin works in his life and in ours:

> *I do not understand what I do; for I don't do what I would like to do, but instead I do what I hate. Since what I do is what I don't want to do, this shows that I agree that the Law is right. So I am not really the one who does this thing; rather it is the sin that lives in me. I know that good does not live in me—that is, in my human nature. For even though the desire to do good is in me, I am not able to do it. I don't do the good I want to do; instead, I do the evil that I do not want to do. If I do what I don't want to do, this means that I am no longer the one who does it; instead, it is the sin that lives in me. So I find that this law is at work: when I want to do what is good, what is evil is the only choice I have. My inner being delights in the law of God. But I see a different law at work in my body—a law that fights against the law which my mind approves of. It makes me a prisoner to the law of sin, which is at work in my body. What an unhappy man I am! Who will rescue me from this body that is taking me to death? Thanks be to God, who does this through our Lord Jesus Christ! This, then, is my condition: on my own I can serve God's law only with my mind, while my human nature serves the law of sin. There is no condemnation now for those who live in union with Christ Jesus. For the law of the Spirit, which brings us life in union with Christ Jesus, has set me free from the law of sin and death.* (Romans 7:15–8:2, GNB)

Paul says that if he were left to his own devices, he would be completely powerless against sin. Despite the fact that his sinful nature (the old man) has been crucified with Jesus, he will become subject to the law of sin if he trusts in his own strength and insight. The message of the Cross, however, is this: just as the law of gravity can be countered only by the law of Archimedes, or buoyancy, the law of sin, which leads to death, can be countered only by a different law, namely the law of the Spirit, who gives us life in Jesus!

> **A Christian is someone in whom the Spirit of Jesus lives and who is therefore no longer powerless.**

A Christian is someone in whom the Spirit of Jesus lives and who is therefore no longer powerless. Jesus in us, who wrestled with our sin in the garden of Gethsemane, is capable of overcoming the sin in us. We do not have to be super-Christians to overcome the law of sin. The only thing we need to do is give Him complete power in our lives and subject ourselves to Him, and He will protect us against the old law of sin. Then we will experience what it is like to be kept, not through our own power, but by the power of God.[193]

FRED

A few months ago, I met Fred. We had several conversations. He did not know God and knew little about the Bible. What he did know was that he was having trouble in different areas of his life. After six conversations, I said: "Fred, even if I were to tell you everything I know, it will not change you. Only if you give your life to God and He comes to live in you, will you change from the inside out." It was several weeks before I heard from him again. I knew Fred was wrestling with this vital decision. Finally, after a long battle, he laid his life in God's hands.

He found it so difficult to let go of his old life: "I know what I have, but I don't know what I'll get! What will happen if I surrender to God?" After he had prayed the sinners' prayer, he looked at me and sighed: "I don't know if I am going to make it."

I looked at him and smiled and said: "Fred, you're right, you will not make it. But thank God that you can't do it yourself. The secret is that Jesus now lives in you. Don't try to change yourself in your own power; let Him do that. He will fight for you. Trust Him to make you completely new from the inside out. You have started a whole new life with Him."

Later we met again. I enjoyed hearing from Fred how he had gone to three former employers whom he had stolen from in the past, to ask for forgiveness and to set things straight. Fred, who always used to put off difficult decisions, did not do this in his own strength. He started to discover that the secret of "Jesus in me" was an inexhaustible source of power, which he could draw on without restrictions.

WRESTLING WITH SIN UNTIL BLOOD FLOWS

You don't have to be a super-Christian to conquer the law of sin. No Christian is condemned to remaining powerless. A Christian is someone who is in Jesus Christ and is therefore no longer powerless. That is why every Christian can be freed from the power of sin. Jesus did not go to the Cross for us to remain unchanged. But we must not boast that we can control or conquer sin by ourselves. Controlling yourself is not victory. We must not think that we can control our sinful nature in our own power! King David tried so hard to control his tongue, but had to conclude that he could not do it in his own strength:

> I said, "I will be careful about what I do and will not let my tongue make me sin; I will not say anything while evil people are near." I kept quiet, not saying a word, not even about anything good! But my suffering only grew worse, and I was overcome with anxiety.

The more I thought, the more troubled I became. (Psalm 39:1–3, GNB)

There is only One who, in the garden of Gethsemane, wrestled with our sin until the blood flowed and who was then victorious: Jesus Christ. If the Bible asks us to "strive against sin unto blood," it means that the Spirit of Jesus, who lives in us, will help us and give us the strength to overcome sin. His victory is our victory! That is why we must keep our eyes on Him in every situation:

... looking to Jesus, the author and perfecter of faith, who for the joy that was set before him endured the Cross, despising shame, and has sat down at the right hand of the throne of God. For consider him who has endured such contradiction of sinners against himself, that you don't grow weary, fainting in your souls. You have not yet resisted to blood, striving against sin. (Hebrews 12:2–4, WEB)

The secret of each Christian is that Jesus has already conquered and that we are more than victorious in Him:

Who, then, can separate us from the love of Christ? Can trouble do it, or hardship or persecution or hunger or poverty or danger or death? As the scripture says, "For your sake we are in danger of death at all times; we are treated like sheep that are going to be slaughtered." No, in all these things we have complete victory through him who loved us! For I am certain that nothing can separate us from his love: neither death nor life, neither angels nor other heavenly rulers or powers, neither the present nor the future, neither the world above nor the world below—there is nothing in all creation that will ever be able to separate us from the love of God which is ours through Christ Jesus our Lord. (Romans 8:35–39, GNB)

The sinful nature always wants to do things its own way, which is precisely what the devil is waiting for. For it is in those areas in which I trust in my own power, my own wisdom and my own abilities that he will gain influence and power over my life.

Someone once asked a young lady how she conquered the devil when he tempted her. She answered: "Before, when the devil would knock on my door, I would say: 'Don't come in! Don't come in!' But the end result was always failure. Now, when the devil knocks on my door I say: 'Lord, would You please open the door for me?' Then when the Lord opens the door, the devil says: 'Pardon me, wrong address!' and runs away." This lady has understood the secret of "Jesus in me" very well. That is why Paul confronts us and asks:

> *Surely you know that Christ Jesus is in you?—unless you have completely failed.* (2 Corinthians 13:5, GNB)

We must understand that it is God's plan and purpose that we are no longer controlled by (the power of) sin. In Romans 6:14 (WEB) Paul says: "For sin will not have dominion over you." Each Christian must be set free from the power of sin, which leads to death! Through the wonder of the Cross God has given us the power to overcome sin. Through the wonder of the Cross we have been set free from slavery to the power of sin, so that we can now experience uninterrupted intimacy with God. It is God's will that we experience complete freedom from our sins!

THE SECRET TO KEEPING
MY SINFUL NATURE CRUCIFIED

I can choose to wrestle against sin on my own, but it will be an endless and a useless battle. I do not have the power in myself to conquer sin or to resist temptation. There is only one way for me to live a blameless life, and that is by living with the Blameless One. If we keep our eyes on Jesus, we have all, but if we turn back to ourselves, we have nothing. Paul discovered the secret of how to keep his sinful nature crucified and how to participate in the power of Jesus:

> *He has said to me: "My grace is sufficient for you, for my power is made perfect in weakness." Most gladly therefore I will rather glory in my weaknesses, that the power of Christ may rest on me.* (2 Corinthians 12:9, WEB)

By glorying in our weakness, we keep our sinful nature crucified, and the power of Christ will be revealed in us.

By glorying in our weakness, we keep our sinful nature crucified, and the power of Christ will be revealed in us. Like Paul, we must learn to glory in our weakness. This is not about false humility, but about becoming aware of our own incompetence and powerlessness. "To glory" means to thank God. Paul says that we must thank God for everything we cannot do ourselves. By confessing this out loud, we thank God that He will reveal His power in us. For instance, we might pray as follows:

> *Lord, thank You that I cannot make it on my own. I thank You that I cannot possibly overcome sin. I am completely powerless. I rejoice in my incompetence. Only You are competent! I thank You that I cannot love my partner. Thank You that I cannot forgive my father. Thank You that I cannot break this bad habit. But in You I am more than a conqueror. In You I can do all things, because You give me power and guide my life. Amen!*

Victory has nothing to do with us, but with Jesus who lives in us! He is the one who is victorious in us; He is the one who helps me to love my partner. He is the one who helps me to forgive my father. He is the one who gives me the strength to break that bad habit. He is the one who wrestled against sin and was victorious. As long as I live in intimacy with Jesus, and remain in conversation with Him, sin has no power over me. How relaxing that is! But as soon as my intimacy with Him is lost, I lose all and I live as an outlaw and sin will catch up with me in no time. Sin comes to us only when we don't have an intimate, personal relationship with God through Jesus.

Victory has nothing to do with us, but with Jesus who lives in us!

When will this battle end? We will be finally freed from this "civil war" inside of us only when we receive a new and glorified body at Christ's return. Then our bodies will be like the body of Jesus, in which sin and death no longer have power (1 Corinthians 15).

The Seventh Wonder of the Cross:
The Wonder of Rebirth

Jesus once spent a night talking to Nicodemus, one of the Jewish leaders, who was a member of the Sanhedrin. He belonged to the party of the Pharisees. Unlike most of the other Jewish leaders, he was not hostile to Jesus. He even once openly defended Jesus during a meeting (John 7:51), which shows that he was a brave man. On this particular night, Jesus spoke with Nicodemus about the Kingdom of God. Jesus said that a man can see and enter the Kingdom of God only if he is born again (*gennethenai anothen*, John 3:3–5). The word *anothen* can mean both "again" and "from above." Both translations are correct. "Being born again" means that we are "born of God," as John puts it in 1 John 3:9.

In talking to Nicodemus, Jesus was actually already speaking of what would happen on the Cross. Nicodemus did not understand this then and he probably still did not understand it when the Roman soldier pierced Jesus' side. Nicodemus generally did not understand what Jesus was speaking about. His way of thinking was different from that of Jesus. Jesus thought and spoke as someone "from above." Nicodemus looked at life from an earthly point of view: "How can an adult be born again? A person cannot be born a second time of his mother." Nicodemus thought in a natural way. That is why Jesus said that he must be born "from above." Then he would see what God sees, speak as God speaks and act as God acts. Jesus did not leave Nicodemus in the dark, but explained to him how he could be born again (from above):

> *"I am telling you the truth," replied Jesus, "that no one can enter the Kingdom of God without being born of water and the Spirit. A person is born physically of human parents, but is born spiritually of the Spirit. Do not be surprised because I tell you that you must all be born again."* (John 3:5–7, GNB)

Being born again is a supernatural miracle. It means that you die to yourself and become part of the Life of Jesus! On the basis of John the Baptist's testimony, Nicodemus might have known that it is necessary to be born of water and of Spirit to enter the Kingdom of God. With this in mind, John baptized with water, saying that the Messiah would baptize with the Holy Spirit,[194] a baptism that was to generate new life in us. "Water and Spirit" together show how we can be born again and enter the Kingdom of God. By our baptism in water we identify with the death of Jesus (our sinful nature has been crucified with Him). By our baptism in the Holy Spirit we are equipped for our new life with Him to continue His work on this earth, because the Spirit of Jesus has come to live in us.

I wonder if Nicodemus, who witnessed the crucifixion of Jesus up close, really understood the profundity of what was going on when the Roman soldier pierced Jesus. Did he understand that God at that moment was making a way for him and us to be born again? Or was he, like all the other witnesses, blind to the wonder of the Cross occurring before his very eyes?

At any rate, Nicodemus loved Jesus so much that he and Joseph of Arimathea arranged for Jesus' body to be taken from the Cross and buried.

Father in heaven,

I realize that I too must be born again to enter the Kingdom
of God. Thank You that I may now give up all hope for my old
nature. Just as You do, I want to see my sinful nature as hopeless and useless. I count myself blessed that I am incompetent
and powerless on my own. Thank You that the blood of Jesus
has taken away my sins and that, through His blood shed on
the Cross, my sinful nature has died with Jesus. Through the
wonder of the Cross I may now be born again, because my old
man was killed the moment Jesus' side was pierced. In Jesus I
have become a new person. You make me completely new on
the inside. I want to lay down my old life by baptism in water.
Lord Jesus, would You baptize me with Your Spirit, so that I
will think as You think, speak as You speak, love as You love
and live as You live?
Thank You that I may identify completely with You.
Thank You for the seventh wonder of the Cross!

Amen.

LOVE FOR HIS BODY

So we, who are many, are one body in Christ.

(Romans 12:5, WEB)

CHAPTER 12

Once the condemned had died, their bodies usually remained on the crosses until wild animals or birds devoured them, or until they fell off through decay. (Golgotha isn't called "the place of the skull" for nothing.) Sometimes the bodies were burned after a crucifixion. This was a thing of great shame for their families. It is quite possible that the high priests wanted to do this to Jesus, so they could wipe out every trace of Him.

It is a curious thing that several men who believe in Jesus are members of the High Court.[195] However, they are afraid of the Pharisees, the greatest opponents of Jesus, and dare not openly confess their faith. Whoever openly confesses his faith in Jesus is likely to be banned from the synagogue.[196] So during the trial, these Jewish leaders do not openly profess their belief. They keep it hidden. The death of Jesus makes such a big impression on them, however, that they begin openly to share their faith in Him. Two of them are mentioned by name: Joseph of Arimathea and Nicodemus.

JOSEPH OF ARIMATHEA

It is almost evening when Joseph of Arimathea goes to the crucifixion site. He is a prominent member of the High Court, a good and just man. He is a follower of Jesus, but has not yet dared to say so publicly, because he is afraid of the Jews. Joseph does not at all agree with the decisions or actions of the other Jewish leaders.[197] He believes that Jesus is the long-awaited Messiah and is eagerly anticipating the Kingdom of God. This Joseph is bold enough to go to Pilate. In doing so, he is risking his position in the High Court. He now dares to testify openly that he is a disciple of Jesus. Because of his high position, he can easily gain access to Pilate. He asks the governor permission on behalf of the family to take the body of Jesus from the Cross and bury it. Emperor Augustus had decreed that the body of the condemned was to go to the family or friends if they asked for it. But Pilate cannot believe that Jesus has already died. He summons the officer who is on duty and responsible for the crucifixion, and asks him about this. The officer confirms that Jesus has indeed died. (A faked death is thereby now ruled out.) Then Joseph, aided by Nicodemus, gets permission to take the body of Jesus.

NICODEMUS

Nicodemus is a member of the High Court, just like Joseph. Three years ago, he went to visit Jesus. Now he openly professes that he is a follower of Jesus. The death of Jesus on the Cross has probably led to this defining moment in his faith. Nicodemus is a wealthy man. Converted into our measurements, the amount of embalming spices he has with him must have weighed about thirty kilos. Such a large amount would in those days normally only have been used for a king. This shows that these two men wanted to honor Jesus in a great way. The spices were made up of a powder mixture of myrrh, which is made from the resin of the myrrh bush, and aloe, a kind of finely ground scented wood. The Jews do not embalm their dead, but wrap them in cloths and bury them. The spices are placed between the cloths to prevent the smell of decay from becoming too penetrating. The cloths are brought by Joseph,[198] the spices by Nicodemus.[199]

FOR THE LOVE OF JESUS

Out of love and compassion for Jesus, Nicodemus and Joseph take His body from the Cross. Very carefully, they try to remove the nails from His hands and feet, as the soldiers and a few passers-by watch. They take His damaged body in their arms, inevitably getting some of His blood on themselves. They try to remove the crown of thorns, which has penetrated deep into His skin. All this speaks of a deep love for and devotion to the man who has changed their lives so radically. Joseph and Nicodemus wrap the body, with the spices, in the linen cloths and carry Him to a garden, not far from the crucifixion site. There is a new and unused grave in the garden, which Joseph has recently had dug out of the rock. He wants to give the best he has. The women who came with Jesus from Galilee go with them to the grave and see how His body is laid inside. They roll a big, round, flat stone into the groove in front of the entrance to the grave and then go home. Friday afternoon has almost passed. The Sabbath is about to start. They plan to rest on the Sabbath, as Jewish law prescribes.

The saddest Passover celebration they have ever had begins for Jesus' followers, if they celebrated it at all. When the exodus from Egypt took place the door to the future was wide open. But now that door has been closed with the crucifixion of their Messiah. At least, that is what they think.

PASSION FOR THE BODY OF CHRIST

Through the seven wonders of the Cross Jesus: 1) forgave our sins; 2) freed us from all accusations and guilt; 3) cleansed our conscience; 4) healed our diseases; 5) freed us from every curse;

6) reconciled us with God the Father; and 7) let us be born again through Him!

Everyone who has personally accepted this wonder of the Cross is part of the Body of Christ, His worldwide church:

> *In the same way, all of us, whether Jews or Gentiles, whether slaves or free, have been baptized into the one body by the same Spirit, and we have all been given the one Spirit to drink.* (1 Corinthians 12:13, GNB)

All of us together are the representatives of Jesus here on earth, called to continue His work as ambassadors of God's Kingdom of love. As children of God, we need each other. The heart of Jesus beats within each one of us and the Spirit of Jesus has come to live in each of us. If we have a passion for Jesus, we will automatically develop a passion for His Body. Joseph of Arimathea and Nicodemus can teach us how. The love shown by them for the lifeless body of Jesus is impressive. See how loving and devoted they are in their care for His body. This is very different from how we often treat the Body of Christ! The Body of Christ is divided here on earth. One part of the Body elevates itself over another part. We call on our traditions, on the size of our church (or on our denomination), on

If we have a passion for Jesus, we will automatically develop a passion for His Body.

the number of converts we've made or the miracles and signs that take place in our midst. Maybe we don't say these things out loud, but the Body of Christ speaks body language. And our actions and attitudes speak louder than our words! We push each other away instead of drawing each other in, proving that the Body of Christ on earth has become desperately ill. Sometimes, we think (and say) that the church hardly has any life left in it. Or even worse: that the

Spirit of Christ is not in it. Let us please be very careful about how we speak of the Body of Christ, especially as it has indeed become so very sick. Let us turn away from the bad things we say about each other. Words of encouragement, uplifting and strengthening are the medication needed to help the Body become healthy and united once again.[200] Let us love each other, because the Beloved lives in us! Let the loving devotion of Joseph and Nicodemus to the lifeless body of their Master inspire us. Then non-believers will acknowledge that God sent Jesus to this world. Then they will want to accept the wonder of the Cross—because they will see the results of it in our lives.

COMPLETE UNITY

Let us become aware of the fact that we can only show the wonder of God's love to the world through "complete unity." This is what Jesus prayed for, not long before He died:

> *The glory which you have given me, I have given to them; that they may be one, even as we are one; I in them, and you in me, that they may be perfected into one; that the world may know that you sent me, and loved them, even as you loved me.* (John 17:22–23, WEB)

People (and churches) can join forces in pursuit of a common goal. This does bring some unity, but only to a certain extent. How often have we not seen that if we alter the way we want to reach that goal, our unity takes a bit of a battering? We move forward, shoulder to shoulder, until we can no longer agree on a certain aspect. And then our unity goes out of the window! Human unity is very relative and very limited. It is a human choice, and who will ever understand the human psyche?

Jesus is not speaking of human unity in this passage, but that "they may be one." The NIV translation speaks of "complete unity!" Only if we are completely united will non-believers acknowledge that God sent Jesus to this world. Then the world will acknowledge that God loves us. His love in us will be tangible! That's why it is so vitally important that we discover how we can bring about this perfect unity in our midst.

Jesus Himself gives us the answer to how we can become completely one in every situation and every circumstance. The secret is hidden in these three words: "I in them!"[201] Complete unity comes about when I see Jesus in you, you see Jesus in me, and we see Jesus in each other. "Jesus in us!" is the secret to achieving complete unity. We are not capable of this on our own. But if—regardless of circumstances and of what is said or done—we recognize Jesus in each other, there will always be unity. That is Jesus' secret for us. In this way, imperfect people can come together in perfect unity—because, under all circumstances, they want to see Jesus in each other, despite the imperfect and sometimes difficult and painful reactions from people.

> **Complete unity comes about when I see Jesus in you, you see Jesus in me, and we see Jesus in each other.**

PATRIA UNITY

We are all children of the same Father. That is why Paul writes in Ephesians 3:14–15: *"For this reason I fall on my knees before the Father, from whom every family in heaven and on earth receives its true name."* We are all named after Him. And even though God does not have a surname, in the original text of the Bible, we find the Greek word *patria*, or lineage, meaning that we are of God's family. The word *patria* comes from the word *pater* (meaning father), just as we come from the will of God, our Father in heaven. We are God's family on earth! And, "so that you, together with all God's people, may have the power to understand how broad and long, how high and deep, is Christ's love. Yes, may you come to know his love" (verses 18 and 19). Only together will we be able to discover how great God's love is for us. We need *patria* unity for this. We need everyone in God's Kingdom, because it is only together that we can discover and make known the love of Jesus. Every generation, every people and every culture is vital in making God, our heavenly Father, visible to the world. We need a childlike openness to go out, youthful enthusiasm to embrace the fact that we have overcome the evil one and the mature love of the fathers and mothers who have come to know God through the various seasons of this life.

> **Every generation, every people and every culture is vital in making God, our heavenly Father, visible to the world.**

Jesus is forming a church from every people and every tribe, because through that great diversity of cultures and identities the wisdom of God in all its forms will be made known. This is God's eternal plan![202] Let us learn from each other and see God's love in the other. Then we will view each other and the world around us in a new way. We have a God who loves diversity!

For Christ himself has brought us peace by making Jews and Gentiles one people. With his own body, he broke down the wall that separated them and kept them enemies. He abolished the Jewish Law with its commandments and rules, in order to create out of the two races one new people in union with himself, in this way making peace. By his death on the cross, Christ destroyed their enmity; by means of the cross, he united both races into one body and brought them back to God.[203]

Father in heaven,

Thank You that I may be a part of the Body of Christ, Your church, here on earth, by being born again. Give me the same love for and devotion to the Body of Christ that Joseph of Arimathea and Nicodemus displayed. Help me to see Jesus at all times in those who, just like me, want to follow Him. That is why I confess that I believe in the unity of Your church, wherever the wonder of the Cross is preached. I choose to be one with those who love You as I do, so that the world may see that Jesus was sent by You to this earth and will acknowledge Him as her Lord and Savior.

Amen.

BETWEEN THE CROSS AND THE RESURRECTION

And in his spiritual existence he went
and preached to the imprisoned spirits.

(1 Peter 3:19, GNB)

CHAPTER 13

We know that Jesus died on Friday 7th April, 30 A.D., around
3:00 p.m. We also know that Jesus—barely forty hours later, early on Sunday morning—appeared alive and well to four women,
who had come to embalm His body. The Bible is clear on this. But
what do we know about what happened between the Cross and the
resurrection? I've noticed that many Christians hardly even think
about what Jesus did for us between the Cross and the resurrection,
let alone about what it means for them personally. Now we must
admit that although the writers of the Gospels were very detailed
in their descriptions of the last eighteen hours of Jesus' life, they
only briefly summarize what happened in the spiritual world after
He died. Actually, the only thing they tell us is what Jesus said:
"Father! In your hands I place my spirit!"[204] However, Jesus did not
go into some kind of "soul sleep" for three days, after which God
woke Him from the dead. It was just the opposite! Jesus did not rest

in peace, but confronted the enormity of death itself, after which He dethroned Satan and stripped him of his power.

Jesus Beat the Devil at His Own Game

If we really want to understand and experience the wonder of the Cross completely, it is necessary to know what happened in the spiritual world after Jesus died:

> *Since the children, as he calls them, are people of flesh and blood, Jesus himself became like them and shared their human nature. He did this so that through his death he might destroy the Devil, who has the power over death, and in this way set free those who were slaves all their lives because of their fear of death.* (Hebrews 2:14–15, GNB)

Many Christians cannot really explain why Jesus became human. It is not that easy to understand, but this translation of Hebrews 2:14–15 makes a lot clear. God had to become man and die in order to dethrone the devil, who had the power over death. These verses tell us quite a lot about what happened between the Cross and the resurrection. Only by becoming human and dying was Jesus able to beat the devil at his own game, in the realm of the dead. In order to understand this, we must know what the Bible says about life after death.

A Prophetic View
of the Realm of the Dead

The ancient religions did not offer people much hope of life after death, but Judaism was an exception to this rule. Jews believed that, after dying, each person would go to the realm of the dead, the place where all people awaited God's judgment (we're talking here of the situation before Jesus conquered death).[205] Jesus Himself acknowledged the existence of the realm of the dead.[206] In this realm, there is no action, no thought, no knowledge, no wisdom.[207] No one praises God there;[208] it is a land of darkness, shadows and confusion.[209] In Psalm 49, we find an interesting prophetic view of the realm of the dead:

> *We can never redeem ourselves; we cannot pay God the price for our lives, because the payment for a human life is too great. What we could pay would never be enough to keep us from the grave, to let us live forever. Anyone can see that even the wise die, as well as the foolish and stupid. They all leave their riches to their descendants. Their graves are their homes forever; there they stay for all time, though they once had lands of their own. Our greatness cannot keep us from death; we will still die like the animals. See what happens to those who trust in themselves, the fate of those who are satisfied with their wealth—they are doomed to die like sheep, and Death will be their shepherd. The righteous will triumph over them, as their bodies quickly decay in the world of the dead far from their homes. But God will rescue me; he will save me from the power of death.* (Psalm 49:7–15, GNB)

The Psalmist believes that God will free him and bring him out of the realm of the dead, where Death is his shepherd (in other words, in control). This is really a prophetic description of what Jesus did between the Cross and the resurrection. But before we try to picture this, we need to look at what Jesus Himself taught about the realm of the dead. In the well-known parable of the rich man and Lazarus, He describes the realm of the dead very similarly to the composer of Psalm 49. And even though it is a parable, Jesus would never have spoken in such detail about this if his description did not resemble the real thing. If we look at this parable closely, we discover that one of His reasons for sharing it was to let us know what would happen between the Cross and resurrection:

If you don't believe when I talk to you about things on earth, how can you possibly believe if I talk to you about things in heaven? (John 3:12, CEV)

THE RICH MAN AND POOR LAZARUS

In this parable, Jesus teaches us more about "heavenly things." He gives us a glimpse into the realm of the dead. It is interesting that Jesus' last words to His hearers in this story are a warning that even if someone were to be raised from the dead and appear to them, they would not believe God (one of His many references to His resurrection from the dead). Let's read the parable first.

Now there was a certain rich man, and he was clothed in purple and fine linen, living in luxury every day. A certain beggar, named Lazarus, was laid at his gate, full of sores, and desiring to be fed with the crumbs that fell from the rich man's table. Yes, even the dogs came and licked his sores. It happened that the beggar died, and that he was carried away by the angels to Abraham's bosom. The rich man also died, and was buried. In Hades, he lifted up his eyes, being in torment, and saw Abraham far off, and Lazarus at his bosom. He cried and said: "Father Abraham, have mercy on me, and send Lazarus, that he may dip the tip of his finger in water, and cool my tongue! For I am in anguish in this flame." But Abraham said: "Son, remember that you, in your lifetime, received your good things, and Lazarus, in like manner, bad things. But now here he is comforted and you are in anguish. Besides all this, between us and you there is a great gulf fixed, that those who want to pass from here to you are not able, and that none may cross over from there to us." He said: "I ask you therefore, father, that you would send him to my father's house; for I have five brothers, that he may testify to them, so they won't also come into this place of torment." But Abraham said to him: "They have Moses and the prophets. Let them listen to them." He said: "No, father Abraham, but if one goes to them from the dead, they will repent." He said to him:

"If they don't listen to Moses and the prophets, neither will they be persuaded if one rises from the dead." (Luke 16:19–31, WEB)

Jesus depicts the realm of the dead as a place that is divided into two sections, separated by an impassable gulf. Lazarus, after his death, is carried by God's angels to the bosom of Abraham. Lazarus is on the "light" side of the realm of the dead, where it is cool and refreshing and where he finds comfort, like a child resting in his mother's or father's lap, or like a guest lying close to the host during a meal. The rich man lifts up his eyes in the realm of the dead after he dies. But for him it is a place of pain and torment. He speaks about being "in anguish" and says that he is suffering in "this flame." And while the rich man suffers much pain, he sees Abraham "far off" with Lazarus at his bosom. There is a great gulf between what I would call the "light" side and the "dark" side of the realm of the dead. Even though they cannot possibly reach each other, it seems that the rich man and Lazarus are able to see each other and communicate. The rich man asks Abraham to send Lazarus to him. If Lazarus could just dip his finger in water and touch his tongue, he might find some relief. This is how terrible the pain is in the flames of fire in this part of the realm of the dead. But Abraham confirms that the gulf between the rich man and Lazarus is impassable. Abraham can do nothing to change the judgment that God has passed; God's judgment is final. But the rich man does not give up. If Lazarus cannot come to him, then maybe he could be sent to his five brothers who are still on earth to warn them, to save them from ending up in this place of torment as well. Abraham then answers: "If they don't listen to Moses and the prophets, neither will they be persuaded if one rises from the dead." Jesus is already foreseeing how the Jewish leaders will react to the message from the Romans guarding the grave and to the apostles' testimony: they will not believe.

GOD DID NOT WANT DEATH

Before Jesus' death and resurrection, the souls of those who died did not go to heaven but to the realm of the dead. God had warned Adam and Eve that if they were to sin, they would die,[210] as the wages of sin is death.[211] And because every human being after Adam also sinned, sin influences all of life. Jesus preached that God loves us. He yearns for us, but cannot have an intimate relationship with us because of our sin. John says the following about the message of Jesus:

> Now the message that we have heard from his Son and announce is this: God is light, and there is no darkness at all in him. If, then, we say that we have fellowship with him, yet at the same time live in the darkness, we are lying both in our words and in our actions. (1 John 1:5–6, GNB)

God did not want death. That is why He sent Jesus Christ, so that He could destroy the power of death. We will never be able to understand and experience the wonder of the Cross fully if we do not have a clear picture of Jesus' victory over death. Even though all people went to the realm of the dead before the victory of Jesus (both believers and unbelievers), God made an exception for three people, which shows His sovereignty as Creator of heaven and earth. We know that Enoch, Moses and Elijah were all brought to God in heaven in a special way. For two of these three men, their transfer to heaven involved a huge spiritual battle (it would seem that Enoch, by contrast, walked right in[212]). The devil knew that he had a right to the lives of these people, as through sin they had come under his power. That is why Elijah had

> **God did not want death. That is why He sent Jesus Christ, so that He could destroy the power of death.**

to be brought to heaven in a flaming chariot, drawn by horses of fire,[213] and Satan and the archangel Michael fought over the body of Moses,[214] after which God Himself buried his earthly remains.[215]

Generally speaking, though, this rule applied to every human being before the Cross: the wages of sin was death.

THE REALM OF THE DEAD: GATEWAY TO HELL

Many Christians confuse the realm of the dead with hell. The realm of the dead is not hell, but the gateway to hell. It is a place of keeping, a kind of in-between zone, where the souls of those who have died are kept until the final judgment; then the realm of the dead will give back its dead:

> *Then the sea gave up its dead. Death and the world of the dead also gave up the dead they held. And all were judged according to what they had done. Then death and the world of the dead were thrown into the lake of fire. (This lake of fire is the second death.) Those who did not have their name written in the book of the living were thrown into the lake of fire.* (Revelation 20:13–15, GNB)

God initially created hell, or the lake of fire, for the devil and his demons. Hell is still empty. When Jesus returns and the dead are judged, Satan and his demons and all those who do not have their names written in the book of life (that is, those who have rejected the sacrifice of Jesus) will be thrown into hell. In Hebrews 2:16, we read that God does not help the fallen angels, but only the descendants of Abraham. Demons cannot turn from their evil ways. The devil disobeyed God. He turned his back on the truth and followed the way of the lie. He has fallen and God has banished him and his followers forever. Jesus says that "eternal fire is prepared for the devil and his angels."[216] Why would God provide a way to buy back the freedom of fallen mankind, but not that of the fallen angels? Didn't man become disobedient as well? Did not man also turn his back on the truth and believe the lie? The difference is this: evil came forth from the devil himself; therefore he cannot be freed from it. Mankind fell for the temptation, and came under the power, of the ruler of this world. Because God became man in Jesus, He could die (taking our sins upon Himself) and beat the devil at his own game in his own territory (the realm of the dead). Jesus gave his life for the "descendants of Abraham," fallen mankind, and not for fallen angels. There is no redemption for them. That is why Jude 1:6 says: "Remember the angels who did not stay within the limits of their proper authority, but abandoned their own dwelling place: they are bound with eternal chains in the darkness below, where God is keeping them for that great Day on which they will be condemned." God will not spare the angels who have been unfaithful to Him (demons). There is no salvation for them. They have no hope, no future. They remain in this state for centuries upon centuries. They know no joy; they have no hope of any change for the better, but exist in the evil certainty of an even more horrible eternal future. They cannot escape the punishment of God. But for the "lost children of God," there is still hope! That is why it is vital that we understand and confess that the wonder of the Cross also means that Jesus has conquered death. Jesus went into the realm of the dead for us to confront death, so that whosoever believes in Him (and accepts His sacrifice) will not die:

Most assuredly, I tell you, if a person keeps my word, he will never see death. (John 8:51, WEB)

JESUS DIED TO DESCEND
INTO THE REALM OF THE DEAD

It may be a strange thought, but Jesus could not die without taking our sins upon Himself. The Bible teaches us this: "The wages of sin is death."[217] Jesus was without sin; He never sinned. This means that His body was never subjected to the results (the curse) of sin! Jesus was completely free from all this. His body could not become sick; His body was not doomed to die. It sounds unbelievable, but Jesus actually "needed" our sins in order to be able to die. By taking our sins upon Himself (by identifying with them), He gave Himself up to the ruler of this world. It was our sins that gave the devil power over Jesus. But don't forget this was God's plan, so that Jesus could confront death in our place in the realm of the dead.

> **It may be a strange thought, but Jesus could not die without taking our sins upon Himself.**

When we speak of "death," we mean the angel of death, who ranks directly under Satan.[218] Paul says that "by the trespass of the one, death reigned."[219] This mighty angel of darkness also has a name: in Greek he is called *Apollyon*; in Hebrew he is called *Abaddon*,[220] which means "the destroyer." He is the "king" of the abyss and the realm of the dead. It was God's plan that Jesus would descend to the realm of the dead to claim the keys of death and its realm[221] and to dethrone the devil, who had power over death. In this way, He freed those who lived their lives in fear of death![222]

JESUS' CONFRONTATION WITH DEATH

Everyone in the realm of the dead was confronted with the mighty angel of death. When He entered the realm of the dead, Jesus was, too. The demons must have screeched with terrible force when Jesus entered the realm of the dead, just as they had screeched at Him on earth.[223] Crazed with anger and fiendish delight, they had cursed and mocked Him during the crucifixion.[224] Now they had Him in their power. Finally, they had brought Jesus, the Son of God, who was supposed to crush the head of the serpent (the devil), to His knees! But their frenzy can have lasted only a short while. For Jesus looked the angel of death straight in the eye. He not only took our sins upon Himself, but confronted the angel of death for us. I am convinced that Jesus bore our sins only as long as necessary. Jesus, the Light of the World, was covered by our sins. But when He threw them into the deepest pit in the realm of the dead, the blinding light of God shone in that dark netherworld. The Lamb of God, who had taken the sins of the world upon Himself, revealed Himself as the Lion of Judah in the realm of the dead! As the Son of God, through whom all things in heaven and on earth are created, the visible and the invisible:

> ... by whom we are set free, that is, our sins are forgiven. Christ is the visible likeness of the invisible God. He is the first-born Son, superior to all created things. For through him God created everything in heaven and on earth, the seen and the unseen things, including spiritual powers, lords, rulers, and authorities. God created the whole universe through him and for him. Christ existed before all things, and in union with him all things have their proper place. (Colossians 1:14–17, GNB)

Jesus' Preaching in the Realm of the Dead

Jesus died to take away our sins and to destroy the power of sin in our lives forever. He has carried the eternal punishment we deserved. Because He carried the punishment (the results of sin) for *all* people (both those who lived before He came to earth and those who were still to be born), Jesus has the power to free each person who believes in Him from the clutches of death.

The apostle Peter writes that Jesus went to the realm of the dead to make known what He had done to those in the first category (those who died before Jesus' redemptive work on the Cross):

> For Christ died for sins once and for all, a good man on behalf of sinners, in order to lead you to God. He was put to death physically, but made alive spiritually, and in his spiritual existence he went and preached to the imprisoned spirits. (1 Peter 3:18–19, GNB)

The World English Bible translation says that Jesus went to the realm of the dead and "preached to the spirits in prison." In the following verses, Peter clarifies whom he is speaking about when he says the "imprisoned spirits." They are, among others, the men and women from the days of Noah, who refused to listen to the warnings of this man of God, even though God patiently waited for them, while Noah built the ark. In the end only eight people were saved; all the others drowned. The "spirits" or "souls" of these people were kept in the realm of the dead, which Peter called "a prison." The prophet Isaiah also described it:

> *They shall be gathered together, as prisoners are gathered in the pit, and shall be shut up in the prison; and after many days shall they be visited.* (Isaiah 24:22, WEB)

When Jesus goes into the realm of the dead and throws off our sins, He starts to speak. And what a speech it is! With a loud voice and with great power He begins to proclaim the good news in the realm of the dead. His voice reaches into every dark corner, into every dungeon of that bleak realm, and everyone can hear it clearly. He preaches the wonder of the Cross to them. He tells them He has given His life for them, too. He has taken their sins, too, so they need no longer remain captive to death! He tells them the Father is waiting for them and that He wants to take them as "captives" into heaven.[225] What an event! And what panic must have broken out in the enemy camp. If they had known this was going to happen, they wouldn't have crucified Jesus—just as the rulers on earth wouldn't have either.[226]

The voice of Jesus has sounded before in the realm of the dead. Before He died, Jesus was in Bethany, a town on the outskirts of Jerusalem. He stood in front of the grave of His deceased friend Lazarus and shouted with a loud voice: "Lazarus, come out!"[227] The words resounded in the very depths of the realm of the dead. This voice had so much power that the angel of death was forced to bow to the will of Jesus. Do not forget that Lazarus had already been in the grave for four days. His soul—like the souls of all other believers prior to Jesus' death—had been "taken captive" by death. He was a prisoner of the realm of the dead. It is hard to imagine what happened in the realm of the dead when Jesus' voice rang through the doors of this "prison": "Lazarus, come out!" At any rate it is clear that death had to let Lazarus go, simply because Jesus had commanded it. And Lazarus was not the only one. The same thing happened when Jesus took the daughter of Jairus by the hand and spoke the words: *Talitha, koum*, which mean, "Little girl, I tell you to get up!"[228] Even then, the voice of Jesus penetrated into the deepest darkness of the realm of the dead and the angel of death could do nothing but release the girl, just as he had been forced to release the young boy in Nain, to whom Jesus had said: "Young man, get up!"[229]

Jesus appears in the realm of the dead as the great Redeemer and Deliverer. He demands the keys of death and of the realm of the dead and opens the dungeons of those held captive by death.[230] The angel of death is completely powerless. He cannot stop Jesus. The deliverance ministry Jesus had on earth is now being carried out in the realm of the dead! Everyone who hears Him now and believes in Him is freed from captivity. Jesus really does have all power in heaven and on earth; yes, His power reaches right into the realm of the dead! Hallelujah! The angel of death knows that he will lose even more souls to Jesus. It's a bad day for death. Since that day, the angel of death has been trying to blind and deafen as many people as he can to the message and the wonder of the Cross, commanded to do so by the lord of darkness. Even though he knows he is fighting a losing battle, he will try to

> **The deliverance ministry Jesus had on earth is now being practiced in the realm of the dead!**

take as many souls with him as he can when at the end of time he is finally thrown into hell.[231]

We don't know how long this "rescue mission" on the part of Jesus lasted, but it had to be long enough to make sure that the criminal on the Cross next to Jesus had arrived in the realm of the dead, so that the promise ("Today you will be with me in paradise") could be kept!

THE GOSPEL OF NICODEMUS

In his famous sermon on the day of Pentecost, Peter calls King David a prophet, who looked into the future and saw and spoke of the resurrection of Jesus: "He was not abandoned in the world of the dead; his body did not rot in the grave."[232] How did King David, and all the other prophets who came after him, react when Jesus appeared in the realm of the dead? The Bible does not say. The apocryphal "Gospel of Nicodemus" (part two) contains an interesting description of how Jesus enters the realm of the dead. It says that there is suddenly a voice like thunder that sounds throughout the realm of the dead: "Open the gates of hell, so that the King of Glory can come in!" At which moment King David stands up and shouts out that he predicted when he was still on earth that:

> *He brought them out of their gloom and darkness and broke their chains in pieces. They must thank the Lord for his constant love, for the wonderful things he did for them. He breaks down doors of bronze and smashes iron bars.* (Psalm 107:14–16, GNB)

Isaiah, too, jumps up and says that he predicted when he was still on earth that:

> *Thy dead men shall live, together with my dead body shall they arise. Awake and sing, ye that dwell in dust: for thy dew is as the dew of herbs, and the earth shall cast out the dead.* (Isaiah 26:19, KJV)

When the righteous dead hear King David and Isaiah speak, they start to shout in chorus: "Open your gates, now you will be defeated, weak and without power." Again a mighty voice resounds: "Open the gates of hell, so that the King of Glory can come in!" When death hears the cries of the righteous dead, he feigns ignorance and says: "Who is this King of Glory?" King David answers: "I know the words of this voice, because I prophesied the same through his Spirit. And now I say to you what I have spoken before":

Who is the King of glory? Yahweh strong and mighty, Yahweh mighty in battle. (Psalm 24:8, WEB)

King David continues: "And now, you most depraved and mean angel of death, open your gates so that the King of Glory can come in!" And while David speaks to death, Jesus appears, full of glory, in the likeness of a man, and He shines His Light into the eternal darkness. He breaks the bonds of death that could not be broken by anyone else. He opens the gates of the dungeons of those held captive in deep darkness and in the shadow of death because of their transgressions and sins. When death and the realm of the dead realize that the Light of the Son has entered their own territory, they are gripped with fear, incapable of doing anything. All is lost for them!

THE GREATEST EXODUS OF ALL TIME!

How many thousands of souls reacted to the good news that Jesus brought? Noah, Abraham, Isaac, Jacob, Deborah, Tamar, Rebecca, Simeon, Hannah and many, many others. According to the "Gospel of Nicodemus," Jesus reaches for Adam and takes him by the hand and they leave the realm of the dead hand in hand, followed by all the righteous who died believing in Him. It must have been the greatest exodus of all time. The angel of death can no longer hold Jesus and His people. A great parade of victors follows in Jesus' footsteps. He died for their sins, too! The way to heaven is open.

> But God raised him from death, setting him free from its power, because it was impossible that death should hold him prisoner. (Acts 2:24, GNB)

Jesus was born for this. Jesus died for this. Jesus could not have beaten the devil at his own game if He had not become a man of flesh and blood.

JESUS ENTERED HEAVEN

How did the holy angels react to Jesus' mission in the realm of the dead? When He created the earth, they were there and they broke out in loud rejoicing.[233] They were there when He came to earth as a small baby[234] and again they broke out in loud rejoicing: "Glory to God in the highest heaven, and peace on earth to those with whom He is pleased!"[235] Now the Son of God returns home, bringing thousands upon thousands of men and women with Him. This must have caused great rejoicing and happiness in heaven— not just among the angels, but also in the heart of God the Father!

In the letter to the Hebrews, we read that Jesus is not only the Lamb that was slain for our sins, but also the high priest who went into heaven with a golden bowl, filled with His blood:

> But Christ has already come as the High Priest of the good things that are already here. The tent in which he serves is greater and more perfect; it is not a tent made by human hands, that is, it is not a part of this created world. When Christ went through the tent and entered once and for all into the Most Holy Place, he did not take the blood of goats and bulls to offer as a sacrifice; rather, he took his own blood and obtained eternal salvation for us. (Hebrews 9:11–12, GNB)

Jesus appears in heaven before the throne of His Father. And on the altar that is in front of the throne,[236] He sprinkles some of His own blood, through which we are now eternally freed from sin:

> For Christ did not go into a Holy Place made by human hands, which was a copy of the real one. He went into heaven itself, where he now appears on our behalf in the presence of God. The Jewish high priest goes into the Most Holy Place every year with the blood of an animal. But Christ did not go in to offer himself many times, for then he would have had to suffer many times ever since the creation of the world. Instead, now when all ages of time are nearing the end, he has appeared once and for all, to remove sin through the sacrifice of himself. Everyone must die once, and after that be judged by God. In the same manner Christ also was offered in sacrifice once to take away the sins of many. He will appear a second time, not to deal with sin, but to save those who are waiting for him. (Hebrews 9:24–28, GNB)

One cannot help wondering how God the Father would have looked at Jesus His Son, on His return to heaven. God had chosen not to intervene as He died. And now He stands eye to eye with His Son, who has brought in the first harvest of souls!

In my mind, I see a smile appear on the face of the Father, and then on that of the Son, who is perhaps thinking: this is what I did it for, to see this smile on the face of my Father. His Father had looked forward to this day: the day that His lost children would be brought home by the Son. The price that Jesus paid was totally worth it. There must have been a deafening outburst of praise and rejoicing when this reunion took place.

WHOEVER BELIEVES IN JESUS WILL NOT SEE DEATH

It is interesting to find out what famous people said and experienced just before they died. One glimpse of a person on his deathbed often says more about him than all his "great" works and deeds combined. The moment death looks us in the face, all our masks are peeled away and only the naked truth remains.

Voltaire, who had always mocked God, had a terrible end. His nurse later said: "Even for all the money in the world I never again want to see an unbeliever die in such a way!" Voltaire called out and screamed all night, begging that his sins might be forgiven him.

The personal doctor of Napoleon wrote: "The emperor dies alone and abandoned. His battle with death is horrible."

Yagoda (chief of the Russian secret service in the thirties) said just before he died: "There must be a God. He is punishing me for my sins." The English philosopher Hobbes spoke fearfully: "I must take a terrible leap into darkness." Nietzsche died completely insane.

Sir Thomas Scott, an English member of Parliament, spoke thus before he died: "Until this moment I thought there was neither a God nor a hell. Now I know and feel that there

> **So many people are afraid of death. But if we have made things right with God, we do not have to be intimidated by the enemy. When a child of God dies, they will not see death.**

are both, and I am doomed to perdition by the just ruling of the Almighty."

Lenin died as a man who had lost his mind, asking chairs and tables to forgive him for his sins.

"Please burn all my books," Jaroslavsky, the head of the International Alliance of Atheists, said just before he died. "See the Holy One! He has waited a long time for me. He is here!"

So many people, including Christians, are afraid of death. But if we have made things right with God, we do not have to be intimidated by the enemy. When a child of God dies, they will not see death. Jesus said:

> *Most assuredly, I tell you, if a person keeps my word, he will never see death.* (John 8:51, WEB)

Jesus has already confronted death for us and gained victory over it! When I die, I will see Jesus. Paul, who had a so-called "third-heaven experience," said:

> *My deep desire and hope is that I shall never fail in my duty, but that at all times, and especially right now, I shall be full of courage, so that with my whole being I shall bring honor to Christ, whether I live or die. For what is life? To me, it is Christ. Death, then, will bring more. But if by continuing to live I can do more worthwhile work, then I am not sure which I should choose. I am pulled in two directions. I want very much to leave this life and be with Christ, which is a far better thing; but for your sake it is much more important that I remain alive. I am sure of this, and so I know that I will stay. I will stay on with you all, to add to your progress and joy in the faith.* (Philippians 1:20–25, GNB)

Thank You, Jesus,

Thank You for loving me so much that You confronted death for me. You bought my life with Your own blood. I thank You that for this reason I will not see death. I believe all power in heaven and earth has been given to You. I no longer need to be afraid to leave this world, because I know that You are waiting for me in heaven. You have prepared a place for me so that I can live with You for eternity. How can I ever thank You for what You have done for me? That is why I lay my life in Your hands and entrust myself to You completely.

Amen.

THE RESURRECTION

And if Christ has not been raised from death,
then we have nothing to preach
and you have nothing to believe.

(1 Corinthians 15:14, GNB)

CHAPTER 14

The first person Jesus appears to after rising from the grave early in the morning on the first day of the week is Mary Magdalene. She has been an eyewitness to the crucifixion, the burial and the empty tomb. She did not miss any of the events in the last eighteen hours of Jesus' life. This shows her devotion, which started when Jesus freed her from seven demons. Mary is the first to meet Jesus alive. He appears to her in a divine body, so she does not recognize Him.[237] The same thing happens to the others to whom Jesus appears: the two men on the road to Emmaus[238] and the disciples.[239] During the forty days after His crucifixion, Jesus is with His disciples at different times and He proves to them in different ways that it really is Him. Again and

According to the apostle Paul, the accounts of Jesus' appearances are not visions, but objective information and historical facts!

again, He speaks to them about the Kingdom of God.[240] The Bible mentions in particular a meeting between Jesus and His half-brother James, resulting in James' conversion.[241] At one point, He also appears to more than five hundred people at the same time![242]

According to the apostle Paul, the accounts of Jesus' appearances are not reports of visions, but objective information about historical facts. At the time when he writes about them (about twenty-four years after the resurrection), Paul says that most of those who witnessed them are still alive. What he means is that anyone could verify the historical accuracy of Jesus' resurrection.

WHY THEY DID NOT RECOGNIZE JESUS

I have thought for a long time about why many of Jesus' followers did not see that it was Him at first. Slowly but surely it became clear to me why even Jesus' best friends did not recognize Him right away.

First of all, we must not forget that Jesus suffered beyond comprehension in the last eighteen hours before He died. All of the disciples still had images in their minds of a severely abused, blood-covered Jesus. Isaiah had prophesied how terribly the Messiah would be treated:

> *Many people were shocked when they saw him; he was so disfigured that he hardly looked human.* (Isaiah 52:14, GNB)

They cannot forget what He looked like then. So when Jesus appears in front of them, without wounds or signs of abuse, it's no wonder they think He is someone else. Mary initially thinks she's talking to a gardener. It isn't until Jesus calls her by name that her heart is touched deeply. She recognizes His voice, just as Jesus said: "The gatekeeper opens the gate for him; the sheep hear his voice as he calls his own sheep by name, and he leads them out. When he has brought them out, he goes ahead of them, and the sheep follow him, because they know his voice."[243]

Second, the disciples do not recognize Him because the Bible says Jesus appeared to them in "another form" (Greek: *morphe*).[244] Jesus has a different body now that He has returned from the grave. This does not just mean that the deep wounds in the body of Jesus are no longer visible: His beaten back, the wounds on His head, hands, feet and side (unless there was a special reason for the wounds in Jesus' hands and side to become visible, for example to convince Thomas, see John 20:27). But it's more than that. Jesus has taken on not only a different appearance, but also a new form of existence. He doesn't just look different from how He did before His resurrection, He indeed *is* different. In one of his letters, Paul recites a song that tells of Jesus' existence with God before creation. This song gives us more clarity about what happened to (the body of) Jesus:

> *Have this in your mind, which was also in Christ Jesus, who, exist-ing in the form of God, didn't consider it robbery to be equal with God, but emptied himself, taking the form of a servant, being made in the likeness of men. And being found in human form, he hum-bled himself, becoming obedient to death, yes, the death of the cross. Therefore God also highly exalted him, and gave to him the name which is above every name; that at the name of Jesus every knee should bow, of those in heaven, those on earth, and those under the earth, and that every tongue should confess that Jesus Christ is Lord, to the glory of God the Father. (Philippians 2:6–11, WEB)*

The words "existing in the form (*morphe*) of God" are a refer-ence to Jesus' existence when He was still with His Father in heav-en. Jesus laid down His power and glory and came as a servant in the body of a human, yet without taking on our sinful nature. He humbled Himself for us and became human and went the way of the Cross for us, to free us from our sinful nature, so that we might partake of His divine nature.

After Jesus went to the realm of the dead in Spirit and preached the gospel,[245] and after He took His blood into heaven as "High Priest of the new covenant,"[246] His Spirit returned to His own body early on that Sunday morning. Jesus' body never saw decay.[247] It was quite the opposite! The moment Jesus returned to His horribly disfigured body, it was transformed in the twinkling of an eye by the glorious power of the Father[248] and the Spirit of God,[249] so that the dead body of Jesus was awoken. His natural body underwent a supernatural change. When Jesus rose from the grave, His natural body was transformed into a supernatural one. The divine nature of Jesus in all its power and glory became visible in His glorified body, now fully subjected to the power of the Holy Spirit. This is why Jesus could move about physically in both the supernatural and the natural world. His resurrection body was not subject to time or space. Although the doors and windows had been closed by the disciples, Jesus could still appear suddenly in their midst,[250] and He could also disappear just as suddenly, becoming invisible.[251] With His resurrection body, Jesus could appear before God in heaven,[252] but also manifest Himself here on earth.[253]

When the Bible says that Jesus appeared to His disciples in a new form (*morphe*), it means He took on the appearance that He had had when He was with God before He came into this world!

When the apostle John has an encounter with Jesus, many years after He has risen from the dead, he describes the Man without sin as follows:

There with the lampstands was someone who seemed to be the Son of Man. He was wearing a robe that reached down to his feet, and a gold cloth was wrapped around his chest. His head and his hair were white as wool or snow, and his eyes looked like flames of fire. His feet were glowing like bronze being heated in a furnace, and his voice sounded like the roar of a waterfall. He held seven stars in his right hand, and a sharp double-edged sword was coming from his mouth. His face was shining as bright as the sun at noon.
(Revelation 1:13–16, CEV)

The moment Jesus returned to His horribly disfigured body, it was transformed in the twinkling of an eye by the glorious power of the Father and the Spirit of God, so that the dead body of Jesus was awoken.

Even though Jesus does not appear to Mary and the disciples in this heavenly form, it is no wonder that they do not recognize Him right away. That explains why Jesus asks them: "Why are you so afraid? And why do you think such thoughts? Look at my hands, my feet: It is me; touch me: a ghost does not have flesh and bones and I do, as you can see." With these words, He shows them His hands and feet. They are so overwhelmed with astonishment and joy that they still cannot believe it, and Jesus asks them: "Do you have something here to eat?" They give Him a piece of fried fish, and He takes it and eats it before their eyes.[254] This account tells us that the glorified body of Jesus can still digest food. By eating the fish, Jesus is proving to the disciples that He has physically risen from the dead. Peter too later informs us that he ate and drank with Jesus, after He was raised from the dead.[255]

> **Our sinful nature will always blur our view of the risen Lord Jesus, too. Our old nature wants us to doubt, to reason and to argue.**

Third, the disciples did not recognize Jesus in His divine form because of their own sinful nature. Luke says that "their eyes were kept from recognizing him."[256] An older translation says "their eyes were holden that they should not know him" (KJV). With their natural eyes they could not recognize Jesus in His glorified form. In some way or other, their sinful nature blinded them to the miraculous transformation that had taken place in the body of Jesus.

Even just before Jesus ascended into heaven, there were a few disciples who doubted once again whether it was really Him![257] Their blindness was taken away by Jesus: He opened their eyes and their minds[258] by opening the Scriptures, so that they understood what Moses and the prophets had prophesied about Him.[259]

Our sinful nature will always blur *our* view of the risen Lord Jesus, too. Our old nature wants us to doubt, to reason and to argue. It cannot believe of its own accord, but must be convicted of sin, righteousness and judgment by the Holy Spirit.[260]

WHY DID JESUS NOT SEIZE POWER?

Another question that a lot of people ask is why the risen Jesus did not go straight to Herod, Pilate and Caiaphas, the secular and religious leaders of the time. That would have been quite something! Why didn't He remove them from their places of power and take over, to rule the world? He said Himself that He had all power in heaven and on earth.[261] He was the man with the capacity to do the job! If anyone was capable of being a pure, honest and resolute leader, it would be Jesus. So why didn't He do it?

First of all, the political and religious leaders who had had Jesus crucified would not have recognized or acknowledged Him. If His own disciples, who spent three and a half years in close proximity to Him, hardly recognized Him, how can we expect these men to have done so? Jesus' appearance in His resurrected body was so totally other and of such a different caliber that it would have been impossible for them to recognize or acknowledge Him. The authorities had had Jesus beaten and abused so severely that even His own mother did not recognize Him! The Jesus they crucified had hung on the Cross as a bloody mass of flesh. If He had appeared to them some forty hours later looking as if the crucifixion had never taken place, they would never have believed it!

Second, Jesus had already answered this question when He told the parable of the rich man and poor Lazarus: "He said to him: 'If they don't listen to Moses and the prophets, neither will they be persuaded if one rises from the dead.'"²⁶² The religious and political leaders were not going to listen to Jesus. They were very stubborn and rebellious. The Bible says that rebellion is like the sin of witchcraft, and stubbornness is like idolatry.²⁶³ Their rebellious attitude was proved when they wanted to kill Lazarus again, after Jesus had just raised him from the dead.²⁶⁴

Jesus did appear to Thomas, who could not believe that He had really risen from the dead, and said to him: "Thomas, come here and touch my hands with your finger. Bring your hand and touch my side, and do not doubt, but believe." And Thomas believed after he had seen Jesus, saying to Him: "My Lord and my God!" Jesus then spoke the words that are so important for us: "Because you have seen me, you have believed. Blessed are those who have not seen, and have believed."²⁶⁵

Third, if Jesus had taken control after He had risen from the dead, He would have become the leader of a world full of people with a sinful nature. After Jesus' resurrection, nothing had changed in the world. If Jesus had remained on earth, our sinful, rebellious nature would have continued to exist, and we would never have been able to accept His leadership. Jesus cannot possibly become our King until the power of sin in our lives is broken. That is why He had to ascend to heaven first, so that the Holy Spirit could be poured out in our hearts and we could be changed from the inside out.

> **If Jesus had remained on earth, then our sinful, rebellious nature would have continued to exist, and we would never have been able to accept His leadership.**

The Spirit of Jesus helps us to crucify the flesh with its passions and lusts.²⁶⁶ When someone's old, sinful nature dies, that person is born again and receives the heart of Jesus within[267] and his or her life becomes more and more tuned to the life and will of Jesus.[268] As we are gradually born again, so the Spirit of Jesus longs for the character (the divine nature) of Jesus to live within us![269] As His Spirit works in us, we become more like Jesus.[270] He is at work making our spirit, soul and body holy, so that the Head will not reject the Body when He returns.[271] For when Jesus returns, we will be like Him.[272] Even our bodies will then be transformed in the twinkling of an eye, just as Jesus' resurrection body was transformed.[273] When Jesus returns, He will take His church to His side like a glorious bride, pure and faultless, without spot or wrinkle or any other imperfection![274] That will be the moment He "takes control" of the earth.

Fourth, the Bible speaks of a time of mercy. Jesus has commanded His disciples down the centuries to make the wonder of the Cross known to those who are burdened by the power of sin and death. Peter said:

> *Don't forget that the Lord is patient because He wants people to be saved. This is also what our dear friend Paul said when he wrote you with the wisdom that God had given him.* (2 Peter 3:15, CEV)

God is waiting until the fullness of the nations has entered His Kingdom. Then Jesus will return! This "complete number" is a predestined amount of people, which only the Father knows.[275] Let our passion for Jesus mobilize us into telling as many people as possible about the wonder of the Cross. The Bible teaches us that we can hasten the return of Jesus by:

1. Dedicating ourselves to bringing the gospel of Jesus to all peoples of the world (Matthew 24:14);
2. Earnestly praying for the return of Jesus (Matthew 6:10 and Revelation 22:20);
3. Leading a holy and godly life. (2 Peter 3:11–12, WEB).

Father in heaven,

Thank You that Jesus died for me and rose again after three days. Thank You for all the wonders of the Cross and the great gift of eternal life that I have received through believing in Jesus Christ. Thank You that I may know You more and more. I want to live each day with Jesus. Teach me to walk with Him in such a way that others will see Jesus through me and I will have the chance to tell them of the wonder of the Cross.

Amen.

LIVING WITH JESUS

I am the vine. You are the branches.
He who remains in me, and I in him,
the same bears much fruit,
for apart from me you can do nothing.

(John 15:5, WEB)

CHAPTER 15

It happened on a Saturday night, our family night. Usually we watch a nice movie together, which my wife has recorded earlier for us. For some reason, things went differently on this occasion and I was not really acting like a family man. While the family was watching one of the television channels, I was reading a book. Later that evening, the boys left the living room and my wife went upstairs with them to wish them goodnight. I remained behind, still reading my book while the television was on. I didn't pay any attention to it until there was a preview of a movie that was going to be broadcast. It showed an erotic scene, lasting just a few seconds. Later, I realized how quickly my body had been aroused by what I'd heard and how my eyes were drawn to the screen. Even though it lasted no longer than three seconds, I could still feel how the adrenaline rushed through my body. On the one hand, I was shocked by how strongly my body reacted to what I saw and heard. On the other hand, these feelings were not unpleasant, and I kept looking at what had been unexpectedly dished up for me. It only took a few seconds, but it was enough to soil me with unclean and impure thoughts. I knew that I had sinned. I had kept on watching and let it sink in, with unsurprising results. I was deeply ashamed and felt very guilty. I had failed. For a long time, I had not had problems with impure thoughts or feelings, and now I had walked into the trap laid for me with my eyes wide open. I was even more ashamed because I was doing an intense study on the last eighteen hours of the life of Jesus. My eyes were opened to what Jesus went through in the garden of Gethsemane; how He wrestled until He bled for my sin. At that moment, it really hit home that the impure feelings that had rushed through my body also rushed through Jesus' body. The Man without sin identified with my lust and sinful desires. It was my sins too that were laid on Jesus by God and which penetrated His soul, spirit and body so forcefully that He began to sweat blood. I was so ashamed. I felt dirty and I was conscious of the fact that I too had betrayed Jesus. Of course, I confessed my sin immediately to God, but I knew I had to confess them to my wife as well.

Ann and I have made a covenant together against sin. If one of us sins in an area in which we are weak, then we confess that sin not only to God but also to each other.[276] We don't want anything to come between God and us. By confessing our sins openly to each other, we are protected not only by God but also by each other. Psalm 25:21 says that goodness and honesty preserve us, so that God will protect us from our enemies. That night, I did not have the courage to confess my sin to my wife. It was shame that kept me from doing it. Even though I knew that shame is a powerful weapon used by the enemy to keep me in his grip, I still went to bed without saying anything.

The next morning, I was going to speak in a church somewhere in Holland. I got up early to prepare myself in prayer. And even though I knew I had to confess something to my wife, I still didn't do it. I got in the car and went to pick up one of our youth leaders, as we had agreed. After a few minutes the Holy Spirit began to speak to me: "Confess your sin to the youth leader." The first thing I thought was: "I wish I had told Ann what happened." But now it was too late for that. I knew I had to obey and I began to confess my sin. I experienced the sensation of the weight that had been crushing me falling off.

So then, confess your sins to one another and pray for one another, so that you will be healed. The prayer of a good person has a powerful effect. (James 5:16, GNB)

Once again, I was able to experience how true this word of God is. We had some extra time that morning so went into some woods to pray together and intercede for the local churches in the city to which we had been invited. During the service, it became evident once again how important it was that I had confessed my sin to God and to one of our leaders. After the sermon, I gave an invitation and several people came forward. The Holy Spirit led me to a young man who was kneeling and wailing in front of the podium. God's Spirit showed me that there was a curse of impurity (!) on his life. I broke this curse over his life in the name of Jesus Christ. The reaction was immediate. He straightened up and grabbed both of my lower arms, while a deep roar came out of him. A spirit of impurity manifested itself violently in this man. My arms were held in a vice-like grip. A thought struck me that they were going to break like matchsticks. But then came the realization that I had complete authority over this unclean demon in the name of Jesus. I commanded it to let go of me and leave this man, in the name of Jesus, and to go wherever Jesus would send it. Immediately, the man was delivered, the demonic violence stopped and the young man started to cry. Impurity had had him in its grip for a long time, but it had been broken that Sunday morning by the power of Jesus. Later on, I wondered what would have happened if I had not confessed my own sin beforehand.

A "COVENANT AGAINST SIN"

On the basis of James 5:16, our leadership team made a "covenant against sin." Of our own free will, we promised God and each other that we would confess our sins not only to God but also to each other. Job is an excellent example of this for all of us.

It was said of Job that he was a blameless and upright man, who feared God, and turned away from evil.[277] Job says in chapter 31:1: "*I have made a covenant with my eyes: how then should I look lustfully at a young woman?*" In verse 4 he says: "*God knows everything I do; he sees every step I take.*" (GNB) He even goes as far as to say that he has made a deal with God, such that if he does sin and fall into lust and desire, God can take everything he owns from him:

> **Of our own free will, we promised God and each other that we would confess our sins not only to God but also to each other.**

> *If I have turned from the right path or let myself be attracted to evil, if my hands are stained with sin, then let my crops be destroyed, or let others eat the food I grow. If I have been attracted to my neighbor's wife, and waited, hidden, outside her door, then let my wife cook another man's food and sleep in another man's bed.* (Job 31:7–10, GNB)

King David also learned the hard way to make a "covenant against sin," in which he included even all those who lived in his household. He says:

> *My conduct will be faultless. When will you come to me? I will live a pure life in my house and will never tolerate evil. I hate the actions of those who turn away from God; I will have nothing to do with them. I will not be dishonest and will have no dealings with*

evil. I will get rid of anyone who whispers evil things about someone else; I will not tolerate anyone who is proud and arrogant. (Psalm 101:2–5, GNB)

David wanted to be faultless in his walk with God. He knew firsthand the destructive power of sin. That is why he made a "covenant" against the sins of impurity, indifference, perversity, gossip, pride and arrogance. He also said: "No liar will live in my palace" (verse 7).

It was Daniel and his friends who had made a "covenant against sin" while they lived in the courts of the king of Babylon. In these extremely occult and unclean surroundings, they decided not to be defiled (Daniel 1:8). Together they stood strong in this environment, which was hostile to God. Their "covenant against sin" had a strong influence on all of them:

God gave the four young men knowledge and skill in literature and philosophy. In addition, he gave Daniel skill in interpreting visions and dreams. (Daniel 1:17, GNB)

The king spoke to them daily and among all his servants he found none like Daniel and his three friends. They were called on in all situations where wisdom and sound judgment were needed. The king noticed that the advice of these men was ten times better than that of all the scholars and astrologers in his kingdom.

WITHOUT JESUS, I CAN DO NOTHING

The wonder of the Cross has changed my life drastically. I realize now more than ever that the Christian faith revolves around one person: Jesus. I want to be a "Jesus person." I have a strong desire to live as He lived. I want to love as He loves. I want to speak as He speaks. I want to believe as He believes. I want to do what He does. I want to breathe in His Spirit every morning and breathe out

His life all day. I want above all that Jesus should become visible in my life. In the way I look at people, in how I react to people, in my daily activities, in everything. I am beginning to understand what Paul means when he says,

> So that it is no longer I who live, but it is Christ who lives in me. This life that I live now, I live by faith in the Son of God, who loved me and gave his life for me. (Galatians 2:20, GNB)

I seek Him all day and pray: "Not me, but You. Not my will, but Your will. Not my plans, but Your plans." And each time I try to ask myself the question: what would Jesus do? What would He say? How would He react? And then I pray the most powerful prayer on earth: "Lord, help." Because I know that I am not capable in and of myself of living as Jesus lived. I am not capable of being like Him.

Through the wonder of the Cross, I have learned to glory (that is, to thank God) in my weaknesses.[278] Every morning, I fill my mouth with words of thankfulness; that I am not capable of doing what God asks of me in my own strength. I am learning to crucify my sinful nature. I have great expectation and faith that He will do it in me. I confess that all my sources are in Him.[279] I accept that in Him I am more than a conqueror.[280]

I want to breathe in His Spirit every morning and breathe out His life all day.

How true are the words of Jesus: "He who remains in Me, and I in him, the same bears much fruit, for apart from Me you can do nothing."[281] These words have been deeply engraved on my heart. Remain in Him! Remain in Him! Then you will bear much fruit, the fruit of the Spirit of Jesus that will show through an intimate relationship with Him:

> But the fruit of the Spirit is love, joy, peace, patience, kindness, goodness, faithfulness, gentleness, and self-control. (Galatians 5:22–23, WEB)

You can tell how closely someone is living with Jesus by the amount of the above-mentioned fruit in their life. How much of His love is visible in me? His joy, His peace, His patience, His kindness, His goodness, His faithfulness, His gentleness and His self-control? Living with Jesus means asking Him to give you all that is in Him and being able to share that with others, as His disciple. People said of the disciples of Jesus after His resurrection that they could recognize them; they could see that they had been "with Jesus."[282]

JOIN JESUS' VICTORY PROCESSION

The secret to a life with Jesus is to spend time alone with Him and be near to Him every day. Then we will carry His "fragrance" with us throughout the day.

Paul compares Jesus' victory with that of a Roman general, for whom they would arrange a triumphant procession through the city. In the Roman Empire, it was common practice that the general would be crowned with a laurel wreath and anointed with fragrant oil before he got into his chariot. Then he was allowed to make a victory procession through the city. In some cases, the wife of the victor was invited to stand next to her husband, and they would both be carried through the streets of the city, where the crowds would cheer them on. At the end of the victory procession, all of her household could smell that she had been near to her (anointed) husband. With this picture in mind, Paul wrote the following words:

> But thanks be to God. For in union with Christ we are always led by God as prisoners in Christ's victory procession. God uses us to make the knowledge about Christ spread everywhere like a sweet fragrance. For we are like a sweet-smelling incense offered by Christ to God, which spreads among those who are being saved and those who are being lost. For those who are being lost, it is a deadly stench that kills; but for those who are being saved, it is a fragrance that

brings life. Who, then, is capable for such a task? (2 Corinthians 2:14–16, GNB)

Indeed, you can "smell" how closely someone lives to Jesus and whether someone is aware of His presence. Listen to the words a person speaks. Are they words of criticism or words of encouragement? Are a person's eyes filled with jealousy or are they full of Jesus' love? Is their heart filled with ambition or with the peace of Jesus? Are their hands building their own kingdom or do we see the healing hands of Jesus that are constructive and bless others? Learn to pray the following prayer daily. Let this be the beginning of a new day every day in an interesting life with Jesus:

> **Indeed, you can "smell" how closely someone lives to Jesus and whether someone is aware of His presence.**

Jesus, fill my heart with Your peace.
Jesus, fill my eyes with Your love.
Jesus, fill my mouth with Your words.
Jesus, fill my hands with Your power and Your blessings
to love You and to serve You as long as I live.
Amen.

THE POWER OF SIN IS BROKEN

God's destiny for us is a life of continual communion with Jesus Christ. Each person is called to live in continual intimacy with Him. We are predestined for good works, which God prepared ahead of time.[283] This is the destiny of every born-again Christian.

Many Christians, however, are living in a vicious cycle of failure, sin and guilt. They try to suppress their sins, to control them, to keep them in check, but discover that this does not work. We must become aware of the fact that Jesus shed His blood to save us not only from hell, but also from the power of sin in our lives.

Each person is called to live in continual intimacy with Jesus.

Through the wonder of the Cross, our old man, who (as a slave to sin) desired to sin, has died. In practice this means that the old master (sin) is still present, but that the slave who served him (my old man), has died and is out of his reach. The old master is still alive, but the slave has died, so that sin has no more power over him.

> *And we know that our old being has been put to death with Christ on his cross, in order that the power of the sinful self might be destroyed, so that we should no longer be the slaves of sin. For when we die, we are set free from the power of sin. Since we have died with Christ, we believe that we will also live **with Him**. For we know that Christ has been raised from death and will never die again—death will no longer rule over him. And so, because he died, sin has no power over him; and now he lives his life in fellowship with God. In the same way you are to think of yourselves as dead, so far as sin is concerned, but living in fellowship with God **through Christ Jesus**.* (Romans 6:6–11, GNB, my emphasis)

"Free from the power of sin" and "dead, so far as sin is concerned" speak of deliverance from the power of sin, which certainly still exists. But because we have been born again, the life of Jesus has been planted inside of us, so that sin no longer has any power over us. Only in Him are we dead to sin. Outside of Him, we immediately fall victim to the old master and slide right back into our old, sinful lifestyle.

It is the Spirit of Jesus that now makes us willing and able to try to live as He lived.[284] We will never be able to live as Jesus lived in our own strength; He will have to work it out in us. He can bring about the wonder of the Cross in you too. It is not something we can teach ourselves, but it is something we may receive in Jesus:

> *It is true that through the sin of one man death began to rule because of that one man. But how much greater is the result of what was done by the one man, Jesus Christ! All who receive God's abundant grace and are freely put right with him will rule in life through Christ.* (Romans 5:17, GNB)

> *But God has brought you into union with Christ Jesus, and God has made Christ to be our wisdom. By him we are put right with God; we become God's holy people and are set free.* (1 Corinthians 1:30, GNB)

Through the wonder of the Cross, the living Jesus has come to reside in us and He will put us right with God, make us holy and set us free. By faith, we can confess that we live in Jesus Christ and that all that is His is ours, too. The devil, of course, wants to sabotage this. He wants to get us away from Christ. He wants us

We will never be able to live as Jesus lived in our own strength.

to try to do things in our own strength, so that we will be destined to fail. He will try to make us feel that we are not really living with and for Jesus. By tempting us and making us go through failure, suffering and trials, he will make us feel uneasy, as if we really are no longer in Him. But our feelings are not the truth in which we live. Jesus Himself is the truth, and if we stay in Him, then the enemy may come, but he will find nothing to disturb our relationship with Jesus. We must learn to trust in Jesus, who lives in us in all circumstances, and not in ourselves. Otherwise, we will find that our sinful nature still makes itself heard in our lives.

Through the wonder of the Cross, an end has come to the regime of the power of sin, so that we can have continual intimacy with Jesus.

LIVING WITHOUT SIN?

The question facing us now is whether we are still living in (the power of) sin, or whether we have been freed from it. Watchman Nee explained this by means of the following illustration:

If someone falls into the water and a life preserver is thrown to him, he will not drown as long as he hangs on to the life preserver. In this case, however, he is not pulled from the water to safety. He may not sink, but he also is not saved. But if someone were to come in a lifeboat, they would pull him out of the water and bring him safely aboard. This is what Jesus did for us on the Cross. He didn't throw us a life preserver, but He came and pulled us out of the water of the power of sin and took us aboard with Him. The biblical salvation will not let us float around in the powerful sea of sin.

> [Jesus] *who gave himself for us, that he might redeem us from all iniquity, and purify for himself a people for his own possession, zealous for good works.* (Titus 2:14, WEB)

> *My children, I am writing this so that you won't sin.* (1 John 2:1, CEV)

This is the message of the wonder of the Cross. It is very straightforward. Both Paul and John say that God wants to protect us from being continually tempted to sin. There is, however, a difference between sinning and living in sin. Living in sin is the same as "living under the power of sin" or "being a slave of sin." It is important that we know the difference.

THE DIFFERENCE BETWEEN SINNING AND LIVING IN SIN

John teaches us the difference between sinning and continual sin (living in sin). He is clear on the fact that all of us, without exception, sin:

If we say that we have no sin, we deceive ourselves, and the truth is not in us. (1 John 1:8, WEB)

Thankfully, John teaches us to live with Jesus through the wonder of the Cross:

If we confess our sins, he is faithful and righteous to forgive us the sins, and to cleanse us from all unrighteousness. If we say that we haven't sinned, we make him a liar, and his word is not in us. (1 John 1:9–10, WEB)

God is faithful, even if we are unfaithful. We make mistakes; we all have our shortcomings and we sin. But despite this, John says that the blood of Jesus cleanses us from all sin (verse 9). With God, there is always a way back. God's mercy, however, is not a permit to carry on sinning. Mercy is not a license from God to continue in sin. This is the other side that John speaks of when he talks about the power of sin in our lives. His teachings are no different from the teachings of Paul on this subject:

> **With God, there is always a way back. God's mercy, however, is not a permit to carry on sinning. Mercy is not a license from God to continue in sin.**

What shall we say, then? Should we continue to live in sin so that God's grace will increase? Certainly not. We have died to sin—how then can we go on living in it? (Romans 6:1–2, GNB)

Living in sin is no different from continuing in a sinful lifestyle, even though you know that it is wrong. You have become a slave to your own sinful lifestyle. It has become a pattern of sin.

You are no longer in control. There is a difference between losing your temper once and getting upset with someone, and having a complete lack of self-control so that no one dares to come near you because you cannot control your temper time and again. There is a difference between catching yourself in a lie and an untrustworthy lifestyle in which the line between truth and falsehood has become very blurred. John warns us about this second lifestyle:

Whoever continues to sin belongs to the Devil, because the Devil has sinned from the very beginning. (1 John 3:8, GNB)

John compares these people to the devil, who sinned from the start and has never stopped sinning. John cannot understand how someone who lives with Jesus can go on living unchanged in his or her sinful lifestyle. Those who continue to sin have become bound like a slave to the power of sin. They live as if the wonder of the Cross has not had any impact on their life.

I have told you this many times before, and now I repeat it with tears: there are many whose lives make them enemies of Christ's death on the cross. (Philippians 3:18, GNB)

The life of Jesus is in us. Therefore, it is impossible for us to continue living in sin.

Paul is speaking here about Christians who are living in sin and do not repent of it. Paul knows what price Jesus has paid for them, but they continue as if they do not care, which causes Paul great grief. He calls them enemies of the Cross. Not enemies of Christ, but enemies of the Cross. This means that the wonder of the Cross cannot take place in their lives, because they have become indifferent to it and continue in their own strength.

John encourages us to continue to live with Jesus when he says:

Those who are children of God do not continue to sin, for God's very nature is in them; and because God is their Father, they cannot continue to sin. (1 John 3:9, GNB)

The life of Jesus is in us. Therefore, it is impossible for us to continue living in sin, because the life of Jesus changes us from the inside out. And when we do sin, His Spirit persuades us to ask God and each other to forgive us. So there can be nothing between Him and us that would damage our relationship.

INTIMACY WITH JESUS IS THE KEY IN OUR STRUGGLE AGAINST SIN

I no longer want to sin. I want to hate sin. Not because I am not allowed to sin (though of course God does not want us to sin!), but because sin separates Jesus and me.[285] I don't want to cause Him pain. I don't want to live without Him. I have chosen a life *with* Him. My "yes" to Jesus implies an immediate "no" to sin. He wants to help me not to fall into sin:

[Jesus] *who gave himself for us, that he might redeem us from all iniquity, and purify for himself a people for his own possession, zealous for good works.* (Titus 2:14, WEB)

And, just as the writer of Hebrews says[286] that I have not yet resisted sin to the point of shedding my blood, I know I would never be able to do this in my own strength. But Jesus lives in me. At Gethsemane, He wrestled with my sin and was victorious. If I stay focused on Him, He will protect me and He will give me the strength to resist temptation. That is why I pray: "Lord Jesus, You wrestled with my sin until You bled, and You were victorious. Thank You that Your victory is also my victory. I want to look to You and trust You because I cannot fight my sinful nature in my own strength. Thank You that when I am weak, Your strength comes over me. In You I am more than victorious."

Intimacy with Jesus is the key in our struggle against sin. Only by walking with the Blameless One will we be able to live without blame.

Intimacy with Jesus is the key in our struggle against sin. Only by walking with the Blameless One will we be able to live without blame. Our heart yearns for Him. Our life revolves around that one Person, the Man without sin. I thank God for the wonder of the Cross, through which we have gained a share in the life of Jesus, and by which we will change from day to day to become more like Him:

All of us, then, reflect the glory of the Lord with uncovered faces; and that same glory, coming from the Lord, who is the Spirit, transforms us into his likeness in an ever greater degree of glory. (2 Corinthians 3:18, GNB)

May the God of peace himself sanctify you completely. May your whole spirit, soul, and body be preserved blameless at the coming of our Lord Jesus Christ. (1 Thessalonians 5:23, WEB)

The world is waiting to see the Son of God revealed in us. We are Jesus' representatives here on earth, destined to make Him visible to the generation we are called to. Through the wonder of the Cross, Jesus' life will become more and more visible in us, so that the world will see that Jesus lives. The apostle Peter calls us to live holy lives by the power of Jesus. You can tell how important this is when he says that the return of Jesus will be hastened by our living a holy lifestyle:

You ought to live holy and godly lives as you look forward to the day of God and speed its coming. (2 Peter 3:11–12, NIV)

Your lives should be holy and dedicated to God, as you wait for the Day of God and do your best to make it come soon. (2 Peter 3:11–12, GNB)

Indeed, the wonder of the Cross has changed my life completely, along with that of millions of others. The wonder of the Cross has taken complete possession of me. My whole life revolves around the Cross. For me, the wonder of the Cross is the miracle of God's love. It is the supernatural intervention of God in this world, in *my* world.

It is my prayer that after you have read this book your life will also revolve around the Cross. I pray that the truth of the wonder of the Cross will no longer sound like nonsense to your ears, but that you will accept God's gift for your life with open hands.

Father in heaven,

Thank You for the wonder of the Cross, through which I can live each day with Jesus. How can I ever thank You enough for this? Thank You, Jesus, that You wrestled with my sins in Gethsemane and that You were victorious. Thank You that Your victory is also my victory. I want to look to You and trust You, so that I will not fight my sinful nature in my own strength. Thank You that when I am weak, your strength comes over me. In You I am more than a conqueror. Jesus, fill my heart with Your peace. Jesus, fill my eyes with Your love. Jesus, fill my mouth with Your words. Jesus, fill my hands with Your strength and Your blessings to love You and to serve You as long as I live.

Amen.

ENDNOTES

PREFACE

1   *If you forgive anyone's sins, they have been forgiven them. If you retain anyone's sins, they have been retained.* (John 20:23, WEB)

2   *Jesus said, "Take away the stone." Martha, the sister of him who was dead, said to him, "Lord, by this time there is a stench, for he has been dead four days."* (John 11:39, WEB)

3   *None of the rulers of this world knew this wisdom. If they had known it, they would not have crucified the Lord of glory.* (1 Corinthians 2:8, GNB)

4   *... looking to Jesus, the author and perfecter of faith, who for the joy that was set before him endured the Cross, despising its shame, and has sat down at the right hand of the throne of God.* (Hebrews 12:2, WEB)

CHAPTER I

5   *... and hope doesn't disappoint us, because God's love has been poured out into our hearts through the Holy Spirit who was given to us.* (Romans 5:5, WEB)

6   *I know your works, and your toil and perseverance, and that you can't tolerate evil men, and have tested those who call themselves apostles, and they are not, and found them false. You have perseverance and have endured for my name's sake, and have labored and not grown weary. But I have this against you, that you left your first love.* (Revelation 2:2–4, WEB)

7   *For when we were in the flesh, the sinful passions which were through the law, worked in our members to bring forth fruit to death.* (Romans 7:5, WEB)

8   *... that you put away, as concerning your former way of life, the old man, that grows corrupt after the lusts of deceit;* (Ephesians 4:22, WEB)

9   *Now the works of the flesh are obvious, which are: adultery, sexual immorality, uncleanness, lustfulness, idolatry, sorcery, hatred, strife, jealousies, outbursts of anger, rivalries, divisions, heresies, envyings, murders, drunkenness, orgies, and things like these; of which I forewarn you, even as I also forewarned you, that those who practice such things will not inherit the Kingdom of God.* (Galatians 5:19–21, WEB)

10   *There is no one on earth who does what is right all the time and never makes a mistake.* (Ecclesiastes 7:20, GNB)

11   *For when we were in the flesh, the sinful passions which were through the law, worked in our members to bring forth fruit to death.* (Romans 7:5, WEB)

12   *Jesus said to them, "I am telling you the truth: everyone who sins is a slave of sin."* (John 8:34, GNB)

13   *I know that good does not live in me—that is, in my human nature. For even though the desire to do good is in me, I am not able to do it.* (Romans 7:18, GNB)

14   *... because the mind of the flesh is hostile towards God; for it is not subject to God's law, neither.* (Romans 8:7, WEB)

15   *Those who obey their human nature cannot please God.* (Romans 8:8, GNB)

16   *In this way He has given us the very great and precious gifts he promised, so that by means of these gifts you may escape from the destructive lust that is in the world, and may come to share the divine nature.* (2 Peter 1:4, GNB)

17   *I exhort the elders among you, as a fellow elder, and a witness of the sufferings of Christ, and who will also share in the glory that will be revealed.* (1 Peter 5:1, WEB)

18   *... who did not sin, "neither was deceit found in his mouth."* (1 Peter 2:22, WEB)

19   *You know that Christ appeared in order to take away sins and that there is no sin in Him.* (1 John 3:5, GNB)

20   *While Pilate was sitting in the judgment hall, his wife sent him a message: "Have nothing to do with that innocent man, because in a dream last night I suffered much on account of Him."* (Matthew 27:19, GNB)

21   *... and said to them, "You brought this man to me and said that he was misleading the people. Now, I have examined Him here in your presence, and I have not found Him guilty of any of the crimes you accuse Him of."* (Luke 23:14, GNB)

22   *"I have sinned by betraying an innocent man to death!" he said.* (Matthew 27:4, GNB)

23   *When the centurion saw what was done, he glorified God, saying, "Certainly this was a righteous man."* (Luke 23:47, WEB)

24   *Which one of you can prove that I am guilty of sin? If I tell the truth, then why do you not believe Me?* (John 8:46, GNB)

25   *Our High Priest is not one who cannot feel sympathy for our weaknesses. On the contrary, we have a High Priest who was tempted in every way that we are, but did not sin.* (Hebrews 4:15, GNB)

26   *For such a High Priest was fitting for us: holy, guiltless, undefiled, separated from sinners, and made higher than the heavens.* (Hebrews 7:26, WEB)

27 *Now the works of the flesh are obvious, which are: adultery, sexual immorality, uncleanness, lustfulness, idolatry, sorcery, hatred, strife, jealousies, outbursts of anger, rivalries, divisions, heresies, envyings, murders, drunkenness, orgies, and things like these; of which I forewarn you, even as I also forewarned you, that those who practice such things will not inherit the Kingdom of God.* (Galatians 5:19–21, WEB)

28 *But the Spirit produces love, joy, peace, patience, kindness, goodness, faithfulness, humility, and selfcontrol.* (Galatians 5:22–23, GNB)

29 *At that time Jesus was filled with joy by the Holy Spirit.* (Luke 10:21, GNB)

30 *When Jesus therefore saw her weeping, and the Jews weeping who came with her, He groaned in the spirit, and was troubled.* (John 11:33, WEB)

31 *Jesus wept.* (John 11:35, WEB)

32 *He took with Him Peter, James, and John, and began to be greatly troubled and distressed.* (Mark 14:33, WEB)

33 *It happened after three days they found Him in the temple, sitting in the midst of the teachers, both listening to them, and asking them questions. All who heard Him were amazed at his understanding and his answers.* (Luke 2:46–47, WEB)

34 See Matthew 22:15–33

35 *But anyone who is joined to the Lord is one in spirit with Him.* (1 Corinthians 6:17, CEV)

36 *So then, confess your sins to one another and pray for one another, so that you will be healed. The prayer of a good person has a powerful effect.* (James 5:16, GNB)

37 *God's Spirit joins Himself to our spirits to declare that we are God's children.* (Romans 8:16, GNB)

38 *... through the hypocrisy of men who speak lies, branded in their own conscience as with a hot iron.* (1 Timothy 4:2, WEB)

39 *I cannot talk with you much longer, because the ruler of this world is coming. He has no power over me.* (John 14:30, GNB)

40 *But Jesus perceived their wickedness.* (Matthew 22:18, WEB)

41 *For I spoke not from myself, but the Father who sent Me, He gave Me a commandment, what I should say, and what I should speak. I know that his commandment is eternal life. The things therefore which I speak, even as the Father has said to Me, so I speak.* (John 12:49–50, WEB)

42 *But Jesus said, "Someone touched me, for I knew it when power went out of Me."* (Luke 8:46, GNB)

43 *But Jesus did not trust Himself to them, because He knew them all. There was no need for anyone to tell Him about them, because He Himself knew what was in their hearts.* (John 2:24–25, GNB)

44 *Woe to you, scribes and Pharisees, hypocrites! For you are like whitened tombs, which outwardly appear beautiful, but inwardly are full of dead men's bones, and of all uncleanness.* (Matthew 23:27, WEB)

45 *Yet some of you do not believe. (Jesus knew from the very beginning who were the ones that would not believe and which one would betray Him.)* (John 6:64, GNB)

CHAPTER 2

46 Literally the day of forgiveness

47 In the original translation by Luther in 1545 the Mercy Seat is called Gnadenstuhl.

48 *... and the Lord would speak to Moses face to face, just like a friend.* (Exodus 33:11, CEV)

49 *This is how those things have been arranged. The priests go into the outer tent every day to perform their duties, but only the high priest goes into the inner tent, and he does so only once a year. He takes with him blood which he offers to God on behalf of himself and for the sins which the people have committed without knowing they were sinning.* (Hebrews 9:6–7, GNB)

50 The difference between the High Priest in Leviticus and Jesus as the High Priest of our confession (Hebrews 3:1) is in the first place the order in which the blood was sprinkled. Jesus, in contrast to the High Priest in Leviticus, first sprinkled the earth with his blood and then entered the heavenly Holy of Holies with his own blood, where He attained eternal salvation for us. The second important difference is that Jesus did not use the blood of a sacrifice, but his own blood, with which He entered the heavenly Holy of Holies. His sacrifice was enough, once and for all, and never need be repeated. The salvation that Jesus attained for us will work eternally for those who believe in Him!

51 *By the sweat of your face will you eat bread until you return to the ground, for out of it you were taken. For you are dust, and to dust you shall return.* (Genesis 3:19, WEB)

52 *From the throne came flashes of lightning, rumblings, and peals of thunder. In front of the throne seven lighted torches were burning, which are the seven spirits of God.* (Revelation 4:5, GNB).
For the seven-branched lamp stand (Exodus 25:31–40)

CHAPTER 3

53   *Jesus spent those days teaching in the Temple, and when evening came, he would go out and spend the night on the Mount of Olives. (Luke 21:37, GNB)*

54   *David went up by the ascent of the Mount of Olives, and wept as he went up; and he had his head covered, and went barefoot: and all the people who were with him covered every man his head, and they went up, weeping as they went up. One told David, saying, Ahithophel is among the conspirators with Absalom. David said, Yahweh, please turn the counsel of Ahithophel into foolishness. It happened that when David had come to the top of the ascent, where God was worshiped, behold, Hushai the Archite came to meet him with his coat torn, and earth on his head. (2 Samuel 15:30–32, WEB)*

55   *The glory of Yahweh went up from the midst of the city, and stood on the mountain which is on the east side of the city. (Ezekiel 11:23, WEB)*

56   *He took with Him Peter, James, and John, and began to be greatly troubled and distressed. He said to them, "My soul is exceedingly sorrowful, even to death. Stay here, and watch." (Mark 14:33–34, WEB)*

57   *Being in agony he prayed more earnestly. (Luke 22:44, WEB)*

58   *His sweat became like great drops of blood falling down on the ground. (Luke 22:44, WEB)*

59   *But the Spirit produces love, joy, peace, patience, kindness, goodness, faithfulness, humility, and selfcontrol. There is no law against such things as these. (Galatians 5:22–23, GNB)*

60   *Now the works of the flesh are obvious, which are: adultery, sexual immorality, uncleanness, lustfulness, idolatry, sorcery, hatred, strife, jealousies, outbursts of anger, rivalries, divisions, heresies, envyings, murders, drunkenness, orgies, and things like these; of which I forewarn you, even as I also forewarned you, that those who practice such things will not inherit the Kingdom of God. (Galatians 5:19–21, WEB)*

61   *The next day John saw Jesus coming to him, and said, "There is the Lamb of God, who takes away the sin of the world!" (John 1:29, GNB)*

62   *But your iniquities have separated between you and your God, and your sins have hidden his face from you, so that he will not hear. (Isaiah 59:2, WEB)*

63   *The sting of death is sin, and the power of sin is the law. (1 Corinthians 15:56, WEB)*

64   See Luke 4

65   *But we see him who has been made a little lower than the angels, Jesus, because of the suffering of death crowned with glory and honor, that by the grace of God he should taste of death for everyone. (Hebrews 2:9, WEB)*

66   *He said to them, "My soul is exceedingly sorrowful, even to death. Stay here, and watch." (Mark 14:34, WEB)*

67   *Every Jewish priest performs his services every day and offers the same sacrifices many times; but these sacrifices can never take away sins. (Hebrews 10:11, GNB)*

68   *But if we live in the light—just as He is in the light—then we have fellowship with one another, and the blood of Jesus, his Son, purifies us from every sin. (1 John 1:7, GNB)*

CHAPTER 4

69   *Judas, the traitor, knew where it was, because many times Jesus had met there with his disciples. (John 18:2, GNB)*

70   *Then Jesus said to the chief priests and the officers of the Temple guard and the elders who had come there to get Him, "Did you have to come with swords and clubs, as though I were an outlaw?" (Luke 22:52, GNB)*

71   *They rose up, dragged Jesus out of town, and took Him to the top of the hill on which their town was built. They meant to throw Him over the cliff, but He walked through the middle of the crowd and went his way. (Luke 4:29–30, GNB)*

72   *After this, Jesus traveled in Galilee; He did not want to travel in Judea, because the Jewish authorities there were wanting to kill Him. (John 7:1, GNB)*

73   *Then they tried to seize Him, but no one laid a hand on Him, because his hour had not yet come. (John 7:30, GNB)*

74   *The Pharisees heard the crowd whispering these things about Jesus, so they and the chief priests sent some guards to arrest him. (John 7:32, GNB)*

75   *Some wanted to seize Him, but no one laid a hand on Him. (John 7:44, GNB)*

76   *For I tell you that the scripture which says, "He shared the fate of criminals," must come true about Me, because what was written about Me is coming true. (Luke 22:37, GNB)*

77   *Yet some of you do not believe. (Jesus knew from the very beginning who were the ones that would not believe and which one would betray him.) (John 6:64, GNB)*

78   *Jesus said to them, "All of you will run away and leave Me, for the scripture says, 'God will kill the shepherd, and the sheep will all be scattered.'" (Mark 14:27, GNB)*

79   *"Listen," He told them, "we are going up to Jerusalem where the Son of Man will be handed over to the chief priests and the teachers of the Law. They will condemn Him to death and then hand Him over to the Gentiles." (Mark 10:33, GNB)*

80   *... and then hand Him over to the Gentiles, who will make fun of Him, whip Him, and crucify Him; but three days later He will be raised to life. (Matthew 20:19, GNB)*

81   *Jesus already knew everything that was going to happen, but He asked, "Who are you looking for?" (John 18:4, CEV)*

82   *No one takes my life away from Me. I give it up of my own free will. I have the right to give it up, and I have the right to take it back. This is what my Father has commanded Me to do. (John 10:18, GNB)*

83   *For I tell you that the scripture which says, "He shared the fate of criminals," must come true about Me, because what was written about Me is coming true. (Luke 22:37, GNB)*

84   *Jesus already knew everything that was going to happen, but He asked, "Who are you looking for?" They answered, "We are looking for Jesus from Nazareth!" Jesus told them, "I am Jesus!" (John 18:4–5, CEV)*

85   *As Saul was coming near the city of Damascus, suddenly a light from the sky flashed around him. He fell to the ground and heard a voice saying to him, "Saul, Saul! Why do you persecute me?" (Acts 9:3–4, GNB, see also Acts 22:7 and 26:14)*

86   *God said to Moses, "I AM WHO I AM," and He said, "You shall tell the children of Israel this: "I AM has sent me to you." (Exodus 3:14, WEB)*

87   *"But all this has happened in order to make come true what the prophets wrote in the Scriptures." Then all the disciples left him and ran away. (Matthew 26:56, GNB)*

88   *When his family heard about it, they set out to take charge of Him, because people were saying, "He's gone mad!" (Mark 3:21, GNB)*

89   *They asked Jesus, "Were we not right in saying that You are a Samaritan and have a demon in You?" (John 8:48, GNB)*

90   *So the Jewish authorities said, "He says that we cannot go where He is going. Does this mean that He will kill himself?" (John 8:22, GNB)*

91   *So Jesus' brothers said to Him, "Leave this place and go to Judea, so that your followers will see the things that you are doing. People don't hide what they are doing if they want to be well known. Since You are doing these things, let the whole world know about You!" (John 7:3–4, GNB)*

92   *They answered, "We do not want to stone You because of any good deeds, but be-
     cause of your blasphemy! You are only a man, but You are trying to make yourself
     God!"* (John 10:33, GNB)

93   *There was much murmuring among the multitudes concerning Him. Some said,
     "He is a good man." Others said, "Not so, but He leads the multitude astray."*
     (John 7:12, WEB)

94   *When Jesus and his disciples came to Capernaum, the collectors of the Temple
     tax came to Peter and asked, "Does your teacher pay the Temple tax?"* (Matthew
     17:24, GNB)

95   *They said this to trap Jesus, so that they could accuse Him. But He bent over and
     wrote on the ground with his finger.* (John 8:6, GNB)

96   *"Isn't this the carpenter, the son of Mary, and brother of James, Josef, Judas, and
     Simon? Aren't his sisters here with us?" They were offended at Him.* (Mark 6:3,
     WEB)

97   *Some people were there who wanted to accuse Jesus of doing wrong; so they
     watched Him closely to see whether He would cure the man on the Sabbath.*
     (Mark 3:2, GNB)

98   *Jesus knew that they were about to come and seize Him in order to make Him
     king by force; so He went off again to the hills by Himself.* (John 6:15, GNB)

99   *So He asked the twelve disciples, "And you—would you also like to leave?"* (John
     6:67, GNB)

CHAPTER 5

100 See Mark 11:15–18

101 *The High Priest questioned Jesus about his disciples and about his teaching.*
     (John 18:19, GNB)

102 *Jesus answered, "I have always spoken publicly to everyone; all my teaching was
     done in the synagogues and in the Temple, where all the people come together. I
     have never said anything in secret."* (John 18:20, GNB)

103 *"Which one of the two did what his father wanted?" "The older one," they an-
     swered. So Jesus said to them, "I tell you: the tax collectors and the prostitutes are
     going into the Kingdom of God ahead of you.* (Matthew 21:31, GNB)

104 *How terrible for you, teachers of the Law and Pharisees! You hypocrites! You are
     like whitewashed tombs, which look fine on the outside but are full of bones and
     decaying corpses on the inside.* (Matthew 23:27, GNB)

105 *Then the chief priests and the elders met together in the palace of Caiaphas, the High Priest, and made plans to arrest Jesus secretly and put Him to death.* (Matthew 26:3–4, GNB)

106 *Then they spat in his face and beat Him; and those who slapped Him said, "Prophesy for us, Messiah! Guess who hit you!"* (Matthew 26:67–68, GNB)

107 *The Lord said to Moses, "Cut two stone tablets like the first ones, and I will write on them the words that were on the first tablets, which you broke."* (Exodus 34:1, GNB)

108 The only unforgivable sin, the Bible mentions, is blasphemy against the Holy Spirit (Luke 12:10.) Some Christians erroneously think that they have committed this unforgivable sin, because even though they have asked God to forgive them, they still suffer from feelings of guilt. They feel guilty and have come to believe that this is because they have not been forgiven. Therefore they have come to the erroneous conclusion that they have committed the "unforgivable sin." They can discover that the wonder of the Cross is more than just the forgiveness of sins. Through the wonder of the Cross we are also freed from the accusations of the evil one and our conscience that accuses us is cleansed with the blood of the Lord Jesus, and the feelings of guilt will really disappear.

109 *There is therefore now no condemnation to them that are in Christ Jesus.* (Romans 8:1, ASV)

110 *But thanks be to God! For in union with Christ we are always led by God as prisoners in Christ's victory procession. God uses us to make the knowledge about Christ spread everywhere like a sweet fragrance.* (2 Corinthians 2:14, GNB)

111 *Or else wouldn't they have ceased to be offered, because the worshipers, having been once cleansed, would have had no more consciousness of sins?* (Hebrews 10:2, WEB)

112 *God will bless you for this, if you endure the pain of undeserved suffering because you are conscious of his will.* (1 Peter 2:19, GNB)

113 *Come back to your right senses and stop your sinful ways. I declare to your shame that some of you do not know God.* (1 Corinthians 15:34, GNB)

114 *So let us come near to God with a sincere heart and a sure faith, with hearts that have been purified from a guilty conscience and with bodies washed with clean water.* (Hebrews 10:22, GNB)

115 *Of course, my friends, I really do not think that I have already won it; the one thing I do, however, is to forget what is behind me and do my best to reach what is ahead. So I run straight toward the goal in order to win the prize, which is God's call through Christ Jesus to the life above.* (Philippians 3:13–14, GNB)

CHAPTER 6

116 *Now there were some present at the same time who told Him about the Galileans, whose blood Pilate had mixed with their sacrifices.* (Luke 13:1, WEB)

117 *They kept on stoning Stephen as he called out to the Lord, "Lord Jesus, receive my spirit!"* (Acts 7:59, GNB)

118 *... you will know the truth, and the truth will set you free.* (John 8:32, GNB)

119 *It was the fifteenth year of the rule of Emperor Tiberius; Pontius Pilate was governor of Judea, Herod was ruler of Galilee, and his brother Philip was ruler of the territory of Iturea and Trachonitis; Lysanias was ruler of Abilene.* (Luke 3:1, GNB)

120 *Jesus answered them, "Go and tell that fox: 'I am driving out demons and performing cures today and tomorrow, and on the third day I shall finish my work."* (Luke 13:32, GNB)

121 *Joanna, whose husband Chuza was an officer in Herod's court; and Susanna, and many other women who used their own resources to help Jesus and his disciples.* (Luke 8:3, GNB)

122 *In the church at Antioch there were some prophets and teachers: Barnabas, Simeon (called the Black), Lucius (from Cyrene), Manaen (who had been brought up with Governor Herod) and Saul.* (Acts 13:1, GNB)

123 *On that very day Herod and Pilate became friends; before this they had been enemies.* (Luke 23:12, GNB)

124 *And at that time there was a prisoner named Barabbas. He and some others had been arrested for murder during a riot.* (Mark 15:7, CEV)

125 *But God has shown us how much He loves us—it was while we were still sinners that Christ died for us!* (Romans 5:8, GNB)

CHAPTER 7

126 *Pilate called together the chief priests, the leaders, and the people, and said to them, "You brought this man to me and said that He was misleading the people. Now, I have examined Him here in your presence, and I have not found Him guilty of any of the crimes you accuse Him of. Nor did Herod find Him guilty, for he sent him back to us. There is nothing this man has done to deserve death."* (Luke 23:13–15, GNB)

127 *He was despised, and rejected by men; a man of suffering, and acquainted with disease: and as one from whom men hide their face he was despised; and we didn't respect him.* (Isaiah 53:3, WEB)

128 *And all that dwell upon the earth shall worship Him, whose names are not written in the book of life of the Lamb slain from the foundation of the world.* (Revelation 13:8, KJV)

129 *When Christ went through the tent and entered once and for all into the Most Holy Place, He did not take the blood of goats and bulls to offer as a sacrifice; rather, He took his own blood and obtained eternal salvation for us.* (Hebrews 9:12, GNB)

130 *He is not like other high priests; He does not need to offer sacrifices every day for his own sins first and then for the sins of the people. He offered one sacrifice, once and for all, when He offered himself.* (Hebrews 7:27, GNB)

131 *This means that every time you eat this bread and drink from this cup you proclaim the Lord's death until he comes.* (1 Corinthians 11:26, GNB)

132 *Think of what He went through; how He put up with so much hatred from sinners! So do not let yourselves become discouraged and give up.* (Hebrews 12:3, GNB)

133 *So Jesus answered them, "I tell you the truth: the Son can do nothing on his own; He does only what He sees his Father doing. What the Father does, the Son also does.... I can do nothing on my own authority; I judge only as God tells Me, so my judgment is right, because I am not trying to do what I want, but only what He who sent me wants."* (John 5:19, 30, GNB)

134 *Let us keep our eyes fixed on Jesus, on whom our faith depends from beginning to end. He did not give up because of the Cross! On the contrary, because of the joy that was waiting for Him, He thought nothing of the disgrace of dying on the Cross, and He is now seated at the right side of God's throne. Think of what He went through; how He put up with so much hatred from sinners! So do not let yourselves become discouraged and give up.* (Hebrews 12:2–3, GNB)

135 *Then Peter came to Jesus and asked, "Lord, if my brother keeps on sinning against me, how many times do I have to forgive him? Seven times?" "No, not seven times," answered Jesus, "but seventy times seven."* (Matthew 18:21–22, GNB)

136 *Lamech said to his wives, "Adah and Zillah, listen to me: I have killed a young man because he struck me. If seven lives are taken to pay for killing Cain, seventy-seven will be taken if anyone kills me."* (Genesis 4:23–24, GNB)

137 *Rejoice with those who rejoice. Weep with those who weep.* (Romans 12:15, WEB)

138 *God was performing unusual miracles through Paul. Even handkerchiefs and aprons he had used were taken to the sick, and their diseases were driven away, and the evil spirits would go out of them.* (Acts 19:11–12, GNB)

139   *... and tasted the good word of God, and the powers of the age to come.* (Hebrews 6:5, WEB)

140   *He said, "If you will obey me completely by doing what I consider right and by keeping my commands, I will not punish you with any of the diseases that I brought on the Egyptians. I am the Lord, the one who heals you."* (Exodus 15:26, GNB)

Chapter 8

141   *Because of the disobedience of Adam and Eve, the ground of the earth is cursed, and has brought forth thistles and thorns ever since. To Adam he said, "Because you have listened to your wife's voice, and have eaten of the tree, of which I commanded you, saying, 'You shall not eat of it,' cursed is the ground for your sake. In toil you will eat of it all the days of your life. Thorns also and thistles will it bring forth to you; and you will eat the herb of the field. By the sweat of your face will you eat bread until you return to the ground, for out of it you were taken. For you are dust, and to dust you shall return."* (Genesis 3:17–19, WEB)

142   *They want to look for nothing but the chance to commit adultery; their appetite for sin is never satisfied. They lead weak people into a trap. Their hearts are trained to be greedy. They are under God's curse!* (2 Peter 2:14, GNB)

143   *God's curse on anyone who makes an idol of stone, wood, or metal and secretly worships it; the Lord hates idolatry. And all the people will answer, "Amen!"* (Deuteronomy 27:15, GNB)

144   In Deuteronomy 27:20–23, 1 Samuel 3:13, and Deuteronomy 23:2 it says that sexual sins can influence up to ten generations.

145   *God's curse on anyone who secretly commits murder. And all the people will answer, "Amen!" God's curse on anyone who accepts money to murder an innocent person. And all the people will answer, "Amen!"* (Deuteronomy 27:24–25, GNB)

146   *God's curse on anyone who leads a blind person in the wrong direction. And all the people will answer, "Amen!"* (Deuteronomy 27:18, GNB; also see Zechariah 5:3–4)

147   *God's curse on anyone who dishonors his father or mother. And all the people will answer, "Amen!"* (Deuteronomy 27:16, GNB)

148   *Parents are not to be put to death for crimes committed by their children, and children are not to be put to death for crimes committed by their parents; people are to be put to death only for a crime they themselves have committed.* (Deuteronomy 24:16, GNB)

The life of every person belongs to Me, the life of the parent as well as that of the child. The person who sins is the one who will die. (Ezekiel 18:4, GNB)
It is the one who sins who will die. A son is not to suffer because of his father's sins, nor a father because of the sins of his son. Good people will be rewarded for doing good, and evil people will suffer for the evil they do. (Ezekiel 18:20, GNB)
Everyone of us, then, will have to give an account to God. (Romans 14:12, GNB)
For all of us must appear before Christ, to be judged by Him. We will each receive what we deserve, according to everything we have done, good or bad, in our bodily life. (2 Corinthians 5:10, GNB)

149 *Like a fluttering sparrow, like a darting swallow, so the undeserved curse doesn't come to rest.* (Proverbs 26:2, WEB)

150 *But if he is found, he shall restore seven times. He shall give all the wealth of his house.* (Proverbs 6:31, WEB)

151 *Don't seek revenge yourselves, beloved, but give place to God's wrath. For it is written, "Vengeance belongs to Me; I will repay, says the Lord."* (Romans 12:19, WEB)

152 *God's plan is to make known his secret to his people, this rich and glorious secret which He has for all peoples. And the secret is that Christ is in you, which means that you will share in the glory of God.* (Colossians 1:27, GNB)

153 *Forgetting the things which are behind, and stretching forward to the things which are before.* (Philippians 3:13, WEB)

CHAPTER 9

154 *Any Israelite or any foreigner living in Israel who curses the Lord shall be stoned to death by the whole community.* (Leviticus 24:16, GNB)

155 *While he was sitting on the judgment seat, his wife sent to him, saying, "Have nothing to do with that righteous man, for I have suffered many things this day in a dream because of Him."* (Matthew 27:19, WEB)

156 *But Jesus kept quiet. Again the High Priest spoke to him, "In the name of the living God I now put You under oath: tell us if You are the Messiah, the Son of God."* (Matthew 26:63, GNB)

157 *Herod was very pleased when he saw Jesus, because he had heard about Him and had been wanting to see Him for a long time. He was hoping to see Jesus perform some miracle. So Herod asked Jesus many questions, but Jesus made no answer.* (Luke 23:8–9, GNB)

158 *When He was accused by the chief priests and elders, He answered nothing.* (Matthew 27:12, WEB)

159 *Pilate said to Him, "You will not speak to me? Remember, I have the authority to set You free and also to have you crucified."* (John 19:10, GNB)

160 *Jesus answered, "You have authority over Me only because it was given to you by God. So the man who handed Me over to you is guilty of a worse sin."* (John 19:11, GNB)

161 *When Pilate heard this, he tried to find a way to set Jesus free. But the crowd shouted back, "If you set Him free, that means that you are not the Emperor's friend! Anyone who claims to be a king is a rebel against the Emperor!"* (John 19:12, GNB)

CHAPTER 10

162 *Simeon blessed them and said to Mary, his mother, "This child is chosen by God for the destruction and the salvation of many in Israel. He will be a sign from God which many people will speak against and so reveal their secret thoughts. And sorrow, like a sharp sword, will break your own heart."* (Luke 2:34–35, GNB)

163 *Mary (who was called Magdalene), from whom seven demons had been driven out.* (Luke 8:2, GNB)

164 *He heals the broken-hearted and bandages their wounds.* (Psalms 147:3, GNB)

165 *Now there was leaning on Jesus' bosom one of his disciples, whom Jesus loved.* (John 13:23, KJV)

166 *They do not believe, because their minds have been kept in the dark by the evil god of this world. He keeps them from seeing the light shining on them, the light that comes from the Good News about the glory of Christ, who is the exact likeness of God.* (2 Corinthians 4:4, GNB)

167 *The wisdom I proclaim is God's secret wisdom, which is hidden from human beings, but which he had already chosen for our glory even before the world was made. None of the rulers of this world knew this wisdom. If they had known it, they would not have crucified the Lord of glory.* (1 Corinthians 2:7–8, GNB)

168 *All the people answered, "May his blood be on us, and on our children!"* (Matthew 27:25, WEB)

169 *For even his brothers didn't believe in Him.* (John 7:5, WEB)

170 *Jesus answered, "You belong to this world here below, but I come from above. You are from this world, but I am not from this world."* (John 8:23, GNB)

171 *When his family heard about it, they set out to take charge of Him, because people were saying, "He's gone mad!"* (Mark 3:21, GNB)

172 *Jesus said to her, "Woman, what does that have to do with you and Me? My hour has not yet come."* (John 2:4, WEB)

173 *Jesus answered him, "Those who love Me will obey my teaching. My Father will love them, and my Father and I will come to them and live with them."* (John 14:23, GNB)

174 *"How can a grown man be born again?" Nicodemus asked. "He certainly cannot enter his mother's womb and be born a second time!"* (John 3:4, GNB)

175 *And so I will give him a place of honor, a place among the great and powerful. He willingly gave his life and shared the fate of evil men. He took the place of many sinners and prayed that they might be forgiven.* (Isaiah 53:12, GNB)

176 *Even the bandits who had been crucified with Him insulted him in the same way.* (Matthew 27:44, GNB)

177 *As the Scriptures say, "When he went up to the highest place, he led away many prisoners and gave gifts to people."* (Ephesians 4:8, CEV)

178 *Not even the chief angel Michael did this. In his quarrel with the Devil, when they argued about who would have the body of Moses, Michael did not dare condemn the Devil with insulting words, but said, "The Lord rebuke you!"* (Jude 1:9, GNB)

179 See Luke 4:1–13

180 *When I was hungry, they gave me poison; when I was thirsty, they offered me vinegar.* (Psalms 69:21, GNB)

181 *"My food," Jesus said to them, "is to obey the will of the one who sent me and to finish the work He gave me to do."* (John 4:34, GNB)

182 *Then the curtain hanging in the Temple was torn in two from top to bottom.* (Matthew 27:51, GNB)

183 *How great is your constant love for me! You have saved me from the grave itself.* (Psalms 86:13, GNB)

184 *Jesus said to them, "I am telling you the truth: everyone who sins is a slave of sin."* (John 8:34, GNB)

185 *For the wages of sin is death, but the free gift of God is eternal life in Christ Jesus our Lord.* (Romans 6:23, WEB)

186 *He says, "Do you think I want all these sacrifices you keep offering to me? I have had more than enough of the sheep you burn as sacrifices and of the fat of your fine animals. I am tired of the blood of bulls and sheep and goats."* (Isaiah 1:11, GNB)

CHAPTER 11

187 *Because the mind of the flesh is hostile towards God; for it is not subject to God's law, neither indeed can it be.* (Romans 8:7, WEB)

188 *Those who obey their human nature cannot please God.* (Romans 8:8, GNB)

189 *One of the soldiers, however, plunged his spear into Jesus' side, and at once blood and water poured out.* (John 19:34, GNB)

190 *I have been crucified with Christ, and it is no longer I that live, but Christ living in me. That life which I now live in the flesh, I live by faith in the Son of God, who loved me, and gave Himself up for me.* (Galatians 2:20, WEB)

191 *When they reached the border of Mysia, they tried to go into the province of Bithynia, but the Spirit of Jesus did not allow them.* (Acts 16:7, GNB)

192 *My dear children! Once again, just like a mother in childbirth, I feel the same kind of pain for you until Christ's nature is formed in you.* (Galatians 4:19, GNB)

193 *They are for you, who through faith are kept safe by God's power for the salvation which is ready to be revealed at the end of time.* (1 Peter 1:5, GNB)

194 *I still did not know that He was the one, but God, who sent me to baptize with water, had said to me, "You will see the Spirit come down and stay on a man; He is the one who baptizes with the Holy Spirit."* (John 1:33, GNB)

CHAPTER 12

195 *Even then, many Jewish authorities believed in Jesus; but because of the Pharisees they did not talk about it openly, so as not to be expelled from the synagogue. They loved human approval rather than the approval of God.* (John 12:42–43, GNB)

After this, Joseph, who was from the town of Arimathea, asked Pilate if he could take Jesus' body. (Joseph was a follower of Jesus, but in secret, because he was afraid of the Jewish authorities.) Pilate told him he could have the body, so Joseph went and took it away. Nicodemus, who at first had gone to see Jesus at night, went with Joseph, taking with him about one hundred pounds of spices, a mixture of myrrh and aloes. (John 19:38–39, GNB)

196 *His parents said this because they were afraid of the Jewish authorities, who had already agreed that anyone who said he believed that Jesus was the Messiah would be expelled from the synagogue.* (John 9:22, GNB)

197   *There was a man named Joseph from Arimathea, a town in Judea. He was a good and honorable man, who was waiting for the coming of the Kingdom of God. Although he was a member of the Council, he had not agreed with their decision and action.* (Luke 23:50–51, GNB)

198   *Joseph bought a linen sheet, took the body down, wrapped it in the sheet, and placed it in a tomb which had been dug out of solid rock. Then he rolled a large stone across the entrance to the tomb.* (Mark 15:46, GNB)

199   *Nicodemus, who at first had gone to see Jesus at night, went with Joseph, taking with him about one hundred pounds of spices, a mixture of myrrh and aloes.* (John 19:39, GNB)

200   *My son, attend to my words. Turn your ear to my sayings. Let them not depart from your eyes. Keep them in the midst of your heart. For they are life to those who find them, and health to their whole body.* (Proverbs 4:20–22, WEB)

201   *I in them and You in Me, so that they may be completely one, in order that the world may know that You sent Me and that You love them as You love Me.* (John 17:23, GNB)

202   *... in order that at the present time, by means of the church, the angelic rulers and powers in the heavenly world might learn of his wisdom in all its different forms. God did this according to his eternal purpose, which he achieved through Christ Jesus our Lord.* (Ephesians 3:10–11, GNB)

203   *For Christ Himself has brought us peace by making Jews and Gentiles one people. With his own body He broke down the wall that separated them and kept them enemies. He abolished the Jewish Law with its commandments and rules, in order to create out of the two races one new people in union with Himself, in this way making peace. By his death on the Cross Christ destroyed their enmity; by means of the Cross He united both races into one body and brought them back to God.* (Ephesians 2:14–16, GNB)

CHAPTER 13

204   *Jesus cried out in a loud voice, "Father! In your hands I place my spirit!" He said this and died.* (Luke 23:46, GNB)

205   *What man is he who shall live and not see death, Who shall deliver his soul from the power of Sheol?* (Psalm 89:48, WEB)

206   *And as for you, Capernaum! Did you want to lift yourself up to heaven? You will be thrown down to hell!* (Luke 10:15, GNB)

207   *Work hard at whatever you do, because there will be no action, no thought, no knowledge, no wisdom in the world of the dead—and that is where you are going.* (Ecclesiastes 9:10, GNB)

208 *In the world of the dead you are not remembered; no one can praise you there.* (Psalm 6:5, GNB)

209 *... a land of darkness, shadows, and confusion, where the light itself is darkness.* (Job 10:22, GNB)

210 *But of the tree of the knowledge of good and evil, you shall not eat of it: for in the day that you eat of it you will surely die.* (Genesis 2:17, WEB)

211 *For the wages of sin is death, but the free gift of God is eternal life in Christ Jesus our Lord.* (Romans 6:23, WEB)

212 *Enoch walked with God, and he was not, for God took him.* (Genesis 5:24, WEB)

213 *They kept talking as they walked on; then suddenly a chariot of fire pulled by horses of fire came between them, and Elijah was taken up to heaven by a whirlwind.* (2 Kings 2:11, GNB)

214 *But Michael, the archangel, when contending with the devil and arguing about the body of Moses, dared not bring against him an abusive condemnation, but said, "May the Lord rebuke you!"* (Jude 1:9, WEB)

215 *The Lord buried him in a valley in Moab, opposite the town of Bethpeor, but to this day no one knows the exact place of his burial.* (Deuteronomy 34:6, GNB)

216 *Then He will say also to those on the left hand, "Depart from Me, you cursed, into the eternal fire which is prepared for the devil and his angel."* (Matthew 25:41, WEB)

217 *For the wages of sin is death, but the free gift of God is eternal life in Christ Jesus our Lord.* (Romans 6:23, WEB)

218 *Since then the children have shared in flesh and blood, He also Himself in like manner partook of the same, that through death He might bring to nothing Him who had the power of death, that is, the devil.* (Hebrews 2:14, WEB)

219 *For if by the trespass of the one, death reigned through the one; so much more will those who receive the abundance of grace and of the gift of righteousness reign in life through the one, Jesus Christ.* (Romans 5:17, WEB)

220 *They have a king ruling over them, who is the angel in charge of the abyss. His name in Hebrews is Abaddon; in Greek the name is Apollyon (meaning "The Destroyer").* (Revelation 9:11, GNB)

221 *I was dead, and behold, I am alive forevermore. Amen. I have the keys of Death and of Hades.* (Revelation 1:18, WEB)

222 *Since the children, as He calls them, are people of flesh and blood, Jesus himself became like them and shared their human nature. He did this so that through his death He might destroy the Devil, who has the power over death, and in this way set free those who were slaves all their lives because of their fear of death.* (Hebrews 2:14–15, GNB)

223 *At once they screamed, "What do you want with us, you Son of God? Have you come to punish us before the right time?"* (Matthew 8:29, GNB)

224 Psalm 22

225 *As the scripture says, "When he went up to the very heights, he took many captives with him; he gave gifts to people."* (Ephesians 4:8, GNB)

226 *None of the rulers of this world knew this wisdom. If they had known it, they would not have crucified the Lord of glory.* (1 Corinthians 2:8, GNB)

227 *After He had said this, he called out in a loud voice, "Lazarus, come out!"* (John 11:43, GNB)

228 *He took her by the hand and said to her, "Talitha, koum," which means, "Little girl, I tell you to get up!"* (Mark 5:41, GNB)

229 *Jesus went over and touched the stretcher on which the people were carrying the dead boy. They stopped, and Jesus said, "Young man, get up!"* (Luke 7:14, CEV)

230 *I have the keys of Death and of Hades.* (Revelation 1:18, WEB)

231 *Then the sea gave up its dead. Death and the world of the dead also gave up the dead they held. And all were judged according to what they had done. Then death and the world of the dead were thrown into the lake of fire. (This lake of fire is the second death.) Those who did not have their name written in the book of the living were thrown into the lake of fire.* (Revelation 20:13–15, GNB)

232 *David saw what God was going to do in the future, and so he spoke about the resurrection of the Messiah when he said, "He was not abandoned in the world of the dead; his body did not rot in the grave."* (Acts 2:31, GNB)

233 *When the morning stars sang together, And all the sons of God shouted for joy?* (Job 38:7, WEB)

234 See Luke 2:13

235 See Luke 2:14

236 *Another angel, who had a gold incense container, came and stood at the altar. He was given a lot of incense to add to the prayers of all God's people and to offer it on the gold altar that stands before the throne.* (Revelation 8:3, GNB)

Chapter 14

237 *Then she turned around and saw Jesus standing there; but she did not know that it was Jesus.* (John 20:14, GNB)

238 *... they saw Him, but somehow did not recognize Him.* (Luke 24:16, GNB)

239 *They were terrified, thinking that they were seeing a ghost.* (Luke 24:37, GNB)

As the sun was rising, Jesus stood at the water's edge, but the disciples did not know that it was Jesus. (John 21:4, GNB)

When they saw Him, they worshiped him, even though some of them doubted. (Matthew 28:17, GNB)

240 *For forty days after his death He appeared to them many times in ways that proved beyond doubt that He was alive. They saw Him, and He talked with them about the Kingdom of God.* (Acts 1:3, GNB)

241 *Then He appeared to James, and afterward to all the apostles.* (1 Corinthians 15:7, GNB)

242 *Then He appeared to more than five hundred of his followers at once, most of whom are still alive, although some have died.* (1 Corinthians 15:6, GNB)

243 *The gatekeeper opens the gate for him; the sheep hear his voice as he calls his own sheep by name, and he leads them out. When he has brought them out, he goes ahead of them, and the sheep follow him, because they know his voice.* (John 10:3–4, GNB)

244 *After that He appeared in another form unto two of them, as they walked, and went into the country.* (Mark 16:12, KJV)

245 *... and in his spiritual existence He went and preached to the imprisoned spirits.* (1 Peter 3:19, GNB)

246 *But Christ having come as a high priest of the coming good things, through the greater and more perfect tabernacle, not made with hands, that is to say, not of this creation, nor yet through the blood of goats and calves, but through his own blood, entered in once for all into the Holy Place, having obtained eternal redemption.* (Hebrews 9:11–12, WEB)

247 *But God raised Jesus from death, and his body did not decay.* (Acts 13:37, CEV)

248 *By our baptism, then, we were buried with Him and shared his death, in order that, just as Christ was raised from death by the glorious power of the Father, so also we might live a new life.* (Romans 6:4, GNB)

249 *If the Spirit of God, who raised Jesus from death, lives in you, then He who raised Christ from death will also give life to your mortal bodies by the presence of his Spirit in you.* (Romans 8:11, GNB)

250 *It was late that Sunday evening, and the disciples were gathered together behind locked doors, because they were afraid of the Jewish authorities. Then Jesus came and stood among them. "Peace be with you," He said.* (John 20:19, GNB)
A week later the disciples were together again indoors, and Thomas was with them. The doors were locked, but Jesus came and stood among them and said, "Peace be with you." (John 20:26, GNB)

251 *Then their eyes were opened and they recognized Him, but He disappeared from their sight.* (Luke 24:31, GNB)

252 *Was it not necessary for the Messiah to suffer these things and then to enter his glory?* (Luke 24:26, GNB)

253 *While the two were telling them this, suddenly the Lord Himself stood among them and said to them, "Peace be with you."* (Luke 24:36, GNB)

254 See Luke 24:38–43

255 *... not to everyone, but only to the witnesses that God had already chosen, that is, to us who ate and drank with Him after He rose from death.* (Acts 10:41, GNB)

256 *But their eyes were kept from recognizing Him.* (Luke 24:16, WEB)

257 *When they saw Him, they worshiped Him, even though some of them doubted.* (Matthew 28:17, GNB)

258 *Then their eyes were opened and they recognized Him, but he disappeared from their sight.* (Luke 24:31, GNB)
Then He opened their minds to understand the Scriptures. (Luke 24:45, GNB)

259 *And Jesus explained to them what was said about Himself in all the Scriptures, beginning with the books of Moses and the writings of all the prophets.* (Luke 24:27, GNB)

260 *When He has come, He will convict the world about sin, about righteousness, and about judgment.* (John 16:8, WEB)

261 *Jesus came to them and spoke to them, saying, "All authority has been given to Me in heaven and on earth."* (Matthew 28:18, WEB)

262 *He said to him, "If they don't listen to Moses and the prophets, neither will they be persuaded if one rises from the dead."* (Luke 16:31, WEB)

263 *For rebellion is as the sin of witchcraft, and stubbornness is as idolatry and teraphim. Because you have rejected the word of Yahweh, he has also rejected you from being king.* (1 Samuel 15:23, WEB)

264 *But the chief priests conspired to put Lazarus to death also.* (John 12:10, WEB)

265 *Jesus said to him, "Because you have seen Me, you have believed. Blessed are those who have not seen, and have believed."* (John 20:29, WEB)

266 *Those who belong to Christ have crucified the flesh with its passions and lusts.* (Galatians 5:24, WEB)

267 *I will give you a new heart and a new mind. I will take away your stubborn heart of stone and give you an obedient heart.* (Ezekiel 36:26, GNB)

268 *I have been crucified with Christ, and it is no longer I that live, but Christ living in me. That life which I now live in the flesh, I live by faith in the Son of God, who loved me, and gave Himself up for me.* (Galatians 2:20, WEB)

269 *But the fruit of the Spirit is love, joy, peace, patience, kindness, goodness, faithfulness, gentleness, and self-control. Against such things there is no law.* (Galatians 5:22–23, WEB)

270 *All of us, then, reflect the glory of the Lord with uncovered faces; and that same glory, coming from the Lord, who is the Spirit, transforms us into his likeness in an ever greater degree of glory.* (2 Corinthians 3:18, GNB)

271 *May the God who gives us peace make you holy in every way and keep your whole being (spirit, soul, and body (free from every fault at the coming of our Lord Jesus Christ.* (1 Thessalonians 5:23, GNB)

272 *My dear friends, we are now God's children, but it is not yet clear what we shall become. But we know that when Christ appears, we shall be like him, because we shall see him as he really is.* (1 John 3:2, GNB)

273 *... in a moment, in the twinkling of an eye, at the last trumpet. For the trumpet will sound, and the dead will be raised incorruptible, and we will be changed.* (1 Corinthians 15:52, WEB)

274 *... in order to present the church to himself in all its beauty—pure and faultless, without spot or wrinkle or any other imperfection.* (Ephesians 5:27, GNB)

275 *There is a secret truth, my friends, which I want you to know, for it will keep you from thinking how wise you are. It is that the stubbornness of the people of Israel is not permanent, but will last only until the complete number of Gentiles comes to God.* (Romans 11:25, GNB)

Chapter 15

276 *So then, confess your sins to one another and pray for one another, so that you will be healed. The prayer of a good person has a powerful effect.* (James 5:16, GNB)

277 *Yahweh said to Satan, "Have you considered my servant, Job? For there is none like him in the earth, a blameless and an upright man, one who fears God, and turns away from evil." (Job 1:8, WEB)*

278 *He has said to me, "My grace is sufficient for you, for my power is made perfect in weakness." Most gladly therefore I will rather glory in my weaknesses, that the power of Christ may rest on me. (2 Corinthians 12:9, WEB)*

279 *They dance and sing, "In Zion is the source of all our blessings." (Psalm 87:7, GNB)*

280 *Who shall separate us from the love of Christ? Could oppression, or anguish, or persecution, or famine, or nakedness, or peril, or sword? Even as it is written, "For your sake we are killed all day long. We were accounted as sheep for the slaughter." No, in all these things, we are more than conquerors through him who loved us. For I am persuaded, that neither death, nor life, nor angels, nor principalities, nor things present, nor things to come, nor powers, nor height, nor depth, nor any other created thing, will be able to separate us from the love of God, which is in Christ Jesus our Lord. (Romans 8:35–39, WEB)*

281 *I am the vine. You are the branches. He who remains in Me, and I in him, the same bears much fruit, for apart from Me you can do nothing. (John 15:5, WEB)*

282 *Now when they saw the boldness of Peter and John, and had perceived that they were unlearned and ignorant men, they marveled. They recognized that they had been with Jesus. (Acts 4:13, WEB)*

283 *For we are his workmanship, created in Christ Jesus for good works, which God prepared before that we would walk in them. (Ephesians 2:10, WEB)*

284 *Because God is always at work in you to make you willing and able to obey his own purpose. (Philippians 2:13, GNB)*

285 *Don't think that the Lord is too weak to save you or too deaf to hear your call for help! It is because of your sins that He doesn't hear you. It is your sins that separate you from God when you try to worship Him. (Isaiah 59:1–2, GNB)*

286 *You have not yet resisted to blood, striving against sin. (Hebrews 12:4, WEB)*

BIBLIOGRAPHY

- Barbet, P., *A Doctor at Calvary: The Passion of Our Lord Jesus Christ as Described by a Surgeon* (New York: P. J. Kenedy & Sons, 1953).

- Bloomquist, E.R., "A doctor looks at the crucifixion," *Christian Herald*, March 1964, 47.

- Bucklin, R., "The legal and medical aspects of the trial and death of Christ," Medicine, Science and the Law, January 1970.

- Bucklin, R., "The shroud of Turin: a pathologist's viewpoint," Legal Medicine Annual, 1981. Humphreys, C.J. and Waddington, W.G., "Dating the crucifixion," Nature 306, 743–746 (1983).

- Davis, Truman C., Dr., "A Physician Analyzes the Crucifixion: A medical explanation of what Jesus endured on the day He died," found online at http://www.evangelicaloutreach.org/crucifix.htm

- McDowell, Josh, Evidence that Demands a Verdict (Authentic Lifestyle; revised edition, 1 Jan. 1999).

- Farrar, Frederick W., The Life of Christ (Dutton, Dovar: Cassell and Co., 1897).

- Green, Michael, Man Alive! (Colorado Springs, Colorado: Inter-Varsity Press, 1968).

- Hengel, M., *Crucifixion in the Ancient World and the Folly of the Message of the Cross* (Philadelphia: Fortress Press, 1977).

- Johnson, C.D., "Medical and cardiological aspects of the passion and crucifixion of Jesus, the Christ," Boletín de la Asociación Médica de Puerto Rico 70(3), 97–102 (1978).

- Mannix, D.P., The History of Torture (New York: Dell, 1983); Wilcox, R.K., The Shroud of Turin (Macmillan Pub. Co.).

- Nee, Watchman, Twaalf manden vol [Twelve Baskets Full], deel 1 (St. Literatuur Evangelisatie, 2002).
- Nee, Watchman, Het normale christelijke leven [The Normal Christian Life], (Pro Mission in samenwerking met St. Literatuur Evangelisatie, 1988).
- Nee, Watchman, Het overwinnende leven [The Victorious Life], (Living Stream Ministry, 1993).
- Scott, C.T., "A case of haematidrosis," The British Medical Journal (1918).
- Wright, J. Stafford, Personen uit de bijbel [Dictionary of Bible People] (Goes, Oosterbaan & le Cointre B.V. , 1980).

SYNOPSIS

DEATH AND RESURRECTION OF JESUS OF NAZARETH

The Bible verses from the four Gospels about the last eighteen hours of Jesus' life before He died, the resurrection, the ascension and the outpouring of the Holy Spirit, were chronologically put together to give you a clear overview of a life with Jesus in the first Christian church.

THURSDAY NIGHT
Jesus Prays in the Garden of Gethsemane
Mark 14:32–36; Luke 22:43–44; Matthew 26:40–42;
Mark 14:40; Matthew 26:44–46

They came to a place called Gethsemane, and Jesus said to his disciples, "Sit here while I pray." He took Peter, James, and John with Him. Distress and anguish came over Him, and He said to them, "The sorrow in my heart is so great that it almost crushes Me. Stay here and keep watch."

He went a little farther on, threw Himself on the ground, and prayed that, if possible, He might not have to go through that time of suffering. "Father," He prayed, "my Father! All things are possible for You. Take this cup of suffering away from Me. Yet not what I want, but what You want."

An angel from heaven appeared to Him and strengthened Him. In great anguish, He prayed even more fervently; his sweat was like drops of blood falling to the ground.

Then He returned to the three disciples and found them asleep; and He said to Peter, "How is it that you three were not able to keep watch with Me for even one hour? Keep watch and pray that you will not fall into temptation. The spirit is willing, but the flesh is weak."

Once more Jesus went away and prayed, "My Father, if this cup of suffering cannot be taken away unless I drink it, your will be done."

Then He came back to the disciples and found them asleep; they could not keep their eyes open. And they did not know what to say to Him.

Again Jesus left them, went away, and prayed the third time, saying the same words. Then He returned to the disciples and said, "Are you still sleeping and resting? Look! The hour has come for the Son of Man to be handed over to the power of sinners. Get up, let us go. Look, here is the man who is betraying me!"

Jesus' Arrest

*John 18:1–3; Mark 14:44–45; Luke 22:48; John 18:4–9; Luke 22:49;
John 18:10; Matthew 26:52–54; Luke 22:51; John 18:11; Matthew
26:55; Luke 22:53; Matthew 26:56; Mark 14:51–52*

After Jesus had said this prayer, He left with his disciples and went across Kidron Brook. There was a garden in that place, and Jesus and his disciples went in. Judas, the traitor, knew where it was, because many times Jesus had met there with his disciples. So Judas went to the garden, taking with him a group of Roman soldiers, and some Temple guards sent by the chief priests and the Pharisees; they were armed and carried lanterns and torches.

The traitor had given the crowd a signal: "The man I kiss is the one you want. Arrest him and take Him away under guard."

As soon as Judas arrived, he went up to Jesus and said, "Teacher!" and kissed Him. But Jesus said, "Judas, is it with a kiss that you betray the Son of Man?" Jesus knew everything that was going to happen to Him, so He stepped forward and asked them, "Who is it you are looking for?" "Jesus of Nazareth," they answered.

"I am He," He said.

Judas, the traitor, was standing there with them. When Jesus said to them, "I am He," they moved back and fell to the ground.

Again Jesus asked them, "Who is it you are looking for?" "Jesus of Nazareth," they said. "I have already told you that I am He," Jesus said. "If, then, you are looking for Me, let these others go." (He said this so that what He had said might come true: "Father, I have not lost even one of those you gave Me.")

When the disciples who were with Jesus saw what was going to happen, they asked, "Shall we use our swords, Lord?"

Simon Peter, who had a sword, drew it and struck the High Priest's slave, cutting off his right ear. The name of the slave was Malchus. "Put your sword back in its place," Jesus said to him. "All who take the sword will die by the sword. Don't you know that I could call on my Father for help, and at once he would send Me more than twelve armies of angels? But in that case, how could the Scriptures come true which say that this is what must happen?" But Jesus said, "Enough of this!" He touched the man's ear and healed him. Jesus said to Peter, "Do you think that I will not drink the cup of suffering which my Father has given Me?"

Then Jesus spoke to the crowd, "Did you have to come with swords and clubs to capture Me, as though I were an outlaw? Every day, I sat down and taught in the Temple, and you did not arrest Me. But this is your hour to act, when the power of darkness rules. But all this has happened in order to make come true what the prophets wrote in the Scriptures."

Then all the disciples left Him and ran away.

A certain young man, dressed only in a linen cloth, was following Jesus. They tried to arrest him, but he ran away naked, leaving the cloth behind.

Friday Morning
Jesus is Interrogated by Annas and Caiaphas
John 18:12–14, 19–23

Then the Roman soldiers with their commanding officer and the Jewish guards arrested Jesus, tied Him up, and took Him first to Annas. He was the father-in-law of Caiaphas, who was High

Priest that year. It was Caiaphas who had advised the Jewish authorities that it was better that one man should die for all the people.

The High Priest questioned Jesus about his disciples and about his teaching. Jesus answered, "I have always spoken publicly to everyone; all my teaching was done in the synagogues and in the Temple, where all the people come together. I have never said anything in secret. Why, then, do you question Me? Question the people who heard Me. Ask them what I told them—they know what I said."

When Jesus said this, one of the guards there slapped Him and said, "How dare you talk like that to the High Priest!"

Jesus answered him, "If I have said anything wrong, tell everyone here what it was. But if I am right in what I have said, why do you hit Me?"

Jesus is Condemned to Death
Mark 14:53; John 18:15–16; Luke 22:55; Mark 14:55–65; Luke 22:65

Then Jesus was taken to the High Priest's house, where all the chief priests, the elders, and the teachers of the Law were gathering.

Simon Peter and another disciple followed Jesus. That other disciple was well known to the High Priest, so he went with Jesus into the courtyard of the High Priest's house, while Peter stayed outside by the gate. Then the other disciple went back out, spoke to the girl at the gate, and brought Peter inside.

A fire had been lit in the center of the courtyard, and Peter joined those who were sitting around it. The chief priests and the whole Council tried to find some evidence against Jesus in order to put Him to death, but they could not find any. Many witnesses told lies against Jesus, but their stories did not agree.

Then some men stood up and told this lie against Jesus: "We heard Him say, 'I will tear down this Temple which men have made, and after three days I will build one that is not made by men.'" Not even they, however, could make their stories agree.

The High Priest stood up in front of them all and questioned Jesus, "Have you no answer to the accusation they bring against you?"

But Jesus kept quiet and would not say a word. Again the High Priest questioned Him, "Are you the Messiah, the Son of the Blessed God?"

"I am," answered Jesus, "and you will all see the Son of Man seated at the right side of the Almighty and coming with the clouds of heaven!"

The High Priest tore his robes and said, "We don't need any more witnesses! You heard his blasphemy. What is your decision?"

They all voted against Him: he was guilty and should be put to death.

Some of them began to spit on Jesus, and they blindfolded Him and hit Him. "Guess who hit you!" they said. And the guards took Him and slapped Him.

And they said many other insulting things to Him.

Peter's Denial
John 18:17–18; Mark 14:66–69; Matthew 26:72; Mark 14:70–72

The girl at the gate said to Peter, "Aren't you also one of the disciples of that man?"

"No, I am not," answered Peter.

It was cold, so the servants and guards had built a charcoal fire and were standing around it, warming themselves. So Peter went over and stood with them, warming himself.

Peter was still down in the courtyard when one of the High Priest's servant women came by. When she saw Peter warming himself, she looked straight at him and said, "You, too, were with Jesus of Nazareth."

But he denied it. "I don't know. I don't understand what you are talking about," he answered, and went out into the passageway. Just then a rooster crowed.

The servant woman saw him there and began to repeat to the bystanders, "He is one of them!" Again Peter denied it and answered, "I swear that I don't know that man!"

A little while later, the bystanders accused Peter again, "You can't deny that you are one of them, because you, too, are from Galilee."

Then Peter said, "I swear that I am telling the truth! May God punish me if I am not! I do not know the man you are talking about!"

Just then a rooster crowed a second time, and Peter remembered how Jesus had said to him, "Before the rooster crows two times, you will say three times that you do not know me." And he broke down and cried.

The Death of Judas
Matthew 27:3–10

When Judas, the traitor, learned that Jesus had been condemned, he repented and took back the thirty silver coins to the chief priests and the elders. "I have sinned by betraying an innocent man to death!" he said.

"What do we care about that?" they answered. "That is your business!"

Judas threw the coins down in the Temple and left; then he went off and hanged himself.

The chief priests picked up the coins and said, "This is blood money, and it is against our Law to put it in the Temple treasury." After reaching an agreement about it, they used the money to buy Potter's Field, as a cemetery for foreigners. That is why that field is called "Field of Blood" to this very day.

Then what the prophet Jeremiah had said came true: "They took the thirty silver coins, the amount the people of Israel had agreed to pay for him, and used the money to buy the potter's field, as the Lord had commanded me."

Friday Morning, 6:00 a.m.
Jesus is Handed Over to Pilate
Matthew 27:1–2; John 18:28–32; Luke 23:2; John 18:33–38;
Matthew 27:13–14; Luke 23:4–7

Early in the morning, all the chief priests and the elders made their plans against Jesus to put Him to death. They put Him in chains, led Him off, and handed Him over to Pilate, the Roman governor.

The Jewish authorities did not go inside the palace, for they wanted to keep themselves ritually clean, in order to be able to eat the Passover meal. So Pilate went outside to them and asked, "What do you accuse this man of?"

Their answer was, "We would not have brought Him to you if He had not committed a crime."

Pilate said to them, "Then you yourselves take Him and try Him according to your own law."

They replied, "We are not allowed to put anyone to death." (This happened in order to make come true what Jesus had said when He indicated the kind of death He would die.)

They began to accuse Him: "We caught this man misleading our people, telling them not to pay taxes to the Emperor and claiming that He Himself is the Messiah, a king."

Pilate went back into the palace and called Jesus. "Are You the king of the Jews?" he asked him.

Jesus answered, "Does this question come from you or have others told you about Me?"

Pilate replied, "Do You think I am a Jew? It was your own people and the chief priests who handed You over to me. What have You done?"

Jesus said, "My kingdom does not belong to this world; if my kingdom belonged to this world, my followers would fight to keep me from being handed over to the Jewish authorities. No, my kingdom does not belong here!"

So Pilate asked him, "Are You a king, then?"

Jesus answered, "You say that I am a king. I was born and came into the world for this one purpose, to speak about the truth. Whoever belongs to the truth listens to Me."

"And what is truth?" Pilate asked.

So Pilate said to Him, "Don't You hear all these things they accuse You of?"

But Jesus refused to answer a single word, with the result that the Governor was greatly surprised.

Then Pilate said to the chief priests and the crowds, "I find no reason to condemn this man."

But they insisted even more strongly, "With his teaching He is starting a riot among the people all through Judea. He began in Galilee and now has come here."

When Pilate heard this, he asked, "Is this man a Galilean?" When he learned that Jesus was from the region ruled by Herod, he sent Him to Herod, who was also in Jerusalem at that time.

Jesus Before Herod
Luke 23:8–12

Herod was very pleased when he saw Jesus, because he had heard about Him and had been wanting to see Him for a long time. He was hoping to see Jesus perform some miracle. So Herod asked Jesus many questions, but Jesus made no answer. The chief priests and the teachers of the Law stepped forward and made strong accusations against Jesus. Herod and his soldiers made fun of Jesus and treated Him with contempt; then they put a fine robe on Him and sent him back to Pilate. On that very day, Herod and Pilate became friends; before this they had been enemies.

The Second Roman Hearing Before Pilate
Luke 23:13–16

Pilate called together the chief priests, the leaders, and the people, and said to them, "You brought this man to me and said that

He was misleading the people. Now, I have examined Him here in your presence, and I have not found Him guilty of any of the crimes you accuse Him of. Nor did Herod find Him guilty, for he sent Him back to us. There is nothing this man has done to deserve death. So I will have Him whipped and let Him go."

Jesus or Barabbas?
Matthew 27:15–22; Luke 23:22–23

At every Passover Festival, the Roman governor was in the habit of setting free any one prisoner the crowd asked for. At that time there was a well-known prisoner named Barabbas. So when the crowd gathered, Pilate asked them, "Which one do you want me to set free for you? Barabbas or Jesus called the Messiah?" He knew very well that the Jewish authorities had handed Jesus over to him because they were jealous.

While Pilate was sitting in the judgment hall, his wife sent him a message: "Have nothing to do with that innocent man, because in a dream last night I suffered much on account of Him."

The chief priests and the elders persuaded the crowd to ask Pilate to set Barabbas free and have Jesus put to death. But Pilate asked the crowd, "Which one of these two do you want me to set free for you?"

"Barabbas!" they answered.

"What, then, shall I do with Jesus called the Messiah?" Pilate asked them.

"Crucify him!" they all answered.

Pilate said to them the third time, "But what crime has He committed? I cannot find anything He has done to deserve death! I will have Him whipped and set him free."

But they kept on shouting at the top of their voices that Jesus should be crucified, and finally their shouting succeeded.

The Ridicule by the Soldiers
John 19:1; Matthew 27:27–30

Then Pilate took Jesus and had Him whipped. Then Pilate's soldiers took Jesus into the governor's palace, and the whole company gathered around Him. They stripped off his clothes and put a scarlet robe on Him. Then they made a crown out of thorny branches and placed it on his head, and put a stick in his right hand; then they knelt before Him and made fun of Him. "Long live the King of the Jews!" they said. They spat on Him, and took the stick and hit Him over the head.

"Crucify Him!"
John 19:4–15; Matthew 27:24–25; Luke 23:24–25

Pilate went back out once more and said to the crowd, "Look, I will bring Him out here to you to let you see that I cannot find any reason to condemn Him." So Jesus came out, wearing the crown of thorns and the purple robe. Pilate said to them, "Look! Here is the man!"

When the chief priests and the Temple guards saw Him, they shouted, "Crucify Him! Crucify Him!"

Pilate said to them, "You take Him, then, and crucify Him. I find no reason to condemn Him."

The crowd answered back, "We have a law that says He ought to die, because He claimed to be the Son of God."

When Pilate heard this, he was even more afraid. He went back into the palace and asked Jesus, "Where do you come from?"

But Jesus did not answer. Pilate said to Him, "You will not speak to me? Remember, I have the authority to set you free and also to have you crucified."

Jesus answered, "You have authority over Me only because it was given to you by God. So the man who handed Me over to you is guilty of a worse sin."

When Pilate heard this, he tried to find a way to set Jesus free. But the crowd shouted back, "If you set him free, that means that you are not the Emperor's friend! Anyone who claims to be a king is a rebel against the Emperor!"

When Pilate heard these words, he took Jesus outside and sat down on the judge's seat in the place called "The Stone Pavement." (In Hebrews the name is "Gabbatha.") Pilate said to the people, "Here is your king!"

They shouted back, "Kill Him! Kill Him! Crucify Him!"

Pilate asked them, "Do you want me to crucify your king?"

The chief priests answered, "The only king we have is the Emperor!"

When Pilate saw that it was no use to go on, but that a riot might break out, he took some water, washed his hands in front of the crowd, and said, "I am not responsible for the death of this man! This is your doing!"

The whole crowd answered, "Let the responsibility for his death fall on us and on our children!"

So Pilate passed the sentence on Jesus that they were asking for. He set free the man they wanted, the one who had been put in prison for riot and murder, and he handed Jesus over for them to do as they wished.

FRIDAY MORNING 9:00 A.M.
The Crucifixion of Jesus
John 19:17; Luke 23:26; Mark 15:21; Luke 23:27–32;
Matthew 27:33–34; Luke 23:33–34; Mark 15:25; John 19:19–27;
Matthew 27:38–43; Luke 23:36–43

He went out, carrying His Cross, and came to "The Place of the Skull," as it is called. (In Hebrews it is called "Golgotha.")

The soldiers led Jesus away, and as they were going, they met a man from Cyrene named Simon who was coming into the city from the country. They seized him, put the Cross on him, and made him carry it behind Jesus. (Simon was from Cyrene and was the father of Alexander and Rufus.)

A large crowd of people followed Him; among them were some women who were weeping and wailing for him. Jesus turned to them and said, "Women of Jerusalem! Don't cry for Me, but for yourselves and your children. For the days are coming when people will say, 'How lucky are the women who never had children, who never bore babies, who never nursed them!' That will be the time when people will say to the mountains, 'Fall on us!' and to the hills, 'Hide us!' For if such things as these are done when the wood is green, what will happen when it is dry?"

Two other men, both of them criminals, were also led out to be put to death with Jesus. They came to a place called Golgotha, which means, "The Place of the Skull." There they offered Jesus wine mixed with a bitter substance; but after tasting it, He would not drink it.

When they came to the place called "The Skull," they crucified Jesus there, and the two criminals, one on his right and the other on his left. Jesus said, "Forgive them, Father! They don't know what they are doing." It was nine o'clock in the morning when they crucified him.

Pilate wrote a notice and had it put on the Cross. "Jesus of Nazareth, the King of the Jews," is what he wrote. Many people read it, because the place where Jesus was crucified was not far from the city. The notice was written in Hebrews, Latin, and Greek. The chief priests said to Pilate, "Do not write 'The King of the Jews,' but rather, 'This man said, I am the King of the Jews.'"

Pilate answered, "What I have written stays written."

After the soldiers had crucified Jesus, they took his clothes and divided them into four parts, one part for each soldier. They also took the robe, which was made of one piece of woven cloth without any seams in it. The soldiers said to one another, "Let's not tear it; let's throw dice to see who will get it." This happened in order to make the scripture come true: "They divided my clothes among themselves and gambled for my robe." And this is what the soldiers did.

Standing close to Jesus' Cross were his mother, his mother's sister, Mary the wife of Clopas, and Mary Magdalene. Jesus saw his mother and the disciple He loved standing there; so He said to his mother, "He is your son."

Then He said to the disciple, "She is your mother." From that time the disciple took her to live in his home.

Then they crucified two bandits with Jesus, one on his right and the other on his left.

People passing by shook their heads and hurled insults at Jesus: "You were going to tear down the Temple and build it back up in three days! Save yourself if You are God's Son! Come on down from the Cross!"

In the same way the chief priests and the teachers of the Law and the elders made fun of him: "He saved others, but He cannot save himself. Isn't He the king of Israel? If He will come down off the Cross now, we will believe in Him! He trusts in God and claims to be God's Son. Well, then, let us see if God wants to save Him now!"

The soldiers also made fun of Him: they came up to Him and offered Him cheap wine, and said, "Save Yourself if You are the king of the Jews!"

Above him were written these words: "This is the King of the Jews."

One of the criminals hanging there hurled insults at Him: "Aren't you the Messiah? Save yourself and us!"

The other one, however, rebuked him, saying, "Don't you fear God? You received the same sentence He did. Ours, however, is only right, because we are getting what we deserve for what we did; but He has done no wrong." And he said to Jesus, "Remember me, Jesus, when You come as King!"

Jesus said to him, "I promise you that today you will be in Paradise with Me."

FRIDAY AFTERNOON 3:00 P.M.

The Death of Jesus

Luke 23:44; Matthew 27:46–47; John 19:28–29; Matthew 27:49;
John 19:30; Luke 23:46; Mark 15:38; Matthew 27:51–54

It was about twelve o'clock when the sun stopped shining and darkness covered the whole country until three o'clock. At about three o'clock, Jesus cried out with a loud shout, "Eli, Eli, lema sabachthani?" which means, "My God, my God, why did You abandon me?"

Some of the people standing there heard Him and said, "He is calling for Elijah!"

Jesus knew that by now everything had been completed; and in order to make the scripture come true, He said, "I am thirsty."

A bowl was there, full of cheap wine; so a sponge was soaked in the wine, put on a stalk of hyssop, and lifted up to his lips.

But the others said, "Wait, let us see if Elijah is coming to save Him!"

Jesus drank the wine and said, "It is finished!" Jesus cried out in a loud voice, "Father! In your hands I place my spirit!" He said this and died.

The curtain hanging in the Temple was torn in two, from top to bottom. The earth shook, the rocks split apart, the graves broke open, and many of God's people who had died were raised to life. They left the graves, and after Jesus rose from death, they went into the Holy City, where many people saw them.

When the army officer and the soldiers with him who were watching Jesus saw the earthquake and everything else that happened, they were terrified and said, "He really was the Son of God!"

A Spear in His Side

John 19:31–37; Luke 23:48–49; Matthew 27:56

Then the Jewish authorities asked Pilate to allow them to break the legs of the men who had been crucified, and to take the bodies down from the Crosses. They requested this because it was Friday, and they did not want the bodies to stay on the Crosses on the Sabbath, since the coming Sabbath was especially holy. So the soldiers went and broke the legs of the first man and then of the other man who had been crucified with Jesus. But when they came to Jesus, they saw that He was already dead, so they did not break his legs. One of the soldiers, however, plunged his spear into Jesus' side, and at once blood and water poured out. (John wrote: The one who saw this happen has spoken of it, so that you also may believe. What he said is true, and he knows that he speaks the truth.) This was done to make the scripture come true: "Not one of his bones will be broken." And there is another scripture that says, "People will look at him whom they pierced."

When the people who had gathered there to watch the spectacle saw what happened, they all went back home, beating their breasts in sorrow. All those who knew Jesus personally, including the women who had followed Him from Galilee, stood at a distance to watch.

Among them were Mary Magdalene, Mary the mother of James and Joseph, and the wife of Zebedee.

FRIDAY AFTERNOON 5:00 P.M.
Jesus' Burial
Matthew 27:57; Luke 23:50–51; Mark 15:43–45; John 19:38–41;
Luke 23:55–56; Mark 15:46; Luke 23:56

When it was evening, a rich man from Arimathea arrived; his name was Joseph, and he also was a disciple of Jesus. He was a good and honorable man, who was waiting for the coming of the Kingdom of God. Although he was a member of the Council, he had not agreed with their decision and action.

It was preparation day (that is, the day before the Sabbath), so Joseph went boldly into the presence of Pilate and asked him for the body of Jesus. Pilate was surprised to hear that Jesus was already dead. He called the army officer and asked him if Jesus had been dead a long time. After hearing the officer's report, Pilate told Joseph he could have the body.

So Joseph went and took it away. Nicodemus, who at first had gone to see Jesus at night, went with Joseph, taking with him about one hundred pounds of spices, a mixture of myrrh and aloes. The two men took Jesus' body and wrapped it in linen cloths with the spices according to the Jewish custom of preparing a body for burial. There was a garden in the place where Jesus had been put to death, and in it there was a new tomb where no one had ever been buried.

The women who had followed Jesus from Galilee went with Joseph and saw the tomb and how Jesus' body was placed in it. Then they went back home and prepared the spices and perfumes for the body. Then Joseph rolled a large stone across the entrance to the tomb.

On the Sabbath they rested, as the Law commanded.

Guards at the Tomb
Matthew 27:62–66

The next day, which was a Sabbath, the chief priests and the Pharisees met with Pilate and said, "Sir, we remember that while that liar was still alive He said, 'I will be raised to life three days later.' Give orders, then, for his tomb to be carefully guarded until the third day, so that his disciples will not be able to go and steal the body, and then tell the people that He was raised from death. This last lie would be even worse than the first one."

"Take a guard," Pilate told them. "Go and make the tomb as secure as you can."

So they left and made the tomb secure by putting a seal on the stone and leaving the guard on watch.

The Resurrection and the Empty Tomb
Mark 16:1; Matthew 28:2–4; Mark 16:2–4;
Luke 24:3–8; Matthew 28:5–8; Luke 24:11

After the Sabbath was over, Mary Magdalene, Mary the mother of James, and Salome bought spices to go and anoint the body of Jesus.

Suddenly there was a violent earthquake; an angel of the Lord came down from heaven, rolled the stone away, and sat on it. His appearance was like lightning, and his clothes were white as snow. The guards were so afraid that they trembled and became like dead men.

Very early on Sunday morning, at sunrise, they went to the tomb. On the way they said to one another, "Who will roll away the stone for us from the entrance to the tomb?" (It was a very large stone.) Then they looked up and saw that the stone had already been rolled back. So they went in; but they did not find the body of the Lord Jesus. They stood there puzzled about this, when suddenly two men in bright shining clothes stood by them. Full of fear, the women bowed down to the ground, as the men said to them, "Why are you looking among the dead for one who is alive? He is not here; He has been raised. Remember what He said to you while He was in Galilee: 'The Son of Man must be handed over to sinners, be crucified, and three days later rise to life.'"

Then the women remembered his words.

The angel spoke to the women. "You must not be afraid," he said. "I know you are looking for Jesus, who was crucified. He is not here; He has been raised, just as He said. Come here and see the place where He was lying. Go quickly now, and tell his disciples, 'He has been raised from death, and now He is going to Galilee ahead of you; there you will see Him!' Remember what I have told you."

So they left the tomb in a hurry, afraid and yet filled with joy, and ran to tell his disciples.

But the apostles thought that what the women said was nonsense, and they did not believe them.

The Lie of the Jewish Council
Matthew 28:11–15

While the women went on their way, some of the soldiers guarding the tomb went back to the city and told the chief priests everything that had happened. The chief priests met with the elders and made their plan; they gave a large sum of money to the soldiers and said, "You are to say that his disciples came during the night and stole his body while you were asleep. And if the Governor should hear of this, we will convince him that you are innocent, and you will have nothing to worry about."

The guards took the money and did what they were told to do. And so that is the report spread around by the Jews to this very day.

Peter and John Go to the Tomb
John 20:3–10

Then Peter and the other disciple went to the tomb. The two of them were running, but the other disciple ran faster than Peter and reached the tomb first. He bent over and saw the linen cloths, but he did not go in. Behind him came Simon Peter, and he went straight into the tomb. He saw the linen cloths lying there and the cloth which had been around Jesus' head. It was not lying with the linen cloths but was rolled up by itself. Then the other disciple, who had reached the tomb first, also went in; he saw and believed. (They still did not understand the scripture which said that He must rise from death.) Then the disciples went back home.

Jesus Appears to Mary Magdalene
Mark 16:9; John 20:11–18; Mark 16:10–11

After Jesus rose from death early on Sunday, He appeared first to Mary Magdalene, from whom He had driven out seven demons.

Mary stood crying outside the tomb. While she was still crying, she bent over and looked in the tomb and saw two angels there dressed in white, sitting where the body of Jesus had been, one at the head and the other at the feet. "Woman, why are you crying?" they asked her.

She answered, "They have taken my Lord away, and I do not know where they have put Him!"

Then she turned around and saw Jesus standing there; but she did not know that it was Jesus. "Woman, why are you crying?" Jesus asked her. "Who is it that you are looking for?"

She thought he was the gardener, so she said to Him, "If you took Him away, sir, tell me where you have put him, and I will go and get Him."

Jesus said to her, "Mary!"

She turned toward Him and said in Hebrew, "Rabboni!" (This means "Teacher.")

"Do not hold on to Me," Jesus told her, "because I have not yet gone back up to the Father. But go to my brothers and tell them that I am returning to Him who is my Father and their Father, my God and their God."

So Mary Magdalene went and told the disciples that she had seen the Lord and related to them what He had told her.

She went and told his companions. They were mourning and crying; and when they heard her say that Jesus was alive and that she had seen Him, they did not believe her.

Jesus Appears to the Two Disciples
on the Road to Emmaus
Mark 16:12; Luke 24:13–35; Mark 16:13

After this, Jesus appeared in a different manner to two of them while they were on their way to the country. On that same day two of Jesus' followers were going to a village named Emmaus, about seven miles from Jerusalem, and they were talking to each other about all the things that had happened. As they talked and discussed, Jesus Himself drew near and walked along with them; they saw Him, but somehow did not recognize Him. Jesus said to them, "What are you talking about to each other, as you walk along?"

They stood still, with sad faces. One of them, named Cleopas, asked Him, "Are you the only visitor in Jerusalem who doesn't know the things that have been happening there these last few days?"

"What things?" He asked.

"The things that happened to Jesus of Nazareth," they answered. "This man was a prophet and was considered by God and by all the people to be powerful in everything He said and did. Our chief priests and rulers handed Him over to be sentenced to death, and He was crucified. And we had hoped that He would be the one who was going to set Israel free! Besides all that, this is now the third day since it happened. Some of the women of our group surprised us; they went at dawn to the tomb, but could not find his body. They came back saying they had seen a vision of angels who told them that He is alive. Some of our group went to the tomb and found it exactly as the women had said, but they did not see Him."

Then Jesus said to them, "How foolish you are, how slow you are to believe everything the prophets said! Was it not necessary for the Messiah to suffer these things and then to enter his glory?" And Jesus explained to them what was said about Himself in all the Scriptures, beginning with the books of Moses and the writings of all the prophets.

As they came near the village to which they were going, Jesus acted as if He were going farther; but they held Him back, saying, "Stay with us; the day is almost over and it is getting dark." So He went in to stay with them. He sat down to eat with them, took the bread, and said the blessing; then He broke the bread and gave it to them. Then their eyes were opened and they recognized Him, but He disappeared from their sight. They said to each other, "Wasn't it like a fire burning in us when He talked to us on the road and explained the Scriptures to us?"

They got up at once and went back to Jerusalem, where they found the eleven disciples gathered together with the others and saying, "The Lord is risen indeed! He has appeared to Simon!"

The two then explained to them what had happened on the road, and how they had recognized the Lord when He broke the bread.

They returned and told the others, but these would not believe it.

Jesus Appears to the Disciples
Mark 16:14; John 20:19; Luke 24:37–41;
Mark 16:14; Luke 24:41–49; John 20:21–25

Last of all, Jesus appeared to the eleven disciples as they were eating. It was late that Sunday evening, and the disciples were gathered together behind locked doors, because they were afraid of the Jewish authorities. Then Jesus came and stood among them. "Peace be with you," He said. They were terrified, thinking that they were seeing a ghost. But He said to them, "Why are you alarmed? Why are these doubts coming up in your minds? Look at my hands and my feet, and see that it is I Myself. Feel me, and you will know, for a ghost doesn't have flesh and bones, as you can see I have."

He said this and showed them his hands and his feet. They still could not believe, they were so full of joy and wonder. He scolded them, because they did not have faith and because they were too stubborn to believe those who had seen Him alive.

So He asked them, "Do you have anything here to eat?" They gave Him a piece of cooked fish, which He took and ate in their presence. Then He said to them, "These are the very things I told you about while I was still with you: everything written about Me in the Law of Moses, the writings of the prophets, and the Psalms had to come true."

Then He opened their minds to understand the Scriptures, and said to them, "This is what is written: the Messiah must suffer and must rise from death three days later, and in his name the message about repentance and the forgiveness of sins must be preached to all nations, beginning in Jerusalem. You are witnesses of these things. And I myself will send upon you what my Father has promised.

But you must wait in the city until the power from above comes down upon you." Jesus said to them again, "Peace be with you. As the Father sent Me, so I send you." Then he breathed on them and said, "Receive the Holy Spirit. If you forgive people's sins, they are forgiven; if you do not forgive them, they are not forgiven."

Jesus Appears to the Disciples
(Thomas is Present)
John 20:26–29

A week later, the disciples were together again indoors, and Thomas was with them. The doors were locked, but Jesus came and stood among them and said, "Peace be with you." Then He said to Thomas, "Put your finger here, and look at my hands; then reach out your hand and put it in my side. Stop your doubting, and believe!"

Thomas answered Him, "My Lord and my God!"

Jesus said to him, "Do you believe because you see Me? How happy are those who believe without seeing Me!"

Jesus Appears to Seven Disciples
John 21:1–14

After this, Jesus appeared once more to his disciples at Lake Tiberias. This is how it happened. Simon Peter, Thomas (called the Twin), Nathanael (the one from Cana in Galilee), the sons of Zebedee, and two other disciples of Jesus were all together. Simon Peter said to the others, "I am going fishing."

"We will come with you," they told him. So they went out in a boat, but all that night they did not catch a thing. As the sun was rising, Jesus stood at the water's edge, but the disciples did not know that it was Jesus. Then He asked them, "Young men, haven't you caught anything?"

"Not a thing," they answered.

He said to them, "Throw your net out on the right side of the boat, and you will catch some." So they threw the net out and could not pull it back in, because they had caught so many fish.

The disciple whom Jesus loved said to Peter, "It is the Lord!" When Peter heard that it was the Lord, he wrapped his outer garment around him (for he had taken his clothes off) and jumped into the water. The other disciples came to shore in the boat, pulling the net full of fish. They were not very far from land, about a hundred yards away. When they stepped ashore, they saw a charcoal fire there with fish on it and some bread. Then Jesus said to them, "Bring some of the fish you have just caught."

Simon Peter went aboard and dragged the net ashore full of big fish, a hundred and fifty-three in all; even though there were so many, still the net did not tear. Jesus said to them, "Come and eat." None of the disciples dared ask Him, "Who are You?" because they knew it was the Lord. So Jesus went over, took the bread, and gave it to them; He did the same with the fish.

This, then, was the third time Jesus appeared to the disciples after He was raised from death.

Jesus' Conversation with Peter
John 21:15–23

After they had eaten, Jesus said to Simon Peter, "Simon son of John, do you love Me more than these others do?"

"Yes, Lord," he answered, "You know that I love You."

Jesus said to him, "Take care of my lambs." A second time, Jesus said to him, "Simon son of John, do you love Me?"

"Yes, Lord," he answered, "You know that I love You."

Jesus said to him, "Take care of my sheep." A third time, Jesus said, "Simon son of John, do you love me?"

Peter became sad because Jesus asked him the third time, "Do you love Me?" and so he said to Him, "Lord, You know everything; You know that I love You!"

Jesus said to him, "Take care of my sheep. I am telling you the truth: when you were young, you used to get ready and go anywhere you wanted to; but when you are old, you will stretch out your hands and someone else will tie you up and take you where you don't want to go." (In saying this, Jesus was indicating the way in which Peter would die and bring glory to God.) Then Jesus said to him, "Follow Me!"

Peter turned around and saw behind him that other disciple, whom Jesus loved—the one who had leaned close to Jesus at the meal and had asked, "Lord, who is going to betray You?" When Peter saw him, he asked Jesus, "Lord, what about this man?"

Jesus answered him, "If I want him to live until I come, what is that to you? Follow Me!"

So a report spread among the followers of Jesus that this disciple would not die. But Jesus did not say he would not die; He said, "If I want him to live until I come, what is that to you?"

The Great Commission
Matthew 28:16–19; Mark 16:16–18; Matthew 28:19–20

The eleven disciples went to the hill in Galilee where Jesus had told them to go. When they saw Him, they worshiped Him, even though some of them doubted. Jesus drew near and said to them, "I have been given all authority in heaven and on earth. Go, then, to all peoples everywhere and make them my disciples. Whoever believes and is baptized will be saved; whoever does not believe will be condemned. Believers will be given the power to perform miracles: they will drive out demons in my name; they will speak in strange tongues; if they pick up snakes or drink any poison, they will not be harmed; they will place their hands on sick people, and these will get well, baptize them in the name of the Father, the Son, and the Holy Spirit, and teach them to obey everything I have commanded you. And I will be with you always, to the end of the age."

Jesus' Ascension
Acts 1:3–7; Luke 24:49; Acts 1:8; Luke 24:50; Acts 1:9–12

For forty days after his death He appeared to them many times in ways that proved beyond doubt that He was alive. They saw Him, and He talked with them about the Kingdom of God. And when they came together, He gave them this order: "Do not leave Jerusalem, but wait for the gift I told you about, the gift my Father promised. John baptized with water, but in a few days, you will be baptized with the Holy Spirit."

When the apostles met together with Jesus, they asked Him, "Lord, will You at this time give the Kingdom back to Israel?"

Jesus said to them, "The times and occasions are set by my Father's own authority, and it is not for you to know when they will be. And I myself will send upon you what my Father has promised. But you must wait in the city until the power from above comes down upon you."

"But when the Holy Spirit comes upon you, you will be filled with power, and you will be witnesses for Me in Jerusalem, in all of Judea and Samaria, and to the ends of the earth."

Then He led them out of the city as far as Bethany, where He raised his hands and blessed them. After saying this, He was taken up to heaven as they watched Him, and a cloud hid Him from their sight.

They still had their eyes fixed on the sky as He went away, when two men dressed in white suddenly stood beside them and said, "Galileans, why are you standing there looking up at the sky? This Jesus, who was taken from you into heaven, will come back in the same way that you saw Him go to heaven."

Then the apostles went back to Jerusalem from the Mount of Olives, which is about half a mile away from the city.

Judas' Successor
Acts 1:13–26

They entered the city and went up to the room where they were staying: Peter, John, James and Andrew, Philip and Thomas, Bartholomew and Matthew, James son of Alphaeus, Simon the Patriot, and Judas son of James. They gathered frequently to pray as a group, together with the women and with Mary the mother of Jesus and with his brothers.

A few days later, there was a meeting of the believers, about a hundred and twenty in all, and Peter stood up to speak. "My friends," he said, "the scripture had to come true in which the Holy Spirit, speaking through David, made a prediction about Judas, who was the guide for those who arrested Jesus. Judas was a member of our group, for he had been chosen to have a part in our work."

(The money that Judas got for his evil act was used to buy a field, where he fell to his death; he burst open and all his insides spilled out. All the people living in Jerusalem heard about it, and so in their own language, they call that field Akeldama, which means "Field of Blood.")

"For it is written in the book of Psalms, 'May his house become empty; may no one live in it.'

"It is also written, 'May someone else take his place of service.'

"So then, someone must join us as a witness to the resurrection of the Lord Jesus. He must be one of the men who were in our group during the whole time that the Lord Jesus traveled about with us, beginning from the time John preached his message of baptism until the day Jesus was taken up from us to heaven."

So they proposed two men: Joseph, who was called Barabbas (also known as Justus), and Matthias. Then they prayed, "Lord, you know the thoughts of everyone, so show us which of these two you have chosen to serve as an apostle in the place of Judas, who left to go to the place where he belongs." Then they drew lots to choose between the two men, and the one chosen was Matthias, who was added to the group of eleven apostles.

The Outpouring of the Holy Spirit of Jesus
Acts 2

When the day of Pentecost came, all the believers were gathered together in one place. Suddenly there was a noise from the sky which sounded like a strong wind blowing, and it filled the whole house where they were sitting. Then they saw what looked like tongues of fire which spread out and touched each person there. They were all filled with the Holy Spirit and began to talk in other languages, as the Spirit enabled them to speak.

There were Jews living in Jerusalem, religious people who had come from every country in the world. When they heard this noise, a large crowd gathered. They were all excited, because all of them heard the believers talking in their own languages. In amazement and wonder they exclaimed, "These people who are talking like this are Galileans! How is it, then, that all of us hear them speaking in our own native languages? We are from Parthia, Media, and Elam; from Mesopotamia, Judea, and Cappadocia; from Pontus and Asia, from Phrygia and Pamphylia, from Egypt and the regions of Libya near Cyrene. Some of us are from Rome, both Jews and Gentiles converted to Judaism, and some of us are from Crete and Arabia—yet all of us hear them speaking in our own languages about the great things that God has done!" Amazed and confused, they kept asking each other, "What does this mean?"

But others made fun of the believers, saying, "These people are drunk!"

Then Peter stood up with the other eleven apostles and in a loud voice began to speak to the crowd: "Fellow Jews and all of you who live in Jerusalem, listen to me and let me tell you what this means. These people are not drunk, as you suppose; it is only nine o'clock in the morning. Instead, this is what the prophet Joel spoke about:

"This is what I will do in the last days, God says: I will pour out my Spirit on everyone. Your sons and daughters will proclaim my message; your young men will see visions, and your old men will have dreams. Yes, even on my servants, both men and women, I will pour out my Spirit in those days, and they will proclaim my message. I will perform miracles in the sky above and wonders on the earth below. There will be blood, fire, and thick smoke; the sun will be darkened, and the moon will turn red as blood, before the great and glorious Day of the Lord comes. And then, whoever calls out to the Lord for help will be saved.

"Listen to these words, fellow Israelites! Jesus of Nazareth was a man whose divine authority was clearly proven to you by all the miracles and wonders which God performed through Him. You yourselves know this, for it happened here among you. In accordance with his own plan God had already decided that Jesus would be handed over to you; and you killed Him by letting sinful men crucify Him. But God raised Him from death, setting Him free from its power, because it was impossible that death should hold Him prisoner. For David said about Him,

"I saw the Lord before me at all times; he is near me, and I will not be troubled. And so I am filled with gladness, and my words are full of joy. And I, mortal though I am, will rest assured in hope, because you will not abandon me in the world of the dead; you will not allow your faithful servant to rot in the grave. You have shown me the paths that lead to life, and your presence will fill me with joy.

"My friends, I must speak to you plainly about our famous ancestor King David. He died and was buried, and his grave is here with us to this very day. He was a prophet, and he knew what God had promised him: God had made a vow that he would make one of David's descendants a king, just as David was. David saw what God was going to do in the future, and so he spoke about the resurrection of the Messiah when he said,

"He was not abandoned in the world of the dead; his body did not rot in the grave.

"God has raised this very Jesus from death, and we are all witnesses to this fact. He has been raised to the right side of God, his Father, and has received from Him the Holy Spirit, as He had promised. What you now see and hear is his gift that He has poured out on us. For it was not David who went up into heaven; rather he said,

"The Lord said to my Lord: Sit here at my right side until I put your enemies as a footstool under your feet." "All the people of Israel, then, are to know for sure that this Jesus, whom you crucified, is the one that God has made Lord and Messiah!"

When the people heard this, they were deeply troubled and said to Peter and the other apostles, "What shall we do, brothers?"

Peter said to them, "Each one of you must turn away from your sins and be baptized in the name of Jesus Christ, so that your sins will be forgiven; and you will receive God's gift, the Holy Spirit. For God's promise was made to you and your children, and to all who are far away—all whom the Lord our God calls to himself."

Peter made his appeal to them and with many other words he urged them, saying, "Save yourselves from the punishment coming on this wicked people!" Many of them believed his message and were baptized, and about three thousand people were added to the group that day. They spent their time in learning from the apostles, taking part in the fellowship, and sharing in the fellowship meals and the prayers.

Many miracles and wonders were being done through the apostles, and everyone was filled with awe. All the believers continued together in close fellowship and shared their belongings with one another. They would sell their property and possessions, and distribute the money among all, according to what each one needed. Day after day they met as a group in the Temple, and they had their meals together in their homes, eating with glad and humble hearts, praising God, and enjoying the good will of all the people. And every day the Lord added to their group those who were being saved.

ABOUT THE AUTHOR

After working for sixteen years as an educator, Wilkin van de Kamp served for ten years as a pastor for the German-Dutch *Euregio Christengemeente* (Euroregion Christian congregation). Since 2010, he has served as pastor-director of *Vrij Zijn* (Being Free), written more than twenty books, and spoken at international conferences drawing thousands of Christians.

Regarding *The Seven Wonders of the Cross*, Wilkin explains, "At the beginning of 2004, I started a year-long intensive study of the last eighteen hours of Jesus's life. I studied what historians, doctors, theologians, and others wrote about the suffering and death of Jesus. I not only wanted to understand why Jesus had to go through such tremendous suffering, but to be close to Him in the most difficult hours of His life."

Wilkin eventually wrote *Het Wonder van het Kruis* (*The Wonder of the Cross*), in forty days, spread out over half a year. The book has become a best-seller in the Netherlands and has been translated into several languages.

Heading a national movement, *Wij Kiezen Voor Eenheid* (We Choose Unity) in the Netherlands, Wilkin hosted the *Nationale Ontmoetingsdag van Verootmoediging en Verzoening* (National Day of Abasement and Reconciliation) in The Hague on October 6, 2012. National leaders and about three thousand Christians from many denominations confessed before God and to each other that they had spoken about and dealt negatively with one another in the past. This day was viewed as a breakthrough in the ecumenism of the Netherlands' churches.

Wilkin is also a co-founder and ambassador for the Christian, humanitarian, non-governmental organization *Pan de Vida* (Bread of Life) in Peru. Children receive a free, healthy meal once a day at thirty-three locations in different slums. Pan de Vida has also established two child care facilities and an orphanage.

Wilkin has felt God's call to help the church make the majesty of the cross its central theme, a symbol of great love and courage that had never been seen before and will never be seen again.

He and his wife, Aukje (Ann), have four sons and four grand-daughters.